Managing Networks
in International Business

INTERNATIONAL STUDIES IN GLOBAL CHANGE

Edited by **Tom R. Burns,** Uppsala University, Sweden, and **Thomas Dietz,** George Mason University, Virginia, USA

This book series is devoted to investigations of human ecology, technology and management and their interrelations. It will include theoretical and methodological contributions to the analysis of social systems and their transformation, technology, risk, environmental problems, energy and natural resources, population growth, public health, and global economic and societal developments.

Managing Networks in International Business

Edited by

Mats Forsgren
and
Jan Johanson

Uppsala University
Sweden

Gordon and Breach

Philadelphia • Reading • Paris • Montreux • Tokyo • Melbourne

Gordon and Breach Science Publishers

5301 Tacony Street, Drawer 330
Philadelphia, Pennsylvania 19137
United States of America

Post Office Box 161
1820 Montreux 2
Switzerland

Post Office Box 90
Reading, Berkshire RG1 8JL
United Kingdom

3-14-9, Okubo
Shinjuku-ku, Tokyo 169
Japan

58, rue Lhomond
75005 Paris
France

Private Bag 8
Camberwell, Victoria 3124
Australia

Library of Congress Cataloging-in-Publication Data

Managing networks in international business / edited by Mats Forsgren
and Jan Johanson
      p. cm. -- (International studies in global change ; v. 2)
   Includes bibliographical references and index.
   ISBN 2-88124-505-6
    1. International business enterprises--Communication systems--Management. 2. Communication--Network analysis. 3. Middle
managers. 4. Intercultural communication. I. Forsgren, Mats.
II. Johanson, Jan, 1934-   . III. Series.
HD62.4.M367   1992
658' .0546--dc20   91-20278

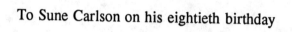

To Sune Carlson on his eightieth birthday

Contents

PART III: UNDERSTANDING NETWORK CHANGE PROCESSES IN INTERNATIONAL BUSINESS

Chapter Eleven: Managing Ownership Internationalization
Henrik Didner

Chapter Twelve: Barriers in International Banking Networks
Lars Engwall

Chapter Thirteen: Power Balancing in an International Business Network
Mats Forsgren and Ulf Olsson

Chapter Fourteen: Entering a Tightly Structured Network—Strategic Visions or Network Realities
Nils Kinch

CONTENTS

Illustrations

Figures

Tables

Introduction to the Series

This series brings together under one banner works by scholars of many disciplines. All of these researchers have distinguished themselves in their specialties. But here they have ventured beyond the frontiers of traditional disciplines and have developed new, innovative approaches to the study of social systems and social change.

Why? What has prompted this foray into uncharted territory? What is the reason for broadening theoretical perspectives and developing new methodologies? The impetus comes from the world we seek to understand. Scholars have traditionally made "boundary" assumptions that limited their scope of inquiry to the concerns of a discipline. Such limitations facilitate concentration, though they have always been artificial. The interpenetration of social, economic and environmental phenomena, and the precipitous pace of change in the late twentieth century make it clear that such convenient intellectual boundaries are not only unrealistic, they are untenable.

How complex waves of change sweep through the contemporary world, altering the natural environment, technology, the economy and social systems; the interaction of these forces, their impact on nations, communities, families and individuals; and the response to them by individuals and collectivities—this is the focus of the research to be presented in this series. The scholars writing in the series are themselves engaged in social change—the restructuring of our way of thinking about the world.

The Uppsala research program on international business, inspired by Sune Carlson, is a particularly appropriate topic for the second volume in this series. As the fifteen chapters in this book demonstrate, the Uppsala approach has always been innovative and interdisciplinary, while grounded in the reality of business experience. The essays presented here emphasize management in a dynamic environment, one in which interactions across networks of companies and individuals require strategies that evolve in more complex ways than would be predicted by simple models.

Tom R. Burns
Thomas Dietz

Preface

This book was written, in part, to assure Sune Carlson on his eightieth birthday that the international business research program that he initiated at Uppsala University in the early sixties is still innovative and productive. Some years before coming to Uppsala, Carlson completed his pioneering study of executive behavior. A quotation from that study exemplifies two key features of the Uppsala international business research program in general, and of this book in particular:

> Before we made the study, I always thought of a chief executive as the conductor of an orchestra, standing aloof on his platform. Now I am in some respects inclined to see him as the puppet in a puppet show with hundreds of people pulling the strings and forcing him to act in one way or another. (Carlson 1951, p. 52)

One feature of this quotation is the emphasis placed upon empirical observation rather that theoretical assumption. When he started the international business research program, Carlson told us that, first and foremost, we had to empirically investigate international business. He taught us that empirical facts are the foundation of systematic knowledge. Through a painful process we slowly learned that business facts are not always consistent with business theory. He taught us to believe in facts rather than theoretical assumptions, so we were forced to organize the facts on the basis of new concepts and theories. Using this inductive approach, the Uppsala program has proceeded with a strong emphasis on the close interplay between empirical observation and theoretical development. Such interplay is perhaps more normal than exceptional, but its empirical foundation is particularly distinct at Uppsala, with its long international business research tradition.

The second feature of the quotation is related to the results reported in Carlson's study. These results demonstrate the importance of lower managerial levels rather than top management in business. In mainstream international business research, the top management perspective dominates. Lower management levels are seen as little more than obstacles to the implementation of top managerial decisions. In our research we have chosen a middle management perspective in which we try to gain an understanding of business situations as seen by these managers. Such an approach opens up a number of important research opportunities. One is access to the world in which business is actually conducted. Swedish business research benefits especially from open companies and interested businessmen on all levels. We thank all those who over the years have helped us in our work by explaining their situations and discussing the facts of international business life as they saw them.

This volume includes fifteen contributions from different researchers in the Department of Business Studies at Uppsala University. It explores the theoretical and empirical bases developed in the department within the fields of international business and industrial marketing. We therefore are greatly indebted to many of the department's researchers and to members of the advanced seminar. We are especially grateful to Margaret Gottlieb for her editorial work and for co-ordinating the contributions of seventeen authors. Without her patience and efficiency this book would not have materialized.

Mats Forsgren
Jan Johanson

1

Managing Internationalization in Business Networks
Mats Forsgren and Jan Johanson

1.1. A New Approach to International Business Analysis

The international business arena is enlarging rapidly as well as undergoing dramatic structural changes. The old international business actors − large and small multinational firms engaged in industry, trade and services − are expanding all over the world. They are developing and modifying their business practices. New actors − private and public − are entering. Some of them come from countries and areas which used to be isolated and economically backward, some come from the old industrialized countries but from business fields which were mainly domestic in most countries. New forms and patterns of business activities are brought to the arena. Sometimes the firms compete on their own, sometimes they co-operate with other actors in ever changing patterns. The traditional distinct roles in the market place as suppliers, customers and competitors are becoming mixed. Competitors in one market co-operate in another and are suppliers and customers to each other in a third. Correspondingly, traditional boundaries between industries are breaking down and firms from different industries meet in new markets.

Parallel with this development there has been a tremendous growth in the research and literature about international business. The number of textbooks about international business, marketing, and finance is increasing exponentially. But their character remains essentially the same despite some minor changes. Thus, in the sixties we witnessed the first textbooks about International Marketing (i.e. Cateora, 1966), in the seventies they were called Multinational Marketing (i.e. Keegan, 1974) and in the eighties we see textbooks titled Global Marketing (i.e. Toyne & Walters, 1989) in the publishers' lists. In spite of the changing titles the basic approach remains the same.

Reflecting the dominant approach in business literature the single firm operating – or potentially operating – internationally is strongly in focus. This firm, in its entirety, is the unit of analysis and a distinct boundary separates it from its environment. The basic task of these books comprises the analysis from a top management perspective. Given the environment of the firm and its own resources, which strategic decisions maximize the company's return and which organization is needed to implement them.

This book is based on a different approach to business analysis. It starts with the assumption that international business takes place in a network setting where different business actors are linked to each other through direct and indirect business relationships. Managing international business, then is a matter of establishing, developing and maintaining the firm's positions in the international business networks.

A corner stone in the network view is that it regards firms as engaged in more or less lasting business relationships with other actors in the business arena, the main managerial task being to handle their interaction. Thus, rather than drawing a sharp line between the firm and its environment this book focuses on the interaction between firms in an attempt to understand how they, in competition and in co-operation, together shape the future conditions for business. Rather than viewing the environment as a set of separate, anonymous forces – political, competitive, legal, cultural, economic, etc. – all the actors are considered bearers of diverse interests, powers and characteristics. It is in the meetings in the international business arena that such factors impinge on the development of business.

Second, as this interaction involves managers on all managerial levels the book lacks the clear top management perspective so dominant in international business literature but focuses on the tasks of middle management in handling the relationships with customers, suppliers, distributors and all kinds of business actors. This implies also that the firm as a whole is not taken for granted. Rather, the firm operating internationally can be seen as composed of different units with different interests and differential possibilities to pursue their interests. Thus managerial problems may as well concern managing relationships with other business units in the same firm as with business units in other firms. In fact, this view implies that managing relationships with superior units is an important managerial task.

Third, rather than focusing single, discrete decisions this book devotes attention to the current activities in the firms and their consequences. It assumes that business relationships are developed and maintained primarily through everyday interaction. This approach implies that business processes, whether they take place within or between firms, should be of prime interest in international business studies. Understanding of the processes whereby the firms develop internationally and maintain their international business positions is more important to managers than models for optimal strategic decisions.

The approach of the book is based on long-term research in international business at Uppsala following two separate but closely related lines which are presented in the next sections of this Chapter. Both lines of research have been pursued in close interaction with business managers and have a strong empirical orientation. The first concerns business networks and the second the internationalization process of the firm. In a third section of the chapter these two lines are integrated and the content of the book is outlined.

1.2. Firms in Business Networks

1.2.1. Business Relationships

In empirical research at Uppsala about Swedish industrial firms in international competition it was found that major marketing problems in the firms concerned establishment, development and maintenance of lasting business relationships with customers, suppliers and other important actors (Johanson, 1966, Forsgren & Kinch, 1970, Kinch, 1974).

This observation has led to a line of research focusing interaction in business relationships (Håkansson & Östberg, 1975, Håkansson, ed., 1982). Relationships with such important customers and suppliers are, according to this research, developed over time through interaction processes. Through the interaction the parties gradually, on one hand, learn about each other's needs, capabilities and strategies and come to trust in each other, and on the other, adapt to each other's way of performing operations and commit resources to the relationship.

Empirical data about some 1000 business relationships in European markets collected in an international research project — IMP Project — show that both industrial suppliers and industrial customers are engaged in lasting relationships, which they consider important (Håkansson, ed., 1982 and Turnbull & Valla, eds., 1986). The data also indicate that most firms operate in markets where a limited number of customers account for a considerable proportion of the firms' sales. The managers often characterize their customer distribution by a 80-20 rule, saying that 20 per cent of the customers take 80 per cent of the firm's sales. In a similar manner the main part of the firms' purchases of inputs come from a limited number of suppliers. They are important as they secure effective sourcing and marketing, and because they form a basis for the firms' competence development. The business relationships are significant, intangible assets of the firms. The average age of the relationships investigated was fifteen years, a considerable number of them were much older.

Business relationships are established and developed by investing time and resources in interaction with each other. Such relationship-specific investments may include adaptations of products, processes and routines. Examples of such adaptations are customized products, just-in-time-delivery systems, and quality assurance programs. Considerable adaptations are also made gradually as a consequence of two firms learning about each other's ways of performing activities. The relationship-investment processes are often mutual.

Most businessmen agree that business relationships are of critical importance. The relationships are, however, hardly visible from outside, as they are subtle phenomena, in which intentions, interpretations, and expectations are important aspects (Håkansson & Johanson, 1988). They are also difficult to grasp for an outsider as they comprise a number of different and complex dependences — technical, logistic, social, cognitive, administrative, legal, and economic — between the parties.

Although the basic nature of business relationships seems to be common there are great differences between different relationships with regard to the interaction processes and the dependences. To some extent such differences are structurally conditioned. There are differences between domestic and international relationships. Likewise there are differences depending on product type, production technology and market structures (Hallén, Johanson & Seyed-Mohamed, 1987).

But the character of business relationships is also a consequence of the interaction strategies of the parties (Cunningham & Homse, 1982). A supplier of a product may pursue different strategies towards different customers. The interaction with one may aim exclusively at sales volume while interaction with another is important with regard to technical development. Correspondingly, a customer firm may have one or a few main, stable suppliers of a product and some other secondary suppliers so as to test the market.

Business in one relationship is often conditioned by relationships with third parties, such as the customer's customers, the supplier's suppliers, consultants, competitors, supplementary suppliers, middlemen, as well as public or semi-public agencies. This leads to the important conclusion that markets are more or less stable networks of business relationships (Hägg & Johanson, eds., 1982). Firms make important investments in such networks. The competitive situation of the firms is a matter of the networks they operate in or may operate in − there is a great difference between being an insider and an outsider − and their relations to those networks. The network is the framework which gives the firms both possibilities and constraints in their business.

1.2.2. Business Networks

Against this background we define business networks as sets of connected exchange relationships between actors controlling business activities (cf. Cook & Emerson, 1984).

Business networks differ from social networks − and from networks in general − by being coupled to business activities. The business network model is therefore based on some assumptions about business activities. In business fields a number of more or less interrelated business activities are pursued. Each activity is more or less dependent on the performance of a number of other activities which must precede or are expected to ensue. Each activity is a link in one or several more or less extensive and closely linked activity chains. The activities are performed more or less repetitively. Over time, through experience, some of the activities are modified and adapted to each other, thus increasing their joint productivity and their cohesion. The interdependence between the activities − in the sense that the outcome of the one is dependent on the performance of the other −

becomes stronger. As two activities become more closely interlinked they are usually separated from some other activities. Thus, change in the performance of one activity may lead to adjustments through activity chains and also cause changes in related activity chains.

Any such business field involves a number of different actors — irrespective of whether they are firms, divisions, business units or individuals. No actor's activities are performed in isolation. They are more or less embedded in the wider web of business activities performed in the field. But the dependence between actors can be more or less specific. There is a specific dependence between two actors if one of them is dependent on the activities of the specific counterpart. There may also be general dependences, which are not related to specific counterparts. Thus, a firm may be dependent on the activities in a certain market irrespective of which firms in the market perform the activities, or on the activities utilizing a specific resource irrespective of which firms utilize the resource.

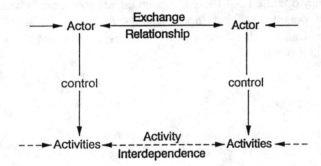

FIGURE 1.1: Relation between Exchange Relationships and Activity
             Interdependence

The exchange relationship can be seen as a mode of handling activity interdependence between two actors (Figure 1.1). The stronger the specific activity interdependence between two actors the more they will be inclined to develop an exchange relationship with each other. Potential gains from just-in-time-deliveries, joint product development, and quality assurance arrangements can be expected to lead to development of strong relationships rather than conducting business in arms-length market relations. Inversely, two actors who are engaged in a close relationship will tend to strengthen their specific interdependence in order to raise the joint productivity of their activities. This implies also that two actors, between whom there is initially no specific activity interdependence but who are involved in a relationship with each other due to earlier activities, will have opportunities to raise their effectiveness by adapting their activities to each other.

Correspondingly, business networks is a mode of handling activity interdependences between several business actors. Other modes of handling or governing interdependences in a business field are markets and hierarchies. The network differs from the market — the invisible hand — with regard to the relations between the actors. In a market model the actors have no specific relations to each other. The interdependences are regulated through the market mechanism which transforms the demands and supplies of the different actors into market prices. In contrast, in the business network the actors are linked to each other through exchange relationships and their needs and capabilities are mediated through the interaction taking place in the relationships. If there are productivity gains through joint arrangements within the framework of exchange relationships business networks will replace arms-length market relations.

The industrial network differs from the hierarchy — the visible hand — insofar as the actors are autonomous and handle their interdependences bilaterally rather than via a coordinating unit on a higher level. Whereas a hierarchy is organized and controlled as one unit from the top the business network is organized by each actor's willingness to engage in exchange relationships with some of the other actors in the network. The networks are more loosely coupled than are hierarchies, they can more easily change shape. Any actor in the network can engage in new relationships or break old thereby modifying its structure. Thus business networks can be expected to be more flexible in response to changing conditions in turbulent business fields, such as those where technical change is very rapid.

It can be concluded that business networks will emerge in fields where coordination between specific actors can give strong gains and where conditions are changing rapidly.

The business networks should not be confused with strategic networks, such as franchising networks or subcontracting networks where one central actor contracts a number of franchisees or subcontractors (Thorelli, 1986). Strategic networks are usually built by one actor whereas the business networks emerge over time through interaction between several, autonomous actors. Strategic networks may well be sections of business networks. Typically, they are based on formal contracts between the actors. In business networks, in contrast, formal contracts between the actors are of only secondary importance.

Exchange relationships are basic elements in business networks. They develop over time as a consequence of exchange between two parties. Several aspects of exchange can be distinguished. In the business networks the business aspect is central but most exchange has a communication and a social aspect too. The exchange relationship can be seen as a set of more or less implicit rules governing the exchange in the same way as language is related to communication. The rules are formed, reinforced and modified through exchange at the same time as they constitute the framework of subsequent exchange (cf. Giddens, 1984). Obviously, this implies that the exchange can be more or less regular and that the relationships can be sleeping.

In business networks exchange relationships are connected, that is exchange in one relationship is conditioned by exchange in others (Cook & Emerson, 1984). The connections may be positive or negative. A positive connection means that exchange in one relationship is facilitated or supported by exchange in the other. Typically, relationships along activity chains are positively connected, while a customer's relationships with competing suppliers usually are negatively connected.

The connections between two relationships can operate via the activities. The logic of activity interdependences obviously has implications for the connections between exchange relationships, as the two simple examples in the paragraph above demonstrates. But the connections may also operate via the actors and their views of the network. The connections are to a large extent a matter of the subjective visions and strategies of the actors. Thus one may view two relationships as complementary while another regards them as competitive.

The patterns and character of the connections between the relationships give the business networks structures. Although the business networks consist of lasting exchange relationships their structures are by no means static. They change continually. New relationships are established. Existing relationships develop through interaction between the parties. Sometimes they are broken. Sometimes they become sleeping by not being used. Other networks are linked to the network, which also may become partitioned into separate sub-networks. It can be assumed that the network structures to some extent are conditioned by technical and cultural factors, but they are also enacted, that is they are formed and modified through the interaction between the actors. The network structure is a result of history.

In the business networks the actors have positions in the sense that they are directly and indirectly linked to specific other actors (Mattsson, 1989). Such positions are established and developed over time through investment processes and are assets on which future action can be based (Johanson & Mattsson, 1985, 1990).

The actors in the networks have different power over the activities. The power is based on the network positions (Markovsky *et al.*, 1988) and on the control over critical resources and activities via the relationships with other actors (Pfeffer & Salancik, 1978). In every network there is a power structure in the sense that different actors have different power to act and to influence the action of others. The power in the network may be more or less concentrated to one or a few actors. The power structure has important consequences for the returns of the actors as well as the future development of the network.

In every exchange relationship, sub-network or wider network there is a potential conflict between the actors concerning the distribution of the surplus and the influence on the future development. At the same time the actors in a relationship, sub-network or wider network have a common interest in making that relationship, sub-network or network effective in relation to those of competitors. Although the firms engaged in a network co-operate with each other in some respects they may very well be in strong conflict in others. Consider, for example, a supplier and customer together developing a new logistic system which makes it possible for them to handle deliveries more economically. They may be in conflict about how much each of them shall pay for installing the new system.

A basic feature of business networks is that they have no objective boundaries. Via the actors they extend without limits. An actor in the network may draw suitable boundaries for managerial or analytical purposes. Such boundaries may be drawn on the basis of technology, country, product type or a focal firm. But all such boundaries are, in principle, arbitrary. They are a result of perspectives, intention, interpretations. In fact, an important aspect of strategic creativity is to draw other network boundaries than those of the other actors in the field. In that way new networks may be linked to each other and the actor creating link may change both his own position and those of other actors. This is very often the reason behind formation of strategic alliances. Such strategic action may entail alliances between firms with different, complementary technologies or firms from different countries.

Another feature of business networks is that they are opaque. This is a consequence of the invisibility of relationships. Every businessman knows that business relationships exist and are important. But no one can have a clear view of other relationships than their own, and no one can have but very vague ideas about distant network sections although every one is aware that they exist. Even the two parties in a relationship may have inconsistent perceptions of their relationship. An actor, or observer, who is not engaged in a network cannot but get a very superficial comprehension of it. Learning a network structure requires interaction with actors in the network.

1.3. The Internationalization Process of the Firm

A common and typical issue in the dominant international business tradition is the firm's choice between different modes of international operations. It is generally assumed that this choice is based on carefully collected information about the potential foreign markets and their macroeconomic environment including such factors as geographical, sociocultural, political, economic conditions (Root, 1987). It is also assumed that the choice of entry mode is made simultaneuosly with marketing-mix decisions about price, products, and promotion. Different entry modes to choose between are various types of representatives or subsidiaries – sales or production subsidiaries or some combination – as well as various contractual arrangements (Young et al 1989).

Empirical studies at Uppsala about this choice indicate that both management and research problems should be framed somewhat differently and be more directed to the internationalization process whereby firms gradually commit themselves to and learn about foreign markets and operations (Carlson, 1966, Hörnell & Vahlne, 1973, Johanson & Wiedersheim-Paul, 1975, Forsgren & Johanson, 1975, Johanson & Vahlne, 1977). The basic conclusion of these studies is that a firm's internationalization is a gradual process which in turn is the result of an interplay between two separate, but closely related processes; knowledge development processes and commitment processes. International expansion is inhibited by the lack of knowledge about foreign markets and such knowledge can mainly be acquired gradually through experience from practical operations abroad. New opportunities and new problems in the foreign markets are discovered as a consequence of operations. Thus internationalization is a gradual process where the firm stepwise expands and defends its foreign operations.

The internationalization of the firm is in this approach a growth process. Because of lack of resources and knowledge about foreign environments the firm first develops its home market operations. Because of internal factors, e.g a need to expand the operations in order to be more profitable, or a surplus of resources that must be used, the firm eventually starts to export. But the first export order can also appear as a consequence of initiative from the market side. Companies abroad ask for offers or give orders directly or through middlemen. A combination of internal and external factors may be the most probable explanation.

Irrespective of the reason for the export start it is rather limited in the beginning. It represents a small part of the firm's turnover, is confined to a few countries and does not imply any major investments there. It can rather be seen as a way to explore other markets than the home market. Usually an independent agent represents the firm abroad. The limited financial and personal resources in combination with uncertainty about foreign affairs impel the firm to avoid undue engagement in the international operations.

Some of the markets abroad for the firm's products will eventually grow, and the knowledge thereof will increase through the experience from the exporting activities. In consequence the possibilities of larger engagements in certain markets will increase. At the same time the need to control the export activities in the larger markets will increase and problems or crises with the representatives, for example, will induce the firm to take over the agents and establish sales companies of its own.

Through its own sales subsidiaries the firm becomes acquainted with foreign markets and is in a better position to evaluate the selling possibilities and the need for market investment. The foreign organization is enlarged in order to support the marketing activities by stock-holding, spare part, and repair services and, eventually, production of certain components.

Parallel to a deeper engagement in the first countries the foreign activities are extended to others. The firm has now gained some experience in starting and operating its own sales companies and encounters less hesitation about such arrangements. In some cases subsidiaries are established without taking over the firm's former agent in the country. Sometimes export to new countries is channeled through a firm's own sales companies from the outset if the market seems large enough to carry such an investment.

The increased knowledge about foreign activities, often acquired through the firm's own sales companies, provides the basis for eventually starting production abroad. Sometimes the trigger consists in difficulties in exporting because of increased custom duties or other trade barriers. Sometimes opportunities to acquire foreign customers or competitors, or an effort by the firm to utilize cheaper production factors, leads to establishment of production units abroad. This step can also be linked to the firm's need to locate its production activities as near as possible to customers.

The critical issue in the internationalization pattern described above is the importance of experiential knowledge and the increasing commitments which are connected to the foreign operations. Through deeper and deeper engagement in a certain country, on the one hand, a firm gains better and better knowledge about the business conditions in that market. On the other hand the firm also becomes more and more attached to that market because of enlarged market investments which are difficult to put to an alternative use. Both factors have a profound influence on the firm's behavior and therefore on the internationalization process. The knowledge factor as well as the commitment means that a firm seldom has a full range of modes of international operations from which to choose in every situation, a very common, and usually implicit, assumption in most other analyses of international business. In the latter the main managerial and research questions concern the optimal mode of operation which the international firm must adopt in order to adjust to the foreign environment. In the "Uppsala School" the important questions concentrate more on finding and understanding general patterns in the process of internationalization at the firm level. This view is based on the idea that managing the internationalization process is more a matter of understanding the forces driving and hindering this process than of making specific strategic decisions about the internationalization. This entails questions regarding the gradual accumulation of international market knowledge, and rather than focusing how to exploit firm-specific competitive advantages, it directs attention to the processes of developing the international knowledge base. It also includes issues regarding the investment nature of current activities in international business as those activities are assumed to have long term implications for international competitiveness. Furthermore, instead of starting from the assumption that the focal firm is the only active firm in the market it maintains that there are innumerable potential actors acting in relation to the focal firm. From that assumption follows that important issues concern how to respond to those other actors and how to organize the firm so as to be able to respond appropriately.

This research also points to the fact that the knowledge about international operations is dispersed in the company's organization. It is mainly acquired and developed by middle management, responsible for operations in the various markets. The character of the internationalization process is consequently due in large measure to the less than perfect executive control of international operations (Carlson, 1951, Engwall & Johanson, eds, 1980). The research indicates that issues concerning the interrelations between different parts of international firms, the relative control of those parts, and the power bases on which they act, are important.

1.4. International Business in a Network Context

The network approach has implications for international business analysis. Instead of characterizing a foreign market in terms of language, culture, industry structure, business practice and so forth, and comparing these factors with corresponding characteristics in the home market in order to analyse the national differences, the network approach means scrutiny of the relevant relationships on a firm level.

This has an influence on the type of concepts and research questions raised in international business research. Investments in foreign markets, for instance, entail investments in specific exchange relationships with customers, suppliers, and competitors located in other countries. Accordingly, foreign direct investments are investments in order to establish, defend or develop positions in foreign networks of such relationships. It is therefore interesting to determine whether or not the firm already has a position in such a network. In the former case the foreign direct investment can be interpreted as an attempt to defend or improve the position, in the latter the aim is to establish a new position. Received international business doctrine regards direct investments as means of entering foreign markets in order to exploit a firm-specific asset. With a network approach this aspect is only one in a far wider spectrum of factors underlying the firm's foreign investments. The investments reflect in large measure the firms' need to reach the demands imposed by the local industrial environment, and to handle the relations in the foreign network by monitoring, influencing, or even incorporating other actors. A newcomer must try to establish a position of some sort, which is difficult in the short run by reason of the long-term, stable relationships in the existing networks. This explains the cumulative nature of the internationalization process (Johanson & Mattsson, 1988, Forsgren, 1989). Market entry in this view is not so much a matter of choosing modes of entry but a laborious process of acquiring a rudimentary understanding of the character of the network, of timing of activities regarding different relationships, and of responding to actions by other actors in the network (Hallén & Johanson, 1989).

Another example is the terms psychic and cultural distance denoting factors that inhibit trade between countries in a wide sense. These concepts are used to catch the less than perfect understanding of actors from one country about conditions in other countries. It is assumed that the greater the differences between the countries concerning institutional, social, cultural, legal and other conditions the greater are the difficulties in understanding each other, and this is a factor inhibiting exchange between the countries. The network model implies that it is more relevant to use the concepts on a firm level. There is a psychic distance between two firms from different cultural settings and this distance is affected by their interaction and it affects their interaction with each other. Thus the distance is a relationship-specific factor. The interaction between, for instance, a buyer and a seller leads to the development of an atmosphere in which the psychic distance is one component. This atmosphere is dependent on the character of the specific relationship rather than on general differences on a country level (Vahlne & Wiedersheim-Paul, 1973, Hallén & Wiedersheim-Paul, 1979).

A third example is the approach to a firm's international strategy. This issue is often described as a firm's decision about allocation of resources world-wide in order to meet the need for multinational integration as well as national responsiveness (Doz, 1986, Porter, 1986, Robock & Simmonds, 1989). In a network approach every firm has a role in a system of exchange relationships. This role is not decided once and for all by the firm but develops over time in interaction with other firms and organizations. It is continually changing through the interaction processes, but it is also strictly constrained by the network structure in which interaction takes place. Thus, the strategic position is more or less determined given the historical role in the network. The international strategy of the firm is more a matter of the pattern of interaction with other network actors than of a strategic decision taken by top management (Håkansson & Snehota, 1989).

The network approach implies a move in international business research away from the firm as the unit of analysis to exchange between firms and between firms and other organizations as the main object of study (c.f. Toyne, 1989). It implies, however, also a move away from transactions to more lasting exchange relationships constituting a structure within which international business takes place and evolves.

1.5. The Structure of the Book

Understanding the premises of international business in a network context is the main theme of this book. To gain an insight into the business relationships in international business, the power of the different actors in these relationships, and how one relationship is connected to others are important issues for every firm with international business. They concern firms with established positions in foreign networks as well as firms trying to create a position in such a network. They are also relevant to the comprehension of how different units within the international firm interact to affect the observable corporate behavior — usually called the firm's strategy — as well as how the position of the firm as a whole is affected by the surrounding network — usually called the firm's environment.

The book applies a different view to the concept of managing than is the practice in the management literature. The underlying perspective is that managing in reality is not a unidirectional process controlled by, and ultimately derived from the top level but rather a multidirectional process covering every level and every corner of the organization. It is more a matter of handling and taking care than of control, a process difficult to understand for an outside observer. Nevertheless, understanding what is going on by empirical research rather than prescriptions about what should be going on is the core of our approach.

Common to the chapters in the book is the analysis of various aspects of international business using the network theory introduced in this chapter as a main tool. The chapters are separated into three groups. The first group aims primarily at gaining an understanding of how specific business relationships are handled in an international network context. Various aspects of customer-supplier relationships, technological co-operation between firms, international licensing and relationships between headquarters and subsidiaries in international firms are described and analysed.

The second group is devoted to networks and aims at gaining an understanding of their nature and management in an international setting. This section comprises chapters dealing with the management of infrastructural international networks. It includes also chapters focusing network contexts in which some different types of international business operations are pursued. They discuss how the character of the network context influences the business activities as well as how these activities reinforce and modify the networks. Countertrade, technical consultancy, and project marketing are the activities discussed.

The third section of the book, finally, focuses change processes in international network settings. In particular, chapters discuss how the network provides both driving and hindering forces in the international development of firms and operations.

PART I
Understanding the Nature of International Business Relationships
Mats Forsgren and Jan Johanson

The first part of the book contains chapters mainly trying to understand the basic structure of one specific relationship in an international business setting. In Chapter Two Mats Forsgren and Jan Johanson discuss how the business relationships with external actors on the subsidiary level affect the relationship between the subsidiary and the rest of the international firm, including its headquarter. The background of the analysis is the development of the large international firm into multi-centre systems, with each centre having its own network identity more or less in conflict with the identity defined by the formal organization and the official policy. The authors propose a political perspective when studying the headquarter-subsidiary relationship as a more relevant approach than the hierarchical one, which is normally used.

Another specific relationship is analysed by Barbara Henders and Håkan Håkansson in Chapter Three, viz. the cooperation in technical development between firms but across borders. Empirical data presented in the chapter show that the international dimension is a vital aspect of firms' technological development. As internationalization proceeds the urgency of maintaining up to date awareness of the technological development around the world increases. Cooperation with suppliers and customers in other countries seems to be one important but difficult way of solving the problem.

In Chapter Four Madelene Sandström gives a new dimension to a fundamental problem discussed by many scholars in international business research; the influence of culture. She starts from the well known assumption in international business research that differences in national culture, often called psychic distance, have a tempering effect on business activities between a supplier and a customer and can only be bridged through the personal knowledge of the respective parties. By using the concept of atmosphere in a relationship she argues that the influence of

17

concept of atmosphere in a relationship she argues that the influence of difference in culture is contingent upon the possibility of the two parties of finding common but implicit rules for carrying out their transactions. If such rules exist the difference in culture on a national level need not be an obstacle to trade between firms in different countries. Sandström's analysis gives new insight into the phenomenon of extensive international trade parallel with a multiplicity of cultural differences between trading partners.

A specific relationship is also at issue in Chapter Five in which Carl G Thunman carries out a thorough analysis of the relationship between a licensor and a licensee in international licensing agreements. The author emphasizes the importance of technical, organizational, cognitive and social bonds in addition to the legal and financial bonds usually described in such agreements. By using two illustrative cases he also discusses how and to what extent, these bonds are contingent upon the business relationships between the two parties and other actors.

2

Managing in International Multi-centre Firms
Mats Forsgren and Jan Johanson

2.1. Towards New Structures in International Firms

In international firms business is conducted by a number of business units operating in different countries. In the literature about international business strategy it is generally assumed that these business units are controlled and co-ordinated by the central headquarters (Doz, 1986, Porter, 1986). Moreover that top management formulates an overall strategy for the group and uses a package of managerial means in its realization thereof. Evidently, however, the realization of such strategies is often less than perfect in practice. Numerous examples show how different units in international groups pursue strategies which are inconsistent with those of the whole group. A classical example is the American Express Office in Paris which despite the company's policy developed the travellers' cheques and tourist business that later became the main business of the company (Grossman, 1987). This chapter discusses some structural traits of international firms which bear on their management. In particular it assumes that firms, when doing business, develop lasting relationships with other firms, thus becoming engaged in wider networks of business relationships. The character of these network engagements have important consequences for management in the global firms. Through their different positions in the networks the different business units are forced as well as enabled to influence the wider strategy of the firm.

Firms can be more or less international in the sense that they are more or less engaged in networks in the different countries, and that these engagements are more or less interrelated. Internationalization of the firm means that it develops positions in networks in a growing number of countries, and that these network positions become increasingly interconnected (Johanson & Mattsson, 1988).

The chapter deals with the latest phase in the internationalization process of the firm. In this phase a partly new situation arises, in which the former centre-periphery structure of the international firms changes to a more complex, reciprocal multi-centred structure. In combination with its network engagement this forms the basis for advocating a more political perspective on the international firm, instead of the hierarchical view which is used in most analyses. The chapter ends with some reflections on the management implications of this perspective. The arguments are illustrated by empirical data from a study of Swedish international firms (Forsgren *et al.*, 1990).

2.2. Overseas Centres in Swedish International Companies

The internationalization of Swedish industry, measured as the proportion of operations outside Sweden, is dominated by comparatively few, large, geographically scattered companies.

Electrolux, for instance, has no less than about 500 companies to supervise, the majority of them outside Sweden and the Nordic countries. Alfa Laval, SKF and Swedish Match have more than 100 group companies, and here too the Swedish units are definitely in the minority. The dispersion among countries is high and the average number of employees per company is not always largest in Sweden. SKF, for example, has very large units in several countries outside Sweden, chiefly West Germany, France, Italy and USA. These are often larger than the largest company in Sweden. Electrolux presents a similar picture save that the number of countries with large subsidiaries is somewhat greater. Alfa Laval and Swedish Match also have subsidiaries abroad which are of the same magnitude as, or bigger than the units in Sweden. Ericsson, Sandvik and Atlas Copco too have subsidiaries in many countries but with very large subsidiaries in far fewer countries. Other companies, e.g. Esselte, PLM, the automobile and pulp and paper companies, are less international in the sense that they have their subsidiaries in fewer countries, but share the attribute that the production outside Sweden comprises companies with many employees.

The issue of interdependence between the parent company and the different geographically and operationally dispersed units can be connected with the internationalization process of the firm. The relation between the centre, the headquarters, and the periphery, the foreign subsidiaries, varies with the degree of internationalization and international experience. At the beginning of this process the overseas subsidiaries are the long arms of their parent companies and are heavily dependent thereon with regard to product and know-how. As the operations of the subsidiaries develop and adjust to the needs of the local market they also assume a more independent position vis-à-vis the parent company. This phase frequently coincides with the subsidiaries' obtainment of their own manufacture and product development. In some cases this phase yields to a situation in which the group's international operation consists of several locally rooted subsidiaries, each having a profound influence on the group's strategy in that market but with no, or very limited, influence on other markets.

Still later, as subsidiaries globalize their operations by exploiting standardization and country-specific assets, units arise which have far greater influence over the group's investment behaviour than the previously locally rooted subsidiaries. The periphery becomes a new centre which competes for influence with the group's traditional centre. Such groups are characterized by their incorporation of several gravity centres in the organization, all of which, by virtue of the resources they control, can claim to influence the group's total strategy, not merely their part thereof (cf. the concept of heterarchy in Hedlund, 1986).

To what extent can we see traces of multi-centre structures in Swedish international companies? A partial answer to this question is given by a study of 22 of the most internationalized firms in 1989 (Forsgren et al., 1990). The concept of a centre is difficult to define operationally. It should reflect the centrality and substitutability of a subsidiary in relation to the firm's operational activities as a whole. It contains a size dimension as well as a dimension of operational dependences between different units of the firm. In the study different types of indicators are used in order to reflect the multi-centre character of the investigated firms.

Five indicators are employed in order to find foreign-based centres, four related to production, marketing, purchasing and R&D respectively and one to the formal organization of the firm. A production centre is defined as a foreign subsidiary manufacturing and selling a product to at least five countries besides the local market. These sales must account for at least 25 per cent of the subsidiary's turnover. To be a production centre the subsidiary must also have product development of its own. Correspondingly, a marketing centre and a purchasing centre signifies a foreign subsidiary with full responsibility for marketing and purchasing respectively of the products within a business area comparing at least five countries. If a foreign subsidiary independently carries out R&D aiming at fulfilling the requirements of the group as a whole (or a large part thereof) it qualifies as a research centre.

These four indicators seek to measure different types of centres of gravity overseas within the operational activities of the international firm. In addition, the way the firm builds up its formal organization can also mirror the existence of such centres. The investigated firms have different forms of multidivisional structure which means that there are "quasifirms" within each. Therefore the extent to which the heads of the firm's business areas (sometimes called divisions) are stationed overseas is used as a fifth indicator of the existence of foreign-based centres of gravity and labeled management centre.

In order to reach a satisfying level of validity by explaining the meaning of the centre concept and the different indicators all data were collected via extensive interviews with the firms. (For details of the methodology see Forsgren *et al.*, 1990.)

The result of the investigation can be summarized as follows. In the 22 firms there are altogether 294 overseas centres. Production centres are most common, 205, followed by marketing and management centres, 40 and 31 respectively. Research centres are less common, only 18 among the firms. Purchasing centres were non-existent. The number of centres varies substantially between the firms but is largest among the engineering firms which began their internationalization long before the Second World War. But there are also a few firms which combine a rather high degree of internationalization with no or only a few foreign-based centres.

The relative importance of a multi-centre structure within production, marketing, research and management abroad is further related to the degree of internationalization of the different firms. The relative importance of centres is then defined as the proportion of the firm's foreign activities which are carried out within centres, using employment, turnover or cost as a variable. The degree of internationalization is measured as the percentage of the firm's employees stationed abroad.

The analysis shows some interesting features. First of all there are several centres of gravity overseas in most of the investigated firms. Secondly, there is a rather close correlation between the degree of internationalization and relative importance of a multi-centre structure abroad for all the indicators used. The existence of overseas centres of any significance is much more common among firms with more than half of their employment abroad. Third, management centres and research centres worthy of mention exist only when the degree of internationalization has reached high levels, 60 to 70 per cent. Fourth, some of the 22 firms are highly internationalized with no or very few overseas centres.

On the basis of knowledge of the firms some tentative conclusions can be drawn. An internationalization of a firm's operations in terms of production and selling precedes, and is a prerequisite for the development of overseas centres. It is tempting to say that an internationalization of a "first degree" is followed by an internationalization of a "second degree" in many firms. But this latter internationalization also conforms to a certain pattern. Production and marketing centres are developed before management and research centres. There is reason to assume that when a subsidiary has reached a certain size in production and marketing efforts will be made to organize it into a separate business area or division with the management stationed abroad. The same line of reasoning is also possible concerning the research centres. It is therefore, reasonable to hypothesize that the latter centres are more or less enforced by the existence of the former.

2.3. A Political View of the International Firm in a Network Setting

The figures above indicate a dispersion of the influence within at least some of the most internationalized companies out from the formal headquarters in Sweden to several other centres of gravity, many of them situated overseas. This justifies an analysis of these firms as political systems rather than as hierarchically controlled systems which is the usual case. This is the more valid the more it is realized that each company within the group through business relationships is engaged in business networks of interdependent companies. Such business networks are not designed by any single business unit according to a master plan or a strategic decision.

Any business unit in the network has a network identity, which refers to the views — both inside and outside the unit — on the unit's role and position in relation to other units in the network. The network identity is formed and developed over time through the transactions with other units. The network identity in turn has strong implications for the development of the unit and its relations to other actors.

Any unit in an international firm, be it a subsidiary or a business unit, belongs at the same time to an owner system—which in fact may be several—and to one or more business networks. Furthermore the units may, besides the external network relations, have more or less important internal network relations, i.e. exchange relationships with other units in the same firm and in the same network. Thus, every unit is subject to pressures from both the business network and the owner system. In some situations these are clearly separate; in most cases, however, units have a number of more or less important exchange relationships with other units in the same firm so that it may be difficult to distinguish network from proprietary pressures.

Correspondingly, every international firm consists of a number of units which, besides the proprietary links, are more or less linked to each other through exchange relationships in which various functional interdependences are handled. Thus, in some companies the activities are concentrated to one or a few business networks, so that the functional links between subsidiaries are fairly extensive, e.g. in vertically integrated companies. In others the activities are spread among many different networks, which implies only proprietary links between many companies in the group. Conglomerate groups fall into the latter category (Forsgren, 1989).

The political view of the firm is based on the idea of power as a relational concept derived from social exchange theory, and the assumption that resource dependence between actors is an important basis of power. Many studies of power have indicated the necessity to distinguish between power based on authority and power based on control of critical resources. Authority is power based on a right to control and a concomitant obligation to obey, i.e. authority involves a position-based power to affect organizational decisions directly. Authority flows downward and is unidirectional, i.e. from parent firm and top management to subsidiaries and divisions. Power based on control of critical resources is multidirectional and can flow upwards, downwards or horizontally, i.e. also from subsidiaries to the parent firm (Larsson, 1985).

In the resource-dependence tradition, the power wielded by a subsidiary in the organization is determined by the criticality of the resources it can provide and the extent to which alternatives are available. In this tradition it is also claimed that the great environmentally derived organizational problem consists of the dependence of one organization on others, based on the relevance of the resources to that organization's task and technology (Pfeffer & Salancik, 1978). From this follows that relationships with external actors in the business networks that surround the organization are important sources of power which can be exercised by a subsidiary within the group and towards the parent firm.

2.4. Tensions between the Corporate Group Role and the Network Role

A manufacturing subsidiary abroad belongs to an business network including other companies inside and outside the group in question. The subsidiary's role in this network is shaped and developed in interaction with these companies, rather than by any specific decision at the top of the formal organization. In this interaction process there is no fundamental difference between those which are sister companies and those which are not; the important thing is that they belong to the same industrial network.

The importance of the formal organization, on the other hand, is related to top management's striving for an overall corporate strategy for the international firm. Implementing an overall strategy means that every unit in the firm is assigned a role in relation to its sister units. The subsidiary's strategic role in the formal organization need not be identical with the subsidiary's role in the business network to which it belongs. On the contrary, there is a fundamental difference. Its strategic identity in the network is assumed to be based on business relationships developed over a fairly long period. Its role within the official strategy is based on formal relationships which can be changed fairly quickly (even if these roles can allow for the business relationships). The tension between these two types of role at the subsidiary level can be considerable. The top management, for instance, can assign to the subsidiary a strategic role that is inconsistent with the one it plays in the business network. Sometimes the network develops into something else than prevailed when the subsidiary's strategic role in the organization was formulated.

The cause of this tension may be interpreted differently by the subsidiary and by top management. The latter's role is supposed to be to strive for a common strategy, in which every unit has its own special position within the international firm. The subsidiary's view is likely to be much more influenced by its business relationships, be they sister companies or not. Against top managements' search for coordination in the group we have the subsidiaries' involvement in business activites based on successive and reciprocal adaptations to other units within the network.

This tension may be complicated by the fact that the subsidiary's network also includes what can be called non-business actors (cf. Boddewyn, 1988). Actors within this field are government and local authorities, trade unions, industrial federations and private-interest associations. These actors do not take part directly in the current economic transactions of the business network as do suppliers, customers and competitors. Still, they support or do not support these economic transactions through authoritative permission or other positive or negative non-economic sanctions, e.g. granting or withdrawal of legitimacy. The foreign subsidiary interacts with these actors using a variety of means: economic (such as monetary contributions to political agents) but also truly political (power), social (solidarity) and cultural (status or respect) (Boddewyn, 1988, p. 342).

These interactions may be as important as business relationships with customers and suppliers or the formal relationships with other units and headquarters at home. It takes time and resources to develop them, they have strong elements of mutual knowledge and trust, and they are important assets. They are also connected to the business relationships. In fact, the relationships with those actors can be seen as part of the industrial network in which the firm is operating.

It can generally be assumed that the longer a subsidiary has been operating in a country, the more its behaviour will be influenced by such links. For instance, in case of disinvestment in a foreign subsidiary the tension between its strategic role and country-specific links often emerges clearly. The foreign subsidiary and local authorities or trade unions often appear as allies against group management and the official corporate strategy. Another example can be seen in the conflict beween the official product policy of an international firm aiming at securing high capacity-utilization in domestic production units and the interest of foreign subsidiaries in choosing their own local suppliers. This wish for freedom in the subsidiaries cannot be explained solely by a general desire for autonomy; it probably also stems from the demand of actors in the industrial network and e.g. local authorities and trade unions.

Tensions arise and shift as a result of changes in the business network, including the non-business relationships or in the formal organization. A sales subsidiary may yield to pressure from the network to supply a wider range of products needed by the customers rather than be a pure distribution channel for products of the parent firm. Such a change calls successively for a different role for that subsidiary in the group, involving a broader product-line, local customer service etc. Tension can also arise because product development in business relationships at the subsidiary level does not harmonize with what is going on in the central R&D function at the group level. Evidently, tensions can arise due to shifts in the non-business relationships. Such shifts are more frequently discontinuous than those in the business relationships. Correspondingly, tensions may evolve because of changes in the top management's endeavour to attain a common strategy. These shifts are also more often of a discontinuous character. For example, the top management in many Swedish international firms have tried to implement a global divisional structure. Such a structure is supposed to embrace the sales subsidiaries abroad in the sense that every subsidiary, or part thereof, belongs to a certain division and reports directly to the manager of that division. By so doing, the top management intends to give the division manager global responsibility for its business—most often a group of related products—including the marketing and sales activities in every local market. In other words, it wants to use the divisional structure as a control device throughout the firm (Hedlund & Åman, 1983).

The implementation of such a transformation has been less than perfect in many cases, however. Many subsidiaries have been opposed to the new structure, arguing that the knowledge about the institutional and business conditions of the local network is too critical to be divided up and subordinated to the division manager in Sweden. From the subsidiary point of view this knowledge, irrespective of the type of product to be marketed, is very much located in the subsidiary which must therefore be kept together and treated as a unit within the group with about the same status as the product division. This opposition is also strengthened by the subsidiary's long-standing direct, rather informal contacts with top management.

Basically, this is a conflict between those who emphasize—and more or less control — the market knowledge and those who emphasize knowledge about the product as such and the production process. This conflict is not always settled in favour of the top management's original intentions. In several cases the conflict has led to a sort of compromise; sales subsidiaries are still treated as independent profit centres reporting to the top management while the division managers have global responsibility for the product with their own sales personnel located in the subsidiary but without full authority in relation to that same personnel. This solution can be interpreted not only as a result of the subsidiary manager's refusal to abdicate from its position but also that it has some possibility to back up its words by power.

This example also illustrates that politics within an organization pertain in large measure to what criteria to use in evaluating the organizational behaviour. The subsidiaries want to be evaluated as independent profit centres with certain discretionary power over sourcing and pricing of products. With respect to the local authorities and the local business environment the subsidiary often seeks to be regarded as an independent company with its own profit and loss statement, not managed from Sweden. Such an evaluation implicitly emphasizes the importance of local market knowledge as a critical resource and therefore strengthens the subsidiary's base for influence within the group.

From the discussion above we may infer that a political perspective on the global firm means that the group is seen as a market for different interests rather than as a hierarchically controlled entity. The top management must work hard to justify the claim to speak of one rather than several firms, while different subsidiaries pursue issues which are formulated in relation to the industrial network including the non-business environment in which they operate. There is no *a priori* evidence that the latter interests are consistent with the strategy formulated on the group level. Further, there is no definite limit for how far a certain special interest can be promoted in relation to the goals formulated by the top management. Or, in other words, a subsidiary can influence the group's investment behaviour as much as the top management.

2.5. Managing in Multi-Centre Firms

The early Uppsala School described the internationalization process as a gradual development of the firms' international operations, keeping pace with a deeper knowledge about the international markets. By using a simple analogy we can say that the process described resembles a ring on the water which is successively spread out into new but more peripheral rings (Johanson & Wiedersheim-Paul, 1975; Johanson & Vahlne, 1977).

This chapter has tried to add some new aspects to this model of internationalization. Today some of the Swedish firms are so highly international and operationally and geographically spread that there are reasons to talk about several rings and several peripheries within one and the same company. The investment behaviour is therefore only partly rooted in the firm's traditional activities in Sweden. They are more and more motivated and shaped by the other centres than the ultimate, domestic one. Therefore, much of the behaviour we still call internationalization does not start from Sweden or pass any border. The foreign subsidiaries have their own strategic motives for investment and organizational change. The more a subsidiary is rooted within a specific country and a specific network the more its view on what should be the corporate strategy is influenced by factors such as local business conditions, relations to suppliers, customers and local authorities and the industrial policy in the host country.

From this follows that decisions about, and implementation of strategy are not developed and controlled solely by the top management. Instead, the organizational behaviour which is called strategic evolves from actions by different actors in the political arena within the firm. The top management is certainly a very important actor in this arena, but not the only one.

The gradual change of the firms from centre-periphery systems to multi-centre systems compels the top management to reduce the Swedish bias of their mental map. The principal force behind this change is the top management's need to maintain its legitimacy within the organization as much as possible. But the way the top management strives for the legitimacy also changes. As long as the foreign subsidiaries' main role was to market the parent firm's products or produce locally what was developed in the parent firm, the parent firm controlled the resources on which the internationalization process was based. In other words, the top management's legitimacy was grounded not only on the formal position but also on control of critical resources. In the new situation, with large, fully-fledged operational units spread over several countries, the top management does not occupy the same type of strategic seat as the former parent company manager. It must therefore rely on other means of acquiring legitimacy.

One such means is symbolic behaviour. Symbolic behaviour emphasizes the importance of language and symbols in organizations and is based on the premise that reality is in large measure socially constructed (Pfeffer, 1981b). While the political perspective emphasizes that investment behaviour is conditioned by tangible resource interdependences, the idea here is that an important management task is to provide explanation, rationalization and legitimization of this behaviour. It is a symbolic, attention-focusing process aimed at creating meaning by way of language, ceremonies and symbols. In a situation where the different subsidiaries or divisions in the international firm to a large extent control the operational activities, the top manager can use what can be called spectacular decisions as one way of showing the organization that it still has the initiative and calls the tune. For instance, an announcement of a merger between two companies, or an acquisition of a large, well known foreign company can serve this purpose. The announcement of such a decision and the surprise it provokes within the organization is as important as the operational outcome of the merger or acquisition as such. The top management has demonstrated its capability and business acumen while the economic consequences of the decision depend on many factors in a complicated context which nobody can accurately foresee.

Of course, a place at the top of the hierarchy of a larger and larger international firm should *ceteris paribus* give more power. But this power works in relation to the non-business environment in general rather than the operations within the different centres of the firm. A reasonable hypothesis is that compared with the earlier stages of internationalization the group management has less influence over the actual business in different parts of the organization but at the same time holds a stronger position in a societal context, as spokesmen for large and powerful organizations. Perhaps it is here fitting to speak of a "politicizing" of the role of top management in large Swedish international firms.

The role of the subsidiary management has also changed. From a former position as bearer of the parent firm's business idea it has become stake-holder within the group, using its resources in terms of relationships with business as well as non-business actors and the corresponding network identity to influence the overall investment behaviour in the global firm.

3

International Co-operative Relationships in Technological Development
Håkan Håkansson and Barbara Henders

3.1. Technological Development in Industrial Companies

Technological development as a key issue for industrial companies is an obvious and unquestioned reality today. Numerous books and articles deal with the subject, and it is the focus of seminars and public debate – and with increasing frequency. In these treatments technological development is normally portrayed either as a menace to the individual company or as its salvation. If the company does not keep up with its competitors in technological development it faces annihilation, if it surpasses them the future is secured. Thus, technology development is seen as the keystone of competitive edge and the need for technological development is accordingly stressed whenever the competitive power of a company is discussed (Porter, 1983).

The underlying reason for this interest in technological development is its effect not only on the company's way of functioning in a technical sense, but, at least as important, on the company's relations to customers and suppliers, and thereby also to competitors.

The increased need for technological development, or better yet the increased need to organize more carefully for or to manage technological development, is one characteristic feature of this problem area. Its importance should act as a bugle call, urging companies into the battle of technical development. But, it is in the nature of things that, at the same time as the importance of handling this area increases so do the difficulties in so doing.

The first of these difficulties is the rising cost of technological development. Product development costs, for instance, have increased in many areas. As a well-publicized example, the development of a new automobile has become an enormous investment. The same applies to other, possibly less glamorous, products, systems and even components. Costs have risen not only for the development of new products, but also for production systems. Increased automation and specialization has added to the cost of both building new production facilities and reconstructing old ones.

A second complication in the handling of technological development is the general growth of complexity, much of which ensues from the combination of technologies. New products are commonly based on several technologies whether, in design (e.g. the computer-assisted design), production (e.g. use of robotics with mechanical engineering in car manufacturing or the combination of chemical, thermal and mechanical technologies in the production of chemi-thermo-mechanical pulp), or the function of the product itself (imagine the effect of the application of computer technology to the mechanics of your car as compared with ten years ago). This general tendency means that the individual company must follow the development in several research areas and at the same time attempt to bring these areas together.

A third factor causing difficulty is the increased integration of activities between companies due to trends such as just-in-time systems, stockless buying, computer links, etc. In consequence, development must be more co-ordinated as changes in the buying or selling company are now more likely to affect its counterpart. Each company has thereby become less free to develop in its own way.

The fourth factor making the development issue more complicated today is greater internationalization. In general internationalization increases the urgency of maintaining up-to-date awareness of technological developments around the world. One of the reasons is that when companies enter the international arena they compete with others (in any one country both domestic producers and other foreign suppliers) which have access to, and utilize a variety of technologies. In these competitive situations, added pressure on technological development can ensue as the competitive edge. This can be particularly problematic for small, perhaps more national-market based companies which can find themselves in competition with multinationals which have greater resources available for technological development.

A second complication from internationalization can be differing customer demand. A very concrete example thereof is in the area of standards, which can differ between national markets. This can involve the need for development of technologies which are flexible enough to be applied to different standards. This can mean developing a basic focal product so flexible as to be adjusted to differing national standards, or one with a basic design compatible with related products of differing standards. The situation can be even more complex when standards are the same, or are being harmonized for several markets or internationally. For example, harmonization of standards in the EC has had a dramatic effect on technological development in certain product areas, such as the mobile telephone, since individual companies have had to alter the course of their product development to meet the new standard. And it is not only a matter of adapting to the standard; involvement in the formation of standards, in the EC or in international committees can be vital for the firm.

This characterization of the technological development issue — the growing need for technological development in combination with increased difficulties in several dimensions — has compelled the individual company to try to find new solutions thereof. For example, the higher cost involved has not only forced companies to make absolutely sure that they are doing the right thing, but also to shift some of the risk and financial burden over to other organizations. The use of co-operative relationships with various counterparts illustrated in these circumstances has been found to be a major mechanism employed to deal with several dimensions of the problem. By sharing development work, the costs to the individual company can be reduced. Furthermore, it will be easier to cover a broader scope of technology, and the need for closer co-ordination in order to handle the integration can more easily be met. Concerning the international issues, the sharing of development work can accumulate a sufficient level of research resources to compete against some of the larger competitors. It can also enhance internationally current awareness of developments.

The use of co-operative relationships in technological development — and especially their international consequences in an internationalizing world — seems to be of such interest, not to say vital importance, to a company that the issue deserves some attention in business research.

The issue will be treated here, with the focus on those co-operative relationships which span international boundaries. While nationally contained relationships also impinge on a company's international competitiveness, those with an international perspective are of special interest, being both inspired by, and perhaps chiefly focused on solving problems encountered in, international involvement.

The impact of technological co-operative relationships on competitiveness has already been elucidated. The following sections describe the possibilities of increased competitiveness conferred international co-operative relationships, and the requirements for building such relationships. While the empirical emphasis is on the involvement of Swedish companies, the findings can be extended to other firms.

3.2. Co-operative Relationships

This section concentrates on some basic issues regarding co-operative relationships. It begins with a discussion of how co-operative relationships develop, then reports on some aspects of the existence of relationships. These aspects include the frequency of co-operative relationships, the counterparts involved in such relationships and, finally, some elements of co-operative relationships which have been found useful in description.

3.2.1. A Learning and Social Exchange Process

Co-operative relationships could be superficially defined as those relationships where the counterparts have realized, and begun to exploit the benefits of working together—the relationship is characterized by co-operative rather than contentious interaction.

Co-operative relationships are built up over time between two parties through interaction characterized by at least a minimum degree of learning and social exchange. Learning brings the parties closer together in multiple ways, helps avoid conflict, and creates opportunities for co-operation. Social exchange is especially important as it implies that a certain degree of mutuality based on trust will develop. This means that over time the two parties realize that they are not just counterparts, but at least partial partners in any of many areas—including technological development.

Both learning and social exchange in interactions can either directly lead to, or support, technological development.

The learning process has several outcomes directly related to technological development (Sahal, 1980). As a direct result of learning about each other, their operations, their technologies, etc., two counterparts mutually adjust in many different technical dimensions. These adaptations increase the efficiency in day-to-day operations of both companies and are normally an important (although not glamorous) share of the total development work. Learning in relationships also has a special interactive character which can result in innovation. Each of the two counterparts is faced with the other's different body of knowledge (technologies or applications) and forced to resolve the discrepancies between them in order to work together. The result —innovation. A final effect of the learning process again pertains to the interface between the two counterparts, but the opposite mechanism. Rather than allowing them to work together, the interface can also enable a better optimal differentiation or specialization of the two parties.

So, the process of learning about the other partner in a relationship can directly result in technological development in the forms of technical adaptation, innovation, and specialization. These can happen indirectly. Through the learning process, each side can successively approach the counterpart's other relationships. This means that learning and its effects occur not only in regard to the counterpart, but also to his friends (and enemies). It is particularly interesting that the specialization mentioned above can be extended to a whole network of companies.

Social exchange also has major implications for technological development, although perhaps more supportively than directly. Social exchange cultivates trust and subsequently the possibility of handling complicated transactions between different units. Whenever technological development is included in a transaction between two companies it increases (often drastically) the complexity of the transaction. Formal agreements can never fully cover all aspects of the proposed relationship, and the parties thus need to have a certain level of trust in each other's abilities and ambitions to carry out the required tasks. The social exchange process is therefore important in constructing a foundation for co-operative relationships.

Secondly, social exchange affects the possibility of mobilizing the other party in favor of or against a specific development phenomenon. Social exchange includes the giving of gifts and countergifts. During this process the firms accumulate favors, markers of gifts they have given to the other firm in the past (see Belshaw 1965). These markers can be recalled in different types of decision-making situations. For example in decision-making situations involving technological development, if the focal firm holds a marker for gifts given in the past the counterpart is more inclined to see the problem from the former's point of view, and, as a countergift, is easier to mobilize as a power for or against a new technical solution.

3.2.2. More Common Than Not

Empirical studies of European companies have shown that the majority of industrial companies are involved in a certain number of co-operative relationships, and that these are essential for the successful functioning of the firms. The proportion of these that includes technical co-operation appears to be high, but no comprehensive picture has yet been drawn. However, in a study of technological development in 123 Swedish companies (The 1-2-3 Study), Håkansson (1989) presents a strong case for the commonness of co-operative relationships in technological development. Data were collected regarding both the companies' total development activities and the proportion executed together with external counterparts. Each of the companies was found to have an average of about 10 close co-operative relationships. The proportion of development executed in conjunction with external parties was about 50% of the total development effort.

However, the use of co-operative partners in technological development showed a very high variation, with some companies showing no and others extensive utilization of co-operative relationships. Different sub-groups were identified from among the companies. These included those which were very isolated, and others having focused interaction (i.e., having co-operative relationships with only one type of counterpart). Yet others had broad, or even very broad, co-operation profiles.

Despite the variation in both awareness and real utilization of co-operative relationships, it can still be concluded that these relationships play a major role in technological development today. Further, the indication is that the significance of this role is increasing.

3.2.3. Counterparts in Technological Development

Obviously several types of counterparts may be of interest to a producing company in the pursuit of technological development. Two of these should both be of special interest for the focus company: suppliers and customers. In the 1-2-3 Study (Håkansson, 1989), customers were found to account for 45 per cent of the important technological development relationships and suppliers for 32 per cent. All other types of counterparts therefore answered for only a quarter (24 per cent). As there were no signs of any systematic difference in the significance of relationships to different counterpart types, the above figures indicate that without doubt customers and suppliers are the most important types of partner.

One category of counterpart which might have been thought especially interesting for technical development comprises universities and other general/independent/non-commercial knowledge-based institutions. In the study mentioned above, 496 important co-operative relationships were analysed in detail. Of these only 16, less that 4 per cent were to research institutes of any kind. In effect, this type of counterpart is seldom used by industry. It is the customer and supplier relationships which are important.

3.2.4. Characteristics of Co-operative Relationships

A general picture of co-operative relationships has been developed through earlier studies. These included analyses of many aspects and features of relationships. Of these, three dimensions have been found to be especially useful as descriptive variables which summarize the "flavor" of relationships— age, degree of formalization and the breadth of the relationship in terms of number of contacts.

The age of relationships is important in that it takes time for relationships to develop. Once developed, time plays a role in that the relationships tend to be permanent. In The 1-2-3 Study cited above, co-operative relationships, on average, were about 12 years old (13 years for relationships with customers and suppliers, and eight years for relationships to others). Similar figures were found in the IMP-project (Hallén, 1986).

Secondly, good relationships do not require, or entail, a high degree of formalization.Very few co-operative relationships are formalized through contracts to any great extent. When contracts are involved, they do not seem to be closely related to protection of company interests, but rather a mechanism for making the relationship more visible (Håkansson & Johanson, 1988). In The 1-2-3 Study, where about 20-30 per cent of the co-operative relationships were formalized in some long-term agreement, the formal agreements were rarely concerned with the technical content of the relationship, but rather commercial aspects such as volume and price.

Thirdly, co-operative relationships normally concern several persons with a variety of functions in the organization. The number of individuals can vary from 2-3 up to hundreds. Both technical and commercial personnel, from a range of hierarchical levels, can be involved. However, while top management might play important roles, the key persons in these relationships are generally from much lower levels.

3.2.5. A Final Word

The main conclusion regarding the development of co-operative relationships is that they evolve organically (Håkansson, 1989, p. 126). The development of the relationship is not planned – it happens. A combination of actors and assets are brought together to perform a task; the combination itself, the activities involved and the assets generated in performing that task, create a group which is suitable for or stimulates its utilization for other tasks. And so it continues. There may be some wishful thinking in the first task, and there may be some extrapolation to possibilities for work together in the future, but the development of the relationship cannot be planned as it arises spontaneously from the entirety of activities of the network.

3.3. International Technological Development Relationships

The first section discussed the increased need to manage technological development as well as the difficulties in so doing. One of these difficulties was increased internationalization. The second section examined the benefits of co-operative relationships for the management of technological development. This third section goes on to suggest that the internationalization of technological development relationships can be beneficial in dealing with not only the difficulties presented by the internationalization of trade, but with others as well.

It is probable that international relationships can equally effectively resolve the general problems of the increasing cost of technological development or the need to handle a broad range of technologies. It could also be assumed that for reasons of increased integration between parties, technological development cooperation should be as important in international as in domestic relationships. And perhaps there are real advantages to international co-operation in keeping up-to-date with technology. On the other hand both social exchange and learning, which reinforce relationships, could be more difficult or costly in international than in domestic relationships.

Working with the information available from the international technological development relationships found in The 1-2-3 Study, the following section will deal with this specific type of co-operative relationship. The questions addressed are how common are international co-operative relationships in technological development, what are the characteristics of these relationships, and how do these relationships differ from those confined to the domestic arena.

3.3.1. Fairly Common

The 1-2-3 Study shows that not a little use is made of the more direct type of international co-operative relationships in technological development. This study involved only small to medium-sized Swedish firms, which might be expected to be less likely to engage in this type of relationship than larger firms with greater resources to invest or perhaps more assets to attract counterparts. Notwithstanding many relationships were found; more firms engaged in international co-operative relationships than did not (60 per cent), and the 74 which did together had a total of over 300 international relationships. Among the subgroup of the most important relationships 22 per cent were international.

TABLE 3.1:Location of Focal Firms' Most Important Technological Development Relationships with Suppliers, Customers and Horizontal Units; Number of Relationships and Percentage of Total for Location.

Counterpart	Location			
	Domestic		International	
	No.	%	No.	%
Supplier	106	34	38	34
Customer	110	35	29	33
Horizontal	97	31	20	23
Total	313	100	87	100

Source: Håkansson (1989)

3.3.2. One European Supplier – Most Likely Counterpart

Almost all technological development counterparts outside of Sweden are located in Europe and North America (Table 3.2). Europe, except the Nordic countries, is the most common location, with more than twice the number of counterparts there as found in the Nordic Countries or North America. The incidences found outside of these three areas account for less than one percent of the total technological development relationships.

TABLE 3.2: Percentage (%) of Technological Development
Relationships Located in Different Geographical Areas.

	Sweden	Nordic Countries	Rest of Europe	North America	Other
Supplier Relationships					
Most important relationships	75	9	13	2	1
All relationships	78	6	12	4	
Purchasing volume	80	6	11	3	
Customer Relationships					
Most important	89	3	11	3	-
All relationships	82	4	11	3	
Sales volume	68	16	11	5	
Horizontal unit relationships					
Most important	89	1	7	3	-
All relationships	87	2	6	5	

Source: Håkansson (1989)

The most common case (for supplier and customer relationships at least) is for individual companies to have a single relationship in any one of the areas outside of Sweden (Table 3.3). This differs from the domestic situation; while about 50 per cent of the companies have two or more relationships in Sweden only only 2-10 per cent have two or more in the other Nordic Countries, and 11-18 per cent in the rest of Europe. Outside of Sweden the number of relationships even seems to be somewhat more limited with customers than with suppliers.

TABLE 3.3: Number of Relationships for Individual Companies in Given Geographic Locations. Percentage.

| | Supplier Relationships | | | | Customer Relationships | | |
	Sweden	Nordic	Europe	Rest of World	Sweden	Nordic	Rest of Europe
Number of Relationships							
0-1	48,1	90,2	82,0	95,0	51,5	98,0	89,0
2-	51,9	9,8	18,0	5,0	48,5	2,0	11,0

Not only do individual companies tend to have a larger number of relationships in Europe than in other international locations, there are more companies with relationships.

TABLE 3.4: Number of Companies Having International Co-operative Relationships.

Counterpart	Nordic	Rest of Europe	World
Suppliers	30	35	22
Customers	10	17	NA

Suppliers were found to be the most common type of counterpart for international co-operative relationships (Table 3.4). Not only do they constitute almost half of the total of international relationships, international relationships are proportionately more common in the technological development relationships with suppliers than with the other two counterpart types. The second most common group are customers, followed lastly by horizontal relationships.

The proportionately greater importance of supplier relationships in international relationships has interesting implications, especially when considered with respect to the correspondence between location of relationships and trade. The use of suppliers for technological development corresponds almost directly with the source of purchases. This implies that the technological development element of buyer/seller industrial relationships is equally important in international relationships as in domestic relationships. This further supports the idea that industrial relationships *demand* co-operative technological development.

Why then is this same correspondence not found in the customer relationships? These include a much higher level of co-operative relationships than sales volume in the domestic market, while the level of relationships in the Nordic countries is correspondingly less, with Europe and other locations being proportional.

The pattern might therefore indicate that co-operation with domestic customers has the same benefits as if with Nordic customers, and is applicable to those customers—but cheaper and easier to handle. This again suggests that technological development relationships with domestic counterparts are more easily handled than international, but that more distant markets have sufficiently specific technological demands or concessions to make this exchange necessary or advantageous. This argument is supported by the fact that if we consider technological development with horizontal units, which are perhaps more directly connected to the technological advantages of exchange with a partner than to other considerations, the same pattern is found as for customers. Another possible conclusion, or influencing factor, is that within the Nordic area many of the international co-operative relationships in technological development are more indirect.

Other than the aspects mentioned above, there is little sign of international co-operative relationships being developed in regions for the sole purpose of acquiring technological information unique to that area. As seen in Table 3.2, the proportion of most important relationships in any given geographic area is equal to the proportion of relationships in that area. This could be interpreted as signifying that no one area is the "source" of technological development, as would have been indicated by an over-concentration of important co-operative relationships in a single area. (This "source" idea might be more likely regarding basic research than technological development.)

Independent of the importance of the area as a source of information, firms must nevertheless be more reliant on single relationships in non-domestic geographic areas for access to information specific to that area due to the smaller number of relationships.

3.3.3. An Aside

It can be pointed out *en passant* that there are several ways for technological development co-operation to be international. The type mentioned above is the more obvious or direct form of international exchange where the organizations are located on different sides of a border which the exchange between them must therefore cross. In a more indirect form at least one of the organizations is located on both sides of the border. The information between the firms is exchanged within the border, and flows across it (the international part) within an organization.

A recent study (IVA, 1989) indicated the importance of these indirect international relationships for large Swedish firms. These firms were found to have 23 per cent of their R&D costs outside of Sweden in installations acquired with foreign companies, or set up in green-field facilities. Political factors and market proximity proved to be the main reasons for the foreign R&D units, but 10 per cent of the activities were associated with the exploitation of foreign R&D resources. Obviously, these foreign R&D facilities can perform the same functions as international co-operative relationships. These findings support the idea of the difficulty in exchange over borders, as well as the demand for information from different areas.

3.4. Implications of International Co-operation in Technological Development

The occurrences and types of international co-operation in technological development presented in this work signify that the international dimension is a vital aspect of firms' technological development. More interesting and specific, however, are the implications of the discrepancy between the use of suppliers and customers in these activities.

The proportional use of international suppliers suggests that by buying abroad a firm can gain access to technological development co-operation with little, if any, increased effort as compared to the use of domestic suppliers. It is the suppliers who must expend the additional energy required to work across borders. This means that foreign suppliers should not only be considered as potential suppliers in those cases where there are no domestic alternatives; buying internationally can be a cost-effective approach to gaining technological information from other areas.

On the other hand, firms selling abroad are confronted with the disadvantage of having to engage in technological development activities with customers at additional cost as compared with activities in the domestic market. This demand can be diminished somewhat by selling standardized products to similar markets; the technological development requirements are then smaller and/or uniform. Commitment to sales of custom-made products, or sales to diverse customers, would seem to be beneficial only if the customer base is large enough, or if there are other, compensating advantages inherent in that market.

A firm can also handle the technological development requirements in foreign markets with its own R&D facilities there. Exchange would be facilitated, but this is probably not a viable alternative for small or medium-sized companies with limited resources. So, while international relationships require more effort than domestic, they are the least resource-demanding alternative which accomplishes the required tasks.

A main point which has been ignored, but supports the discussion above, is that while international co-operation is important for technological development, relationships with domestic firms still predominate.

The Culture Influence on International Business Relationships
Madelene Sandström

4.1. Culture in International Business

Culture is often considered to be a factor causing difficulties in international business. The business research about negotiations, the managing of subsidiaries abroad, the relationship between headquarters and the foreign subsidiary, the establishment in a new national market, the transfer of technology and training of personnel, international marketing, mass communication, public relations, etc. all identify problems which are called cultural. However, the business relationships between companies in different countries which persist despite identified cultural differences are legion. Culture is then used as a concept including language, traditions, religions, political ideology, etc.

In Swedish research difficulties in international business caused by what is designated as culture have been summarized under such headings as cultural distance (Carlson, 1966) and psychic distance (Johanson & Wiedersheim-Paul, 1975; Hallén & Wiedersheim-Paul, 1982). Measurements of psychic distance have been used to rank countries on the basis of factors preventing or disturbing the transfer of information between the company and its market.

On the whole, the literature on business problems due to what the authors define as culture focuses on the differences in the cultural environment. It is often claimed that difficulties in international business are caused by these observable differences. Culture is used as a common explanation as to why the other business party does not find certain proposals or deals attractive, since nationality is the most clearcut characteristic that the companies do not have in common. Cultural characteristics are often in daily business life mentioned in very stereotypical ways, such as "typically dull Swedish" or "all Italians are disloyal" if there are problems in the relationships. To identify culture as a factor connecting all the inhabitants of a country, as this traditional business literature often does, is in itself misleading. Nations are seldom culturally homogeneous and business life contains within its frames several subcultures To single out culture as the main cause of problems in international business is therefore inadequate.

However, some recent international business studies do indicate differences in organizations and management practices between companies in different countries (Hofstede, 1980). In such studies cultures are grouped according to general characteristics which can be found among the set of values, beliefs, structures and attitudes that make up the cultures within the national borders.

These traditional studies, treating culture as a factor jeopardizing the possibilities of the company to work unimpeded all over the world, tend to use culture as a concept on a national ground; thus, to include all the differences which characterise countries. These studies have a "from above" perspective which makes it possible to compare such factors as law, religion, language and politics, structures of the society, business life, organizations, ways of motivating employees, etc. (Terpstra & David, 1985). Due to influence from anthropology and social anthropology culture, in business and management research, is also defined as "mental maps", i.e values and attitudes learned during life (Hofstede, 1980). Analysing organizations and relationships with this perspective opens up possibilities of better understanding what happens in international business.

Business is exchange between people. Persons in their role as employees are bound to each other in exchange relationships and companies have bonds to each other, i.e activity interdependence. Both persons and companies can be considered to be actors in relationships. Persons play the roles of actors within the frames established by the organization to which they belong. Thus, business relationships are in focus for the discussion viz., relationships where the company is the actor although the activities are performed by persons in their professions. In business relationships the exchange takes place at a personal level.

Topics on how, when and why cultural differences exert influence can be understood if a perspective is used which focuses on the actors and the activities, the purpose of the relationship, the costs connected with the establishment of a new relationship and the dependence and the interests of both parties.

The actors adapt their attitudes and views to the exchange relationship as they gradually develop rules which imply a mutual orientation, including mutual trust and interest awareness (Johanson, 1989, p.73)

The exchange between actors does not take place within an emotionally neutral setting. The emotional setting of a relationship is called atmosphere (Williamson, 1975) and is the combination of the feelings of both parties. Atmosphere is the tool needed for the analysis of cultural influence on international business relationships, i.e. culture in the form of values and attitudes.

However, when analysing cultural influence with a relationship perspective a distinction is made between the virtual cultural differences and the feelings of cultural distance. The latter includes the important determinants for the establishment and development of business relationships while the former represents factual conditions such as values based on religion, social structure and business life etc. The consequence of focusing the relationship implies that cultural differences only influence the relationship to the extent of the perception of the actor in an international business relationship, i.e his awareness of a cultural distance in the relationship.

4.2. What are Cultural Differences?

Although it is the feelings of distance which influence the relationship the concept culture must be defined as different levels of the cultural environment affect and/or are present in the interaction.

Culture can be defined on a national, business, organizational, and personal level.

-National level

National culture is perhaps the first to come to mind when culture is mentioned. The values upon which the laws and institutions are based and which constitute the framework for the people are often called the national culture. Culture on the national level includes the language, the social structure, the manifestation of power, the religions and the philosophies which permeate the attitudes of the society. The structure of society also indicates the degree to which business life and government organisations are interconnected and for what purpose.

-Industry level

Industry culture is a subculture in the sense that it involves a set of ideas which are generated by values in the national culture but differ from it in certain respects. What we call industry culture is better seen as values and norms connected with the type of activities performed in the industry, a kind of common agreements among the actors in the industry. Thus, each subculture has its way of handling situations so that some activities are "allowed" in business life but not in social life. Sometimes it is therefore possible to refer to a common language of an industry.

The group of industry cultures in a country have in common some characteristics from what can be called the national culture. The power distance between the hierarchical levels, willingness to take responsibility, business behaviour, the value of agreements, the degree of formalisation, the extent to which business is socially bound, the ownership, etc. are largely determined by the national culture. However, the industry culture may influence this particular industry in several countries.

-Organizational level

The culture of the organization has come to be a concept used to explain the pattern of basic assumptions developed by one group, in this case the organization.

The tolerance and expectations of the exercise of power and prestige within the organization and between higher or lower levels in the hierarchy is a part of the organization culture. The hierarchy also shows the division of responsibility among superiors and subordinates. This culture is often permanent in character, containing stories about "how we solve this kind of problem" etc.

-Personal level

It is on the personal level that the attitudes and values are formed. It is also on the personal level that the culture is determined by the exchange between the interacting parties. Culture on the personal level is both national culture and subcultures. However, when persons interact with others, when they perform a role in a relationship, the values and attitudes representing national culture are present but not always expressed. Differences in the attitudes, values, motives etc. are called cultural distance.

4.3. The Function of Atmosphere in Business Relationships

Atmosphere, the emotional setting in which the interaction takes place, is influenced by culture but not determined by it. Atmosphere in a relationship indicates why it is in the interest of both parties to reduce factors which could damage the relationship. Mutual orientations towards targets, and more or less irretrievable adaptations in the relationship are important explanations.

Thus, in the following discussion a definition of what is meant by the concepts business relationship, atmosphere and rules helps to explain how atmosphere can neutralize the feeling of cultural distance.

4.3.1. Business Relationships

A business relationship must, for its contingency, have a mutual orientation. Due to the mutual orientation two or several companies establish a mutual intention to continue an exchange and thus become bound to each other. The orientation is seldom towards targets in common but all parties consider that the connection and exchange between them will increase their possibility to reach their specific objectives.

The interaction between a supplier and his customer signifies that the interacting parties invest resources in the relationship which are hardly placeable elsewhere (Håkansson,1986). These are investments in the form of technical, commercial, social or financial adaptations. At the same time close interaction often leads to the establishment of bonds between the parties.

A change of supplier or customer often causes considerable resource losses in the form of time, money and effort, when another relationship has to be established or an old one extended. The loss of a relationship also means a loss of important connections, network positions and connected networks.

The existence of this "risk" modifies the impulse to express strong feelings when problems arise in the relationship. In order to control the "risk" rules are established; rules determined by the atmosphere.

4.3.2. Atmosphere

Atmosphere is a concept meant to define an emotional setting (Williamson, 1975). Atmosphere emerges in the relationship as a product of the interaction.

Atmosphere is an important, intangible aspect of a relationship. The atmosphere differs from feelings inasmuch as feelings are the interpretations made by a party to a relationship on the basis of what he knows or assumes about the activities performed by the other party in the interaction. The atmosphere on the other hand is produced by the feelings of both parties. The atmosphere forms an entity where the different feelings of each are adapted to the signals from the other party to form a balance, i.e feelings are unilateral — refer to one party and atmosphere is bilateral — refers to both parties.

Atmosphere may be divided into six dimensions, each representing a status of feelings about the other party and the relationship (Hallén & Sandström, 1988). These are feelings of trust in the other party, commitment to the relationship, cooperativeness, understanding of each other's motive and situation, power balance in the relationship, and feelings of cultural distance, i.e perceptions of the other party as strange.

The atmosphere is always related to exchange on the personal level, i.e among individuals. But when relationships are established between companies the atmosphere is transferred to company level. However when the interaction between companies is described, the atmosphere is discussed on the personal level. It determines the tone for further exchange in the relationship as it dictates which rules will be established by the parties for this specific relationship and the future activity interdependence.

4.3.3. Developing Rules and Routines

Activity interdependence is influenced by rules — rules in the form of unspoken, spoken, unwritten or written agreements, based on established mutual attitudes expressed in procedures in activities connected with the informational, social and product exchange taking place between the parties, concerning how to interpret spoken communication, action and failure to act.

These rules can be related to exchange in the same way as language can be related to communication (Giddens, 1984, pp. 21-22, 24). These rules emerge out of the day-to-day business exchanges. They are specific rules which ensued from the process of exchange in the particular relationship, i.e. an exchange of spoken communication and translation of activities. However, the rules result from previous interaction and environmental conditions. These rules create a frame for future activities, i.e how to interpret and respond to spoken communication, actions and failure to act.

The activities performed by the actors within the relationship as well as the manner in which they are performed are evaluated on the basis of the expectations the parties have on each other, due to the atmosphere of the relationship. No actions are performed "in general" as each relationship has its own characteristics, pattern, ways of communicating, rules and language. This applies to activities within the relationship as well as to relationships with other actors, i.e relationships connected to the one in focus. This importance of the rules is visualized in Figure 4.1.

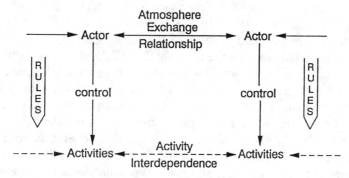

FIGURE 4.1: Relation between Exchange Relationships Activity Interdependence, Atmosphere and Rules. Based on Fig. 1.1.

A smoothly functioning relationship is characterised by the "right" responses to the "right" stimuli. "Right" here is judged with respect to the rules and routines defining the relationship, which both parties accept and try to follow (Gudykunst & Kim,1984). The business activities performed must abide by the rules and thus the atmosphere of the relationship. An example from the pulp industry illustrates the situation. A Swedish pulp company tried to make a good profit at an old customer's expense by increasing the price without warning, this specific way of cheating being rather common in the pulp-network. However, in this industry it was a rule to give six weeks warning of a price rise. When the old customer became very upset and punished the supplier financially the Swedes replied that other suppliers often did the same. The customer answered " we did not expect you to act in that way, we thought you would be better than the other suppliers". This incident was reported by a sales director in the Swedish paper industry. What we saw here was an example of breaking the rules of the relationship, to show a wrong reaction to a right stimulus. However, we can also observe that right in the network can be wrong in the relationship due to its specific atmosphere.

4.3.4. The Connections between Atmosphere, Latitude of Choice and Action Profile

The rules mentioned above shape the preconditions of the relationship. These rules form a latitude of choice, which gives directions about what can or must be done in the relationship. The latitude of choice is defined by the agreements, the remembered history of the relationship, the adaptations, and the thoughts and plans for the future of the relationship. The latitude of choice constitutes a framework for the atmosphere established between interacting actors, as the atmosphere in the relationship on the company level steers the latitude of choice of the actor. Atmosphere on the company level can be compared with rules in as much as it is inherited in the organization, i.e. "We have always had a good co-operation with this customer". The atmosphere of the company then hinders the employee from expressing other feelings, and gives him a notion how to steer the future to some degree. To the interacting persons the atmosphere on the company level is in some respect more of a tradition than a result of the current situation, i.e some kind of latitude of choice. Figure 4.2 shows how atmosphere influences the activities and how the latitude of choice influences the atmosphere and the activities.

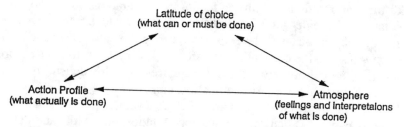

The Action profile refers to the actions performed by the actors. The actors are the persons and groups of persons between whom the interaction takes place. The atmosphere refers to the feelings in the interaction process. The latitude of choice indicates activities and structures.

FIGURE 4.2: The Function of Atmosphere in Business Relationships
(Source: Hallén & Sandström, 1989)

The latitude of choice is also made up of structural conditions such as the access to alternatives. The latitude of choice includes those factors which influence the ability of the interacting parties to intensify the relationship. At the same time the rules of the relationship become a part of the latitude of choice for further interaction. Thus, the company, the connected relationship and the rules of the focal relationships based on the atmosphere form the latitude of choice. The atmosphere influences as it generates the willingness to find possibilities or restrictions to continue the relationship.

The atmosphere and the latitude of choice give the activities their characteristics and meaning and eventually also a motivation as to why they are necessary, who should perform them and how they should be executed.

4.4. The Cultural Influence on Business

Cultural distance remains an obstacle when the parties in a relationship fail to develop common rules to guide the relationship and the activities. This difficulty might be most pronounced when the difference between national cultures is great, but such is not always the case.

When the rules are broken the activity impinges on the atmosphere of the relationship and it changes from its status quo. As atmosphere is often an important factor in the relationship the change in the former influences and modifies the rules of the latter. However, prior to that the culture comes into the relationship. Strong feelings and situations where no rules are established create good possibilities for culture to expand and thus feelings of cultural distance develop. How strong the cultural reaction will be depends also on the cultural characteristics. To break a rule can be more serious in some cultures. But the consequences can also depend on how central the culture has been for the relationship.

The relationship is a whole and appraised as a whole. A Swedish electric equipment company had a long-lasting relationship with an Italian customer. The customer bought two products from the Swedish firm. One year the customer stopped buying one of the products from the supplier but continued to buy the other in the same quantities as before. The person responsible for this business relationship within the supplier company now felt a low trust in the customer and problems arose. The change made her perceive a large degree of cultural distance in her business relationship with the Italian customer although it was of long standing (20 years) with a good continuance. She had been responsible for the Italian market for six years and had previously felt a familiarity with the customer.

It is obvious that the actions are determined by the rules and routines developed in the relationship in which pieces of the cultural values could be found. Activities may express cultural characteristics as long as they do not interfere with the exchange in the relationship and thus generate feelings of cultural distance. Thus, the customer or supplier might be allowed to have some peculiar characteristics in their actions as long as these do not interfere with the exchange. However, if there is a problem in the relationship "a habit" with cultural characteristics performed in activities over the years can be a source of misinterpretations and irritation and finally cause an end to the relationship.

The rules and routines developed through the exchange between those involved are influenced by the culture. However, they allow no scope for characteristics that cannot be shared, understood or ignored.

In general culture in the form of values and attitudes select information from the environment and dictate its translation and interpretation. This information is important and explains other parts and connections, what is logical and what is not. This transformation is created by expectations about how things ought to be done; the same applies to culture at the industry level. However, an atmosphere characterised by understanding and trust will neutralize these prescriptive expectations as new expectations are developed in the rules based on the atmosphere, i.e the feelings of the parties.

Such a situation will probably generate feelings to an extent often culturally determined. Atmospheres can be more or less central for the relationship in different cultures, i.e feelings are more important in some cultures than in others. If the balance of the atmosphere is disturbed and not corrected by the latitude of choice the cultural characteristics and the personalities will determine the activities. There is probably also a cultural factor calculating how much the future of the relationship is worth in such a situation. We once again refer to the case of the pulp industry in which the Spanish customer felt that the need to express his hurt feelings was more important than assuring himself and his company of deliveries in the future.

Established rules neutralize the feelings of cultural distance, neutralize as far as the future of the relationship is given priority before cultural characteristics. It frequently happens that two companies are able to complete a business exchange although they belong to very different cultural traditions and although problems have occurred in the relationship. This is possible because the companies stick to the rules once established and thus are able to continue the relationship.

4.5. Cultural Influence on Types and Complexity of Relationship

A common mistake when discussing cultural differences and their influence on international business consists in mixing culture with different levels of technical development. Persons involved in international business identify cultural problems instead of shortage of energy, suitable input materials to production and trained personnel. Irritation due to this shortage, often influence the relationship. The parties become upset, different targets evolve and no mutual orientation exists in the relationship.

The impressions of cultural differences which the persons involved in business relationships obtain from the exchange with other actors vary depending on the degree of involvement. If a manager of one of the parties seldom takes part in a relationship he might not be aware of the rules and routines developed by the actors who perform the activities and have a more intensive relationship. His actions might then violate expectations inherent in the atmosphere of the relationship.

Relationships may also have different faces. These may pertain to decisions and meetings at high levels in the hierarchy of a company, or handling day-to-day personal contacts by telephone but not in person with well known people in another firm, or contacts with strangers via a computer network.

As contacts intensify, and the areas which need to be considered in the relationship multiply, more aspects of the atmosphere become important. Extensive relationships, which involve several levels of the hierarchy, several departments, and many personnel, including various activities such as co-operation and technical development increase the number of rules and routines on which the parties involved must agree. The complexity limits the possibility of reducing the feelings of cultural distance, e.g due to difficulties in developing mutual orientations.

Difficulties due to culture may not be diminished because of an intensification of the relationship. On the contrary an intensification might increase the fields in which the parties co-operate and are dependent on each other, which also leads to an increase in the sum of grounds for misunderstanding, situations where the two parties simply cannot find a satisfying solution because their targets and/or interests cannot be reached; situations where it is difficult to develop rules for the relationship and where the willingness to continue the relationship is low. The increased interaction will either bring basic differences to the forefront, or reduce them due to greater understanding. An example is the huge mass of unsuccessful joint ventures which develop unsatisfactorily and end with an agreement to separate. However, working together in joint ventures seems to be difficult even for companies from the same country (Laage-Hellman, 1989).

4.6. Conclusion

In this chapter the focus is on business relationships between customers and suppliers where goods are transferred across national borders. A view where culture is recognised as a stereotyped factor does not cover the situation properly, as and exchange processes, decision-making and discussions take place between individuals, not between nations or organizations.

The focus on relationships has enabled understanding of how thousands of actors can perform activities in international relationships over several years although they belong to different cultures. The relationship and the factors constituting a relationship explain why this can be so. The most important factor is the atmosphere of the relationship as it largely determines what rules will be established, rules which will control the activities and the activity interdependence.

The atmosphere is defined as the feelings emerging from the impressions which the actor receives from the activities or lack of activities in the relationship. The relevant activity can either be directed towards the other party concerned or influence its position in the network. In this Chapter a distinction has been made between cultural differences and the cultural distance as perceived by the actors in the relationship. A positive atmosphere and the rules of the relationship protect the actors from feelings of cultural distance.

The possibilities of developing an international business relationship where exchange is not hampered by cultural differences will be entirely dependent on the attitudes of the actors. In order to bridge differences in values and modes of conduct, i.e. the basic cultural differences, both parties must wish to continue the relationship, i.e a mutual orientation. The parties must have the capacity to establish a jointly accepted, unique set of rules, routines, and modes of conduct in both current and extraordinary situations; rules developed by the interacting parties, rules which are often tacit. Joint acceptance of these rules does not necessarily imply that both parties have had equal influence on their design. The relationship may be adjudged to be so valuable by one party that it accepts what the other prescribes.The atmosphere created through interaction between the parties creates the framework for action. The atmosphere can be disturbed by other actors connected to the focal relationship and outside the control of either party. Such actors can be found both within and outside the formal organizational structures of the focal parties.

A central argument in this chapter stresses the impact of culture on business via the actors involved. Studies of relations between people from different cultures indicate that cultural differences can be neutralized by favourable atmospheres which have emerged as a result of interaction between the parties. The atmosphere and the rules repress the feelings of cultural distance.

The culture becomes important to the relationship if the rules are broken or if the situation in the relationship shifts in some other way, e.g changes in the network linked to the relationship through connected relationships. Cultural diffrences blossom as the atmosphere alters from one type to another as this cancels out the rules. However, it is possible that relationships will be broken less by national culture than by violation of industry culture, as industry culture is more of a "rule setter" than national culture when it comes to business relationships.

5

Managing International Licensing Relationships[1]
Carl G. Thunman

5.1. Lasting Relationships in International Licensing

One of the important issues in international business is the choice between different modes of entering different markets (for an overview of such criteria concerning licensing see e.g. Contractor, 1981, and Caves, 1982). Licensing has not been regarded as a principal alternative but as a residual type of activity for most firms, and used mainly to penetrate markets where direct foreign investment is not feasible or attractive, or to gain control of markets through restrictive agreements. The assumption is that the most profitable exploitation of the firm-specific advantage occurs within the multinational firm which generated the advantage in the first place (cf. Buckley & Casson, 1976; Casson, 1979; Caves, 1982 and Rugman *et al.*, 1985). However, interest has shifted in the last few years towards more arms-length approaches to foreign markets with technology transfer as an important ingredient. These "new" internationalization strategies include licensing and other contractual devices for inter-organizational co-operation. It has been pointed out that licensing is a greatly underrated and under-utilized method of foreign market expansion (Zenoff, 1970 and Carstairs & Welch, 1981; Welch 1983 and 1985). Future development may even be directed to make the large multinational firm simply a supplier of technology and other information to essentially national companies which are responsible for the physical production (cf. Robinson, 1980).

[1] International licensing is defined here as a form of external production where the owner of technology or a proprietary right (licensor) agrees to transfer this to an un-affiliated (no ownership connection) firm in another country which is responsible for local production (licensee). In the simplest legal form a licence is the right to make use of, *inter alia,* a trade mark, a patent or know-how for a fee. It is assumed here that licensing involves actual transfer of technology. The author gratefully acknowledges the financial support for this work from Helge Ax:son Johnson's Foundation.

In the licensing literature it is only, en passant, that licensing has been regarded as, e.g. a "continuous and long-lasting relationship" (Caves, 1982, p. 200) or "a continuing working partnership" (Lovell, 1969, p. 7). Some contemporary researchers have, however, recognized licensing in terms of long-term relationships (Wiedersheim-Paul, 1982; McCall & Warrington, 1984; Welch, 1985 and Thunman, 1988). An important concern is then how to manage the establishment and maintenance of an effective licensing relationship.

A great many writers on licensing have addressed the important question of the choice of entry mode and indicated interesting problems in the choice, e.g. the cost associated with handling and policing the patented firm-specific advantage when it is licensed out. In this chapter the focus has shifted from the choice of mode of entry to the problem of managing the relationship between the licensing parties. This also means that the long-term aspects will be emphasized. Costs and revenues will then have a somewhat different meaning and the problems of managing the relationship are dependent not only on how the relationship is established but also on its function in a broader context.

Interactive relations can be identified between firms in industrial markets, especially buyer-seller relationships (cf. Håkansson (ed.), 1982). In fact, the whole industrial system of firms engaged in production, distribution and use of goods and services can be seen as networks of exchange relationships (cf. Johanson & Mattsson, 1985). There is a division of labour in the network whereby the firms' activities are dependent on those of others. The necessary co-ordination in the network is neither via central planning nor the price mechanism but by the interaction between the firms. When the firms (freely) choose to co-operate, market forces come into play, including the influence of price. The parties' characteristics will influence the interaction process between them.

The central focus of this Chapter is on the management of the relationships between the parties in a licensing agreement. Licensing is characterized by interaction between the firms in the market. The interaction proceeds by a single, or a series of, business transactions, by exchange of information, by social exchange, by technical adaptation of products and processes, or by organizational adjustments of responsibilities and routines. When such relationships between the firms are established and developed the integration of the market system is to a great degree between the pure market relations and the pure administrative hierarchies. A transaction between two parties will influence the next transaction between them and create obligations, expectations and interpersonal involvement. The long-term relationship becomes a stable structure involving both parties and constitutes the framework in which transactions and activities are pursued. The successful transfer of technology between parties often requires the establishment of stable, functional relationships. Therefore, transactions in the earlier stages of the relationship must aim at creating long-term bonds within which the exchanges can proceed. The licensing agreement between two parties is, therefore, more than an isolated business deal. It is the process of developing the counterpart with which long-term relationships will be established, sometimes close in nature with an in-group unit.

The process of interaction extends over a number of years, from the first contacts between the parties to the completion of (and beyond) the technology transfer. The relationship between licensor and licensee results in a complex pattern of interaction which has various functions and issues of focus over time. On a short-term basis a number of exchanges take place, e.g. exchange of technical information about the licensed product or process, training activities, payments in various forms etc. The exchanges often require strategic or tactical adaptations in production operations or organization by one or both parties. The adaptations can occur during a single exchange, or throughout the relationship, involving a great many different aspects of exchanges. Long-term relationships are created between the parties and influence the possibility of effecting exchanges. For example, the exchange of know-how not protected by patents is normally only possible after the establishment of a strong legal bond between the parties, a licence contract. Technical adaptations made by the parties create technical bonds between them and interlock them in ways which influence their future exchange. If there is low regularity and frequency of exchanges between licensor and licensee the long-term bonds serve to sustain the relationship. In these situations social exchange is particularly important in maintaining the confidence of the parties in each other.

5.2. Licensing in Business Networks

The relationship discussed so far is a dyad between licensor and licensee but the discussion can also be extended to several interacting parties in a system of relationships. The other parties which influence the licensing interaction process have different functions and in some situations the interaction with them is crucial for the development of the licensing relationship and the licensing parties.

Such other parties are licensee customers, distributors, suppliers, banks, competitors, technical consultants, governments, unions and other organizations. This set of organizations may be situated in the country of one of the parties or in a third country.

Relations to an organization also give bridges to other organizations, e.g. a licensor gains access to the licensee's network of customers. The approach is illustrated in Fig. 5.1. In some situations the licensor may create a network of licensees in a number of markets which all act as a family ("licensing families") to develop the technology (cf. Thomsen, 1974).

The network is specific to an organization, whereas a more general environment is essentially the same for all organizations in a given country and industry. When the parties are situated in countries with major differences in political or cultural environment, the exchanges between them are likely to include difficulties and friction which differ in kind from those between parties in similar environments.

Licensing firms have to take a number of considerations into account when the deal is agreed. Not only will the direct involvement with the licensing partner have to be managed, also other parties and the general environment can have decisive effects on the development of the relationship.

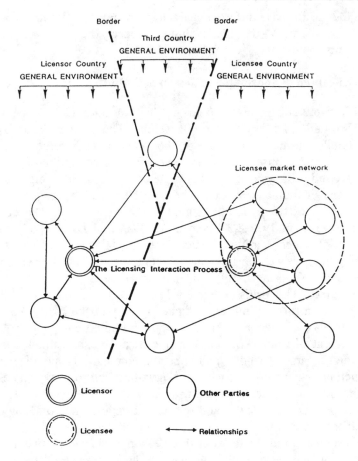

FIGURE 5.1: An Example of a Licensing Network

5.3. Two Cases of International Licensing

In this section two short cases of international licensing will be presented to illustrate the content of the relationship which is developed between the licensing parties. The first case concerns a Swedish-Indian licensing deal and the second a contract between a Swedish licensor and licensee where the latter was responsible for international marketing. The first case includes the total transfer of basic technology for foreign production while the second demonstrates the transfer of a newly innovated technology.

Since the parties have different characteristics and the relationships exhibit particular features the descriptions expose the heterogeneity and complexity in licensing.

5.3.1. Hägglund & Söner AB and Jessop & Co Ltd

The Licensor. Hägglund & Söner AB in Örnsköldsvik is, since 1972, an wholly-owned subsidiary of the ABB Group. The company started in 1899 as a family business and through the years manufactured a variety of products: trucks, buses, airplanes, electrical engines, military equipment, underground rolling stock, military vehicles etc. Hydraulic ship deck cranes have been manufactured since the mid-60s, as a consequence of the development of the hydraulic engine in the early 1960s. The number of employees was in 1972 2,200 and in 1983 2,900. The company has three divisions of which Marine produces cranes. Hägglund's products for the shipping industry were in 1986 manufactured under licence in six countries: India, Japan, Yugoslavia, Bulgaria, Spain and China.

The Licensee. The British company Jessop & Co Ltd was established in 1788 and transformed into an Indian subsidiary of the British company in 1902. In 1941 it was converted into a public limited company. In 1965 the Government of India acquired 50 per cent of the shares and in 1973 the company became a wholly public sector company. It has diversified its production activity from coach and wagon-building to heavy cranes, paper making machinery, aerial ropeway, road rollers and tractors. It has two workshops, one in Calcutta and one in Durgapur. The company employs 10,000 people.

The Development of the Relationship. Jessop & Co was in 1976 the largest crane manufacturer in India, and had produced almost all types of crane, e.g. workshop cranes, dockside cranes, ship-building cranes, for more than 50 years. In September 1976 the Government of India suggested that Jessop undertake the manufacture of ship-deck cranes which had not previously been made in the country. The initiative for this kind of production came originally from a shipyard in Calcutta, under the Defence Ministry, which hoped to start this production themselves. But as Jessop & Co was the traditional crane builders the Government wanted them to assume responsibility. Jessop then approached, and held discussions with, all crane manufacturers in Japan and Germany, and Hägglund from Sweden. This evaluation showed that Hägglund had the best market reputation and additionally was the only manufacturer to have designed and built its own hydraulic equipment (including the motor which is a special type for this application). Jessop was keen on acquiring this hydraulic part of the technology as well as the other more conventional mechanical knowledge. Moreover, Hägglund was able to agree to the terms offered by the Government which the other suppliers rejected. The second on the list was a Japanese firm which neither manufactured the hydraulic part nor agreed to the Government's terms. Consequently Hägglund was chosen to license the technology to Jessop.

Prior to this decision Hägglund had taken part in discussions with the customers, pointing out the advantages of hydraulic over electric cranes. The basic idea in manufacturing ship-deck cranes and the other types of crane is the same in the mechanical aspects. The new aspect in this type was the application of hydraulics which was totally new to Jessop.

Only a few letters were exchanged before the terms of the collaboration agreement were agreed in mid-November. The first draft of the contract was ready in mid-October. The changes were only minor. The Government agreed to the terms prior to the first draft. The licence agreement was signed in December 1976. The whole procedure took a very short time and the contract was formally accepted by the Government in January 1977.

Hägglund sent the drawings and other details of the type of cranes demanded in the first order. The shipyard mentioned above had at that time orders for six ships and wanted the cranes (instead of importing them). But as the ships could not wait until Jessop learned how to manufacture the cranes the first six were imported from Hägglund and assembled in India. Later Jessop obtained the drawings for two more types of crane but manufactured only two types (although the contract covers all types of Hägglund cranes).

No adaptations of drawings were made for Jessop, but it had permission to use Indian material or adjust to Indian standards when required. No change in design was made because the ships carrying the cranes would sail all over the world, and consequently must rely on services and spare parts at Hägglund service stations. Even such components as electric fittings must be inter-changeable.

Hägglund sent a number of engineers to supervise the assembly of the first crane at the end of 1977. From Hägglund ten individuals were involved and came to stay at the Jessop plant for two to four weeks from time to time when technical problems arose. Altogether seven technical officers from Jessop were involved in the new technology. They went for training in Sweden and normally stayed two months each time. This training was continuous from 1977. In some years no one went but in others up to three individuals went to Hägglund for training. The training covered different areas such as assembly, hydraulics and servicing.

Hägglund did not give any guarantee on the products other than that the drawings were correct and that the components they shipped were of the highest quality. Jessop is itself responsible for the quality of the final product.

Production started in mid-1977. Hägglund ran a six-week training course at the Jessop workshop where, beside the Jessop employees, customers took part. Initially there were some problems in the manufacturing process as the hydraulic concept was totally new to Jessop. The problems concerned workshop conditions and workmanship requirements, and particularly the standard of cleanliness required by the hydraulic technology, in terms of dustfree environment which is hard to achieve in a standard engineering workshop. It was also difficult to teach the workers how to clean the tubes and cleanly to assemble the hydraulic parts. Hägglund's supervisors guided this work to show the standards. However, some of the first jobs failed.

The first Indian crane was sold in November 1978 when the agreement came into force. The total sales of these cranes has up to now been six to eight per year depending on how many ships are built in India. They account for a few per cent of Jessop's total sales. In some cases Jessop was not able to deliver in time to the ship-builder and cranes then had to be imported from Hägglund. In 1983 Jessop imported all the hydraulic equipment for the cranes.

When a service engineer from Hägglund comes to Jessop he supervises some installations and also goes round the plant and asks workers if they have questions or need further advice. Hägglund has made no charge for these visits as its engineers were in that part of the world and went to stay for five or six days at Jessop. Also when a tender is to be made, Hägglund representatives come and talk to the customers. Jessop employees have become good friends with the individuals at Hägglund who dealt with them, "so now when anything happens we just pick up the phone and talk to him".

Discussions are in progress (1983) to prolong the contract for another five years to gain access to Hägglund's development in this area but also because Jessop is setting up a separate plant in the next three years to make hydraulic components for a number of products, as well as for the cranes. Jessop has also other agreements with British firms for products which require hydraulic cranes. As a direct outcome of involvement with the Hägglund's hydraulic cranes Jessop have developed a design of a hydraulic roadroller and built their own prototype for the Hanover Show.

5.3.2. Gullspång Elektrokemiska AB and Gränges Engineering

Gullspång Elektrokemiska AB (GEA) is a fairly small smelting works (160 employees). The customers, the large Swedish steelworks, earlier used GEA as a subcontractor. The steelworks supplied scrap-iron from the production of stainless steel and GEA delivered cast steel. When the prices of raw material rose the steelworks kept their scrap-iron themselves and GEA had to buy the raw material elsewhere, mostly from abroad.

During the 1960s GEA developed a new small-scale casting process (The Turn-Cast Method). The new process had some particular advantages and GEA built its own pilot plant. The GEA people envisaged a growing world market for the process, especially in developing countries, but they had no construction capacity of their own and no experience at all in selling casting plants. It was therefore necessary to co-operate with another company which possesed these capabilities. GEA decided that the appropriate partner would be a Swedish company with competence in steel production. Since the steel industry in Sweden is rather small the news of the pilot plant spread rapidly and interested parties appeared.

In 1970 a licence agreement was signed with Gränges Engineering (GE) which was a small engineering division of Gränges Hedlund which in turn was part of the Gränges Group. GE, with worldwide operations, was working in three technical fields; filter, machinery, and casting. As regards casting, GE had long represented the Swiss company Concast, which led the world in the field of continuous casting. The first effort by GE to sell the Turn-Cast plant worldwide was an agreement with Concast, whereby Concast would sell the Turn-Cast plants throughout the world. In nine cases out of ten the Turn-Cast method competed with Concast's own method and sales consequently failed to materialize. The agreement was then revoked and GE assumed responsibility for sales. The present buyers of the Turn-Cast plant are mostly small private iron producers.

When a plant was sold all projections were made in Sweden in accordance with the buyer's specifications. The vital components of the plant were produced in Sweden by firms within the Gränges Group. All other parts were produced locally by agency of the buyer. During construction, a GE supervisor controlled the work.

The licence agreement, which assures GEA a royalty per plant sold, has been sold in *inter alia* Italy, Spain, Turkey, and the Far East. The two companies co-operate closely in continuously developing the process and Gränges have on their own developed some additional patents.

5.4. Bonds in Licensing Relationships

The creation of a licensing relationship results in the two organizations being tied together in various dimensions. These dimensions will here be discussed in terms of seven distinct bonds between the licensing parties. The effects in relation to the broader context, the network, will also be elaborated. The two cases will illustrate the discussion.

5.4.1. Legal Bond

A large amount of interest in the literature has naturally been concentrated on the licensing contract. This is a legally binding agreement between the organizations. Studies have indicated that the important aspects of the contract consist not so much in the legal aspects but in that the negotiating process has given mutually acceptable rules for future exchange (Thunman, 1988). The contract signifies the start of the more substantial technical exchanges between the companies. In the two cases the contract is the natural beginning of mutual action, although some of the following dimensions will be of greater importance. The legal contract is thus only one limited aspect of licensing. The first licence contract is after some years renewed or supplemented with extended contracts.

5.4.2. Technical Bond

One of the principal bonds in international licensing pertains to technical matters. The licensor's technical design will be introduced to the market (including effects on connected markets). In case number one the licensor can add one more shipyard installing its cranes. The licensee will become dependent on the licensor in its capacity as service organization for this particular type of crane at all ports in the world. In the second case GEA uses Gränges' international network to put its technology to work all around the world. Gränges' engineers become more and more involved with this technology and as a consequence also develop auxilliary patents. In the ship-deck cranes case the licensee is dependent on the surrounding technical systems. In case two the licensor is dependent on the licensee's contacts with the final customers. In case one the licensor augments his worldwide production potential with another production site. He thereby increases his capability of production and marketing in other environments. This was not the case for GEA because most experience of the implementation of the technology stayed with Gränges and GEA basically performed the function of a development department. In Hägglunds' case the need for quality control systems further enhanced its technological dominance.

5.4.3. Knowledge Bond

The long-term relationship between the organizations increases their respective knowledge of the other party, its technology and environment. The needs and problems of the one party influence the problem-solving of the other and consequently enlarge the experience. This experience creates a potential for extended business in the future: not only between the partners themselves, but also with other companies because the perception of distance to a market decreases and knowledge of institutional factors increase. In the two cases this increase of knowledge occurs to a varying degree. The licensor acquires knowledge of the licensee's market and other operations. The licensee learns of the licensor's capabilities and how to utilize them. In case two Gränges increased their own capacity by absorbing technology and developing supplementary patents. Such further developed parts of the licensed object can also be transferred back to the licensor (cf. Telesio, 1979). On the long-term scale such exchange of product or process improvements could be profitable for both parties. It seems, however, that more consideration ought to be given to the value of this exchange of information.

5.4.4. Organizational Bond

In licensing between un-affiliated parties the non-existence of organizational bonds would be presumed. However, in order to execute the whole licensing deal the parties have to learn how to communicate and how each other's organization and routines work. The signing of the contract normally opens up flows of information between individuals and departments in the two organizations. Different problems have to be handled by different functions and personnel. In case one the service engineers of Hägglunds visited the licensee without charge as if it had been their own subsidiary. In the second case, GEA had the function of a development department for Gränges regarding this product. The possession of close relationships on many levels with another organization are instrumental in future problem-solving and exchanges in various matters.

5.4.5. Planning Bond

A number of activities have to be performed in order to implement the agreement. These activities are often dependent on the successful execution of a prior activity. For example, in case one, the assembly of the cranes is not possible without an efficient training and supervision programme. The parties must be able to manage systems for carrying through a complex transfer of technology including training on various sites, e.g. regarding the products and the manufacturing process, deliveries of equipment and components with the surrounding know-how, adjustment of blueprints and drawings etc. In case two the ties based on consecutive activities were less because of the level of technology where the applications were made by the licensee.

5.4.6. Financial Bond

When the contract is signed there is a claim for future payments from the licensor. The payment can either take the form of a lump sum or continuous royalties. The payments are requirements for the relationships rather than directly influencing the exchange between the parties. When a satisfactory agreement has been reached regarding the financial aspects it is only in cases of non-payments that this will influence the relationship (the relationship can even continue despite non-payment, cf. Thunman, 1988).

Payments other than those directly related to the licence, e.g. payments for components and equipment (compare the hydralic components and the cranes in case one) are sometimes of great financial significance (cf. Håkansson, 1980). The licensing agreement can, thus, create potential for extended business exchanges and payments (Carstairs & Welch, 1979).

5.4.7. Social Bond

This type of bond is probably the most underestimated in licensing research although a few writers have commented on its importance (Lowe & Crawford, 1984 and Thunman, 1988). This is surprising because all exchanges are mediated between individuals. The social dimension is also frequently mentioned in discussions with corporate staff involved in licensing. In both the cases the social dimensions worked well between individuals in the organizations. When there are cultural distances between the countries of the parties the social bond is particularly important. The people at Jessop could easily telephone the right person at the licensor to solve emerging problems. The involved people of the parties in case two, being in the same country, were spared the need to cope with this distance. The reasoning can be inverted to say that without a personal trust between the major actors in a licensing deal it is not possible to effect the often delicate actions in different stages of licensing. The personal bonds with individuals in the other organization are instrumental in solving emerging and future problems.

5.4.8. The Business Network

When discussing the different bonds it is apparent that the licensing interaction process influences and is influenced by parties and circumstances outside the licensor – licensee relationship. In the Hägglund case the licensor was in direct contact with licensee customers to market the product and to solve technical problems. In the GEA case Gränges was the link to the international markets. Indeed, one of the basic functions of licensing for the licensor is to "subscribe" to another party's closeness to a network.

In case one Hägglund was in direct contact with both the installing company (the licensor) and the users, i.e. ships plying international routes, which demanded local service. This situation is an example of a powerful licensor network in which the focal relationship is just one additional link. The conditions in the licensing deal concerning technical and quality requirements, components used etc, are then set by the requirements of the international shipping business. In most aspects there are no real alternatives for the licensee than to adhere to the intra-trade requirements. In such cases the scope for the parties' discretion is limited and consequently the impact from other actors, such as governments, suppliers, banks etc, is less important.

The situation is different in case two where the licensee controls the international network. The licensee acts as a sales agent situated in the same country as the licensor and all contacts with the end users are mediated through the licensor. This is a consequence of the nature of the content of the licensing deal. The licensor serves merely as supplier of newly developed technology which has to be applied to users' conditions by the licensee. However, a point which has not been discussed here, licensors in this position can have access to another type of network facilitating the technical development work. This is one example of the kind of symbiosis which can prevail within licensing relationships.

The management of a licensing relationship is, thus, determined by a larger national or international framework. In many cases, the focal relationship can be functional only insofar as it assumes the role given within the total network.

PART II
Understanding the Nature of Networks in International Business
Mats Forsgren and Jan Johanson

In Part II understanding the structure of a whole network in an international business setting rather than a specific relationship is the object of study. Chapters Six and Seven discuss the infrastructural character of certain networks in international business. A network can be considered infrastructural insofar as it is created in order to provide a possibility of communication but not to link specific individuals or organizations with regard to prespecific tasks. Such a network has a non-task character but influences the framework within which business is conducted, or offers communication channels where regular paths are not so well trodden. Using empirical data from interviews with board members and executives Lars Hallén in Chapter Six analyses such networks, dividing them into four different types: organization-centered or person-centered, planned or spontaneous. One typical feature of the infrastructural network is its impermanence, another its spontaneity. Hallén points *inter alia* to the contradiction inherent in the last feature; an infrastructural network may be effective simply because it does not seem to be organized for the practical purposes of information gathering, influencing etc. for which it is actually used.

The infrastructural aspects of networks in international business is also an important part of the study of international travelling carried out by Björn Axelsson, Jan Johanson and Johan Sundberg, reported in Chapter Seven. Structured questionnaires were distributed to passengers on sixteen SAS flights in order to discover who travels, whom do they meet abroad, what do they do when they meet, and what gives rise to the meetings. The authors find that the purpose of the trips is usually some kind of action, but an almost equal number of visits are made for information or network cultivation purposes. It is a continuous activity building the foundation for

75

future business where the non-task oriented feature of the network is as important as the task-oriented.

The task-oriented feature of specific network structures is treated in Chapters Eight, Nine and Ten. Doing business in under-developed countries often means managing the countertrade systems used by these countries. It is important to understand how actors, including producers, trading houses and different goverment bodies, in the under-developed country as well as their counterparts in the industrial country are interrelated in a countertrade network. In Chapter Eight Hedvig Brorsson analyses such a network in Indonesia. The case illustrates, *inter alia*, the importance of identifying not only those relationship in a countertrade system which are long lasting and stable but also which actors in the network are in a position to guide the activities in certain directions.

In Chapter Nine D. Deo Sharma analyses the behavior of technical consultancy firms when they internationalize their activities. The business networks to which the firms belong play a major role in this process as they have a strong tendency to reactivate more or less "sleeping" relationships when performing international consultancy. Sharma argues, on the basis of empirical data, that these circumstances imply a promotion of exports from the consultants' home countries because of the domestic character of such firms' networks.

The reactivation of relationships in an business network is also a significant aspect of Amjad Hadjikhani's analysis in Chapter Ten of how package deal projects are organized and executed. He finds that a project manager is greatly concerned in mobilizing relationships of already established networks. By so doing, the cost of the package deal will be reduced compared with a situation when new relationships are formed, even if the latter would involve better technical solutions. New relationships arise only when new technical requirements are needed. Hadjikhani concludes that the normal approach of looking upon a package deal project as a temporary organization, should be modified inasmuch as an underlying network influences the management of the project.

6

Infrastructural Networks in International Business
Lars Hallén

6.1. Infrastructural Networks

"The major function of international personal contacts is not to make business. What is most important is to use them to explain and soothe agitated feelings caused by statements from politicians. There is a need for people who placate negative feelings and assist in opinion formation, i.e. who act as good-will ambassadors and meet with opinion creators. Another important task is to inform about the actual stability and solidity of Swedish firms, as the foreigners, e.g. the Wall Street Journal, cannot read the financial reports from Swedish companies. Some companies employ former ambassadors for international tasks. However, their function is different. They can be used to open doors at a pre-business stage, particularly in developing countries. But neither here is it a matter actually of making business.

The networks get superimposed on each other, and you never know when they may get activated. And you cannot claim that certain contacts or networks are used for certain purposes, as any network can be used for any purpose. You might want to find a person with a specific competence or certain connections, and thus you ask someone whom you might meet or pretend to call for another purpose: 'By the way, do you know anyone who could help us with a certain matter – it is quite secret – do not mention it to anyone else...'. Whether or not this produces results in a specific case is a matter of serendipity, but with many contacts you get many chances." (Chairman, Financial Group)

Contact nets, such as those described in the above quotation from one of the grand old men of the Swedish business world, are associated with high status and a considerable amount of mystique. They are an integral part of the industrial networks, which link business firms to each other, and can be seen as infrastructural to the business networks in about the same sense as telecommunications, railways, road transport systems etc., i.e. they provide underlying preconditions and support for industrial and business activities. For instance, a railway network is not built to link specific individuals or organizations with regard to pre-specified tasks but to provide a possibility of communication. Similarly, the infrastructural contact networks are not designed for specific business deals. Instead, they are used to acquire advance information, to influence the framework within which business is conducted, or to give communication possibilities where regular paths are not so well-trodden.

The influence of factors beyond the direct business issues has been discussed in many contexts, e.g. as non-task factors influencing purchasing (Webster & Wind, 1972) or as non-market relationships, i.e. relationships and environment which do not involve the firm's buying and selling relationships (Boddewyn, 1988). The distinction between task and non-task refers to the degree of orientation towards the actual business deals, i.e. the distinctiveness of the business purpose of the activity, whereas the market/non-market dichotomy indicates whether the counterpart is inside or outside of the business world.

The present paper focuses on non-task relationships. These non-task relationships, which include business actors as well as non-business (non-market) actors, are seen to constitute networks which are infrastructural to the business networks.

On the basis of the task orientation, at least three different levels of the business networks can be defined. Level 1 includes the inter-firm relationships which directly concern the business deals. These include not only links between actual customers and suppliers but also relations to many third parties connected to the business relationships, e.g. other suppliers or customers of the business parties in question, other companies which assist in bringing about business deals (such as banks, law firms, marketing or technical consultants). However, all these contacts are task-oriented. Thus, there is an impact on the business relationships by task-oriented parties which are not directly in contact with the customer and supplier involved in a specific business transaction: important task-oriented relationships might very well be unknown to the central parties, e.g. suppliers or customers further upstream or downstream the manufacturing chain. These indirect relationships as well as those task-oriented relationships which are directly connected to the customer-supplier relationship create a business network structure, which forms a major part of the industrial network of connected interfirm exchange relationships (cf. Johanson & Hallén, 1989).

The relationships with non-business actors such as government and local authorities, trade unions, industrial federations, and private-interest associations may be as important as the business relationships, and represent important assets to the firm. They can be connected to the business relationships, and if so constitute part of the business network. However, they can also form an important part of a secondary structure, with the properties of an infrastructure, which has emerged as an effect of the primary functions. This emergence can either be spontaneous or brought about more or less by plan. Basically, the infrastructure is assumed to be generated by the processes in the primary structure. These infrastructural networks can grow either around the company's business activities (organization-centred infrastructural networks—level 2) or

TABLE 6.1: Business Networks and Infrastructural Networks

NETWORK ACTORS

			Business	Non-Business	Level
TASK ORIEN-TATION	High	Business Networks	business relations	non-market relations	1
		Infra-Structural	organization-centred infrastructural relations		2
	Low		structural relations		3

around specific individuals in their capacity both as professional businessmen and as private persons (person-centred infrastructural networks—level 3). The distinction between the last two levels depends on whether the network connections are basically created by and related to the company of the person disposing of the contacts, or if they are related to him personally: created by him at various stages of his career and retained—although perhaps as dormant contacts—over the years. The infrastructural networks as defined on level 2 can mostly be expected to be transferable to other individuals, whereas this normally would not be the case with regard to those on level 3. The company is the focal actor on level 2; the individual plays the corresponding role on level 3. This is summarized in Table 6.1.

The definition of the business and the infrastructural networks on the basis of the task-orientation of the relationships results in corollaries regarding their strength and function.

The strength of the ties, defined in Granovetter's terms (1973) as the amount of time, the emotional intensity, the intimacy (mutual confidence), and the reciprocal services which characterize the tie, can be assumed to decrease as the degree of task orientation decreases. Thus, a larger number of links — be they bridges or not — can be kept alive if they can be maintained with weak rather than strong interaction. For certain periods, they may even be dormant but still be capable of resuscitation when required.

The function of the ties can also be expected to be related to the network levels. Business relationships can be considered to connect the resources, the activities, and the actors of the different parties (cf. Håkansson (ed.), 1986), whereas the non-market relationships only link the activities and the actors of the parties. In the case of lobbying, for instance, there are obvious actor connections as well as connections between activities, i.e. the activities of the lobbyist influence — or at least are intended to influence — those of the agency which is the object of the lobbyist's efforts. The reverse activity connection is also clear, as there would be no need for the lobbyist to try to influence the agency if the latter's activities would not have any impact. No resources are, however, jointly mobilized to obtain results in production, development, marketing or other business areas.

Finally, infrastructural relationships are defined as only involving connections between actors. The absence of a common task to be performed is seen as the denominator, and this disinterestedness gives these relationships their particular usefulness.

Table 6.2 summarizes the argument concerning the function of relationships on the different network levels.

TABLE 6.2: Network Level and Relationship Function

RELATIONSHIP FUNCTION	NETWORK LEVEL		
	Business Relationships	Non-Market Relationships	Infrastructural Relationships
Resource Connection	X		
Activity Connection	X	X	
Actor Connection	X	X	X

The infrastructural networks are important in handling links to parties with whom the company has no direct or indirect business relationships, i.e. in cases where no products are bought or sold or paid for. Without having any business transactions with e.g. competitors, government agencies, potential customers, or opinion leaders, firms are dependent on their actions (or failure to act). With some of these actors business transactions are impossible by definition, and the dependence on them takes the form of adaptations to the rules of the game and the framework for action. With other such parties business exchange may just be non-existent for the time being, although potentially possible.

In order to handle dependence in situations where commercial transactions are excluded as a possibility, information is required—preferably advance information. Involvement in political or social activities, which have a bearing on opinions, is another, more direct way of handling such dependence. In situations where firms are dependent on parties with whom business is possible but at present non-existent, e.g. potential customers, it is also useful to be able to influence opinions, although in such cases within a narrower circle. A common approach in such situations is to use well-placed contacts as "door-openers".

The role of public agencies for the handling of such dependence seems to be important and apparently increasing. But also private companies and their organizations are involved in such influencing activities, e.g. by employing former ambassadors, activities within industrial federations, and participation in the public debate both in articles and in advertising campaigns.

The handling of dependence can be specified further with regard to the target of the influencing activities. A basic difference exists between influence through mass communication (e.g. public relations) on the one hand and individual contacts on the other. Additionally, a distinction can be made between influence activities for different purposes: marketing purposes or long-term influence on the framework for company action. In all these cases, however, the infrastructural networks provide avenues for action.

The purpose of this chapter is to discuss infrastructural networks which are not directly designed for business purposes, using the distinction between person-centred and organization-centred networks made above. This is illustrated with empirical data derived from interviews with senior officials on the boards or in the executive offices of six major Swedish industrial groups and in two private-interest organizations. Furthermore, the managing directors of two foreign subsidiaries of Swedish companies (one German, one Australian) were interviewed. One of these managers was Swedish, the other one was a native. Finally, interviews were held with four officials of international organizations. These officials—all of them Swedes—did not represent Sweden within these organizations, but as they were of Swedish nationality it was assumed that by virtue of their positions they might nevertheless influence the attitude or behaviour of their environment in a manner relevant to the circumstances of Swedish business abroad.

In all, seventeen interviews were held in 1983 and 1984, dealing with individual international contacts well placed to influence the general conditions for Sweden's international business by creating understanding of Sweden's position, and to "open doors" for Swedish firms in various contexts. It was stressed that it was not a matter of finding out how specific business deals had been handled.

6.2. Organization-Centred and Person-Centred Networks

The infrastructural networks are described with regard to the nodes to which the focal actors are connected via one or two links. These nodes, around which the networks are built up, often derive from the network actors' previous assignments or tasks. Individual contacts may thereby have been obtained that have either survived or else hibernated in such a manner that they can be revived when required. Furthermore, the nodes may be organizations of which the actor is or was a member in non-task contexts. The nodes may also be related to the company in which he now works, and in such a case the nets are often organizational rather than individual. Thus, the central descriptive aspects are the characteristics of the focal actor (individual or organization), and the nodes that relate the focal actor to the connected networks.

A major function of the network is to provide contacts to be used when required. The capability of the network to fulfil such functions is dependent on the extent of actual connections, i.e. how many relevant contacts are connected to the node, and their character in terms of their further connections as a second or third link as seen from the node, as well as the relative position or strength of influence of different actors in the network. A major purpose of the networks which are not directly related to business, i.e. networks on levels 2 and 3 (organization- and person-centred networks), is to handle information flows to and from the company regarding matters that are extraneous in some sense, be they unforeseen, outside of normal areas, environment-related in general, etc. The function of the networks to provide contacts for such unforeseen purposes imposes special requirements on them. Firstly, they should be diverse, i.e. incorporate many different types of contacts, again to provide for the unforeseeable. Secondly, they should include many loosely joined contacts. Weak ties can be expected to have a cohesive power in connecting different subnetworks to each other (Granovetter, 1973). Bridges between networks are in the form of weak ties, and new data and valuable haphazard information is likely to flow via such weak links.

Business relationships in industrial markets often have the character of strong ties. Customers and suppliers invest in their relationship in the form of adaptations in the technical, commercial, or social spheres, which strengthens the relationship between them and involves high switching costs due to the cost sunk in the relationship. Such strong relationships have many advantages, e.g. by providing the security required for technical collaboration or efficient handling of the product exchange. However, there might also be risks involved: for instance, the parties may thereby become insulated from new ideas and impressions. Using a sociological analogy, the set of strong customer-supplier ties can be likened to a Gemeinschaft, whereas the set of weak ties involves the firm in a Gesellschaft. Thus, persons "enmeshed in a Gemeinschaft may never become aware of the fact that their lives do not actually depend on what happens within the group but on forces far beyond their perception and hence beyond their control. The Gemeinschaft may prevent individuals from articulating their roles in relation to the complexities of the outside world. Indeed, there may be a distinct weakness in strong ties" (Coser, 1975). The cloistered features of social structures of this kind not only insulate the actors from new information but may also generate inflexibility and a sense of infallibility.

However, not all weak ties are of this special value by connecting the individuals to the Gesellschaft: "only bridging weak ties have this function; the significance of weak ties is that they are far more likely to be bridges than are strong ties" (Granovetter, 1982). Thus, by providing bridges to other networks, the infrastructural relationships can be crucial for securing long-term survival for companies otherwise mostly involved in tightly knit day-to-day business relationships.

Furthermore, Granovetter (1982) concludes "that occupational groups that make the heaviest use of weak ties will be those whose weak ties do connect to social circles different from one's own. In Langlois's Canadian study, the most frequent users are managers and professionals, just the persons who, to use Robert Merton's terms, are most likely in an organization to be 'cosmopolitans' rather than 'locals' — most likely to deal with acquaintances in other organizations or other branches of the same organization". One would thus expect infrastructural networks which provide many bridges to be centred around persons with a diverse career background rather than around those whose networks originate with their present employment.

6.3. Network Examples

Person-centred and organization-centred infrastructural networks are exemplified in Figures 6.1 and 6.2. The networks are characterized by the orientation of the connections, e.g. towards journalists, bankers, politicians, industrialists, etc. The interviewed manager is in the centre of the diagram, and surrounding him are the "nodes" from which the infrastructural networks are built up. These networks are summarily described in the diagram in terms of type of organization, connections, and in one of the examples their geographical extension, i.e. whether it provides contacts particularly in the U.S., Western Europe, the Scandinavian countries, etc.

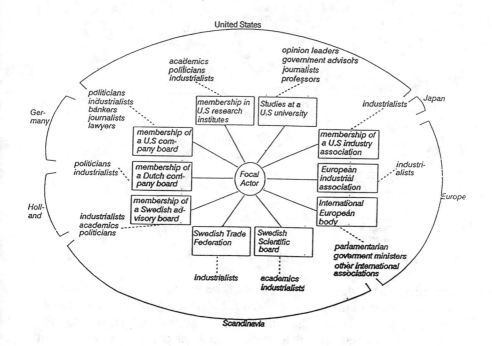

FIGURE 6.1: A Person-Centre Network

The example in Figure 6.1 summarizes the infrastructural network of a former bank chairman with previous professional experience from abroad and several subsequent memberships of boards and committees in private, public, and international entities. The connections are private in character, i.e. they are mostly his own and not his company's. It is possible to specify geographic dimensions of the networks, as the connections of the other individuals involved are mostly to be found in specific regions of the world.

The example in Figure 6.2 is different. The focal actor is the deputy managing director of a rather large company in a high technology industry. The contacts are established and mediated through the focal company, and it is likely that most of them could easily be transferred to other persons in the firm if and when this is necessary. Here it is not meaningful to specify a geographical dimension. Either the contacts are truly world-wide, as in the case of the professional conferences, or else they are similar in most

FIGURE 6.2: An Organization-Centred Network

countries. The nodes in Figure 6.2 are types of organizations, not specific organizations as in the person-centred network in Figure 6.1. This to some extent explains why the number of units depicted in the organization-centred network is smaller than in the person-centred one, but there is certainly a real difference as well. There is a larger number of individual ties in the person-centred network, and these ties are undoubtedly closer. However, the institutional ties in the organization-centred network have proved very efficient, e.g. in the introduction of new products and techniques. The network is of higher density than shown in the diagram.

Person-centred networks may be planned on an individual level, but many of the contacts of course result from chance. These chances, however, seem to have been well utilized in the case illustrated here. In contrast, the organization-centred network is to a large extent planned, e.g. regarding the organization of subsidiaries, contacts with user associations. In this case, too, contact development through gradual involvement in various activities is very important. Thus, the spontaneity versus planning difference should not be exaggerated when comparing the two network types.

The two types of infrastructural networks are unevenly distributed between the respondents. In Table 6.3 the respondents, divided into the functional groups of chairman, managing director, and functional director, are classified with regard to the distinction between person-centred and organization-centred networks. The organization-centred networks are more common. Moreover, the two types are unevenly distributed between the functional groups.

TABLE 6.3: Person- and Organization-Centred Networks

	Person-centred nets	Organization centred nets	Total
Chairman or Ex-Chairman	3	2	5
Managing Director or Deputy	1	5	6
Functional Director	0	6	6
Total	4	13	17

Thus, a striking observation from Table 6.3 is the impact of the traditional division of labour between chairmen of the board on the one hand and executives on the other (cf Stewart 1987). The person-centred networks in the sample are controlled either by the chairman (3 cases) or by the managing director of a subsidiary abroad (1 case). These contacts were acquired during long careers in several jobs and in several countries, and the persons in question consider it to be their duty more or less specifically to provide this kind of general contact to their companies. This attitude is illustrated by the chairman of the board of one of the foreign subsidiaries. He specifies his function as follows:

"The role of chairman of the board includes the normal functions, i.e. chairing the board, as well as other functions between meetings. This means acting as a second opinion for the chief executive, to act as a sounding board regarding both internal and external relations. The company would expect its chief executive to understand the business scene, the organization, the products, pricing etc. Certainly he would be able to deal with all the internal factors. Therefore he is kept up to date regarding policies, practices, and organization. He will obviously also build up external relations. The chief executive does, however, not necessarily know all about external relations. In the case of the two Swedish firms in my country, where I am chairman, these Swedish firms have let their chief executive stay with their firms here longer than e.g. U.S. firms normally do. There is thus no immediate need for me to intervene. Still I assist in business introductions and introductions to business negotiations, and I have a wider knowledge of the business environment in this country regarding economic conditions as these affect markets. I provide my assessments of what may happen in the future regarding such matters as inflation, exchange rates, interest rates, and regulation. I can give a feeling of what may happen. I can also help with remunerations and fringe benefits, as the foreign firm is probably not quite familiar with the practices that go with business in my country. This may concern a company car, regular company loans to executives, or expenses that are reimbursable. I have a long experience of when and how these practices apply." (Managing Director, Foreign Subsidiary)

This example not only points to the role of the chairman in using his personal contacts for the company, but also to the role of nationals on the boards of subsidiaries abroad. The infrastructural network of such national members of the boards of subsidiaries is illustrated by this statement of the managing director of a Swedish firm in a Latin country:

"You should start building your contact net in the country where you are operating by means of a contact of rather high status. It does not matter whether he is a politician, a businessman or a professional of some other kind. Such contacts can be established e.g. at lunches organised by the Chamber of Commerce, but it is of course always a lottery with whom you may happen to be seated. It is also useful to have a social position of one's own, e.g. a membership of the board of the Chamber of Commerce. In this way you get a possibility to approach highly placed officials. In the country where I have been working it is necessary to approach such a person through an intermediary, thus organising for instance a lunch for three. Such an intermediary is called an 'enchufe', literally a 'plug for a wall-socket'. This system is typical for Latin countries." (Managing Director, Foreign Subsidiary)

Thus, national culture, business habits and traditions impinge on the role of infrastructural networks. For instance, contacts of the kind described above are often crucial not only in Latin countries but also elsewhere, e.g. in South-East Asia (cf. Jansson, 1988).

6.4. Planned or Spontaneous Growth of Infrastructural Networks

It is a difficult task to establish and manage infrastructural networks in a planned and systematic manner, and an inherent feature is that they cannot easily be built up systematically in detail. They are specifically to be used for purposes which cannot be determined clearly in advance. However, it is conceivable to handle both person-centred and organization-centred networks either as planned or as emerging systems. Combining these two dimensions gives the matrix shown in Table 6.4. There is no clear dividing line between planned and spontaneously emerging networks, as some combination of intention and chance is probably present in all situations. However, the basic approach could be intentional or laissez-faire.

Furthermore, in the case of a planned approach, there is also the issue of whether the network is planned by the organization or by the concerned individual himself.

TABLE 6.4: Planning of Infrastructural Networks

	Planned	Spontaneous
Organization-Centred	1	2
Person-Centred	3	4

The last quotation in Section 4 above is an example of a planned person-centred network, and indeed planned by the individual himself. There are several such examples, but all are likewise planned by the individuals themselves. But as a totality these networks have emerged more or less spontaneously, as any curriculum vitae is beyond complete planning. Organizational planning of person-centred networks, on the other hand, is considered dubious by many of the interviewed managers:

"Every dynamic person in business has contact nets of his own. The best known and most extensive were probably those of Marcus Wallenberg, not least through the International Chamber of Commerce. Today for instance P. G. Gyllenhammar is systematically building up such nets. Many have tried to make business on providing nets, e.g. via conferences, institutes or informal movements. However, this type of nets often emerges spontaneously, and they are closely tied to the individuals." (Chairman, Industrial Group)

"It is difficult to understand how business were to get organised to produce people with the kind of contacts that Wallenberg had. But such people are certainly needed. It is necessary for the business world to be seen and heard internationally. Thus, people should be given opportunities to widen their horizons. For instance, a future trade secretary should first be trained at the Foreign Office, or at least work for some time at a subsidiary abroad. But it is difficult to recruit people for such purposes. When private companies are approached with the purpose of temporary recruitment of candidates for service abroad, the good candidates are often only available for service for at most a year, whereas the candidates that are offered for this broadening of their networks are people that the companies really do not want to have back after the assignment." (Managing Director, International Agency)

Thus, is it possible to organize this kind of network and transfer them to other members of the organization when necessary? The chairman of a large industrial firm with a previous career as an ambassador has this to say:

> "This kind of network is created through spontaneous processes. Of course you want your network to include a certain mixture of people, but you cannot contact e.g. an American banker for the sole purpose to include him when you find that such a person is missing in your network. A precondition for this kind of network is voluntary. If a certain type of person is missing, that box may stand open for many years. But on the whole, the networks are probably bigger than required, because it is fun to meet people.
>
> The contacts are personal, not the company's. I can of course introduce people in my company to my contacts, but they can only be kept viable if the personalities are compatible. But the need to transfer contacts may not be so great. As you get older, your contacts do so as well. Wallenberg's network decreased in importance during the last 10-15 years of his life, as many of his important contacts were already dead. But one must keep in mind that personal contact nets do not only serve the company but also the individual himself—they may be a tool for the development of his own trajectory. This personal ambition— rather than the establishment of potentially valuable contact nets for the company—may explain many non-business activities, such as for instance the sponsoring of symphony orchestras." (Chairman, Industrial Group)

6.5. Concluding Remarks

A typical feature of the infrastructural networks is their impermanence. Individual contacts grow and strengthen as those involved interact with each other, and their potential value also increases as the position of contact persons within their own networks is strengthened. The number of contacts is also likely to multiply over time. Paradoxically, the value to the companies of the contact nets seems to decrease as the actors reach senior positions and when the nets are widespread and include many well-known names. At this stage the counterparts partially or completely retire from active service and thus lose touch with the current issues. To use an apt image, the networks which previously formed inner circles instead form outer circles without their previous access to information and influence but still having much prestige.

This impermanence has the advantage of making the difficult task of transferring individual contact nets less important. Transfer of infrastructural networks implies a linking between network levels 2 and 3 as defined above, i.e. transferring person-centred to organization-centred networks, as the person who takes over the contacts would not do so in his individual capacity but as a member of a certain company. It also means changing from spontaneous growth to planned network management, or in terms of Table 6.4, going from cell 4 to cell 1, i.e. from one extreme to another.

If one of the aims is to maintain infrastructural networks which originated as networks of the type represented by cell 4, it may be simpler to allow them to grow as indicated by cells 2 or 3. The planning of person-centred networks as represented by cell 3 would involve enabling individuals to establish networks of their own by sending them on various international assignments. The difficulties of such practices are however evidenced by many: either the wrong persons are sent out, or else the company loses people in the process, e.g. as they are naturalized abroad (cf. Borg, 1988). Allowing spontaneous growth of organization-centred infrastructural networks (i.e. cell 2) may be easier, but involves both motivational and control problems: how should non-business related contact creation and maintenance within the framework of ordinary business operations be stimulated?

Furthermore, the notion of managing infrastructural networks is in a sense inherently contradictory. The strength of these networks often consists in that they are neither planned nor managed. To be effective, they must not appear opportunistic. In other words, they may be effective for the very reason that they do not seem to be organized for those practical purposes— information-gathering, influencing etc.—for which they are actually used. Organizing may deprive the network connections of their usefulness.

Can the usefulness of the infrastructural networks be assessed? In a general sense, this is hardly possible, but still some observations can be made. As mentioned above, the usefulness of the infrastructural networks built up around individuals probably declines when they reach their widest extent and highest prestige. At the same time as this seems advantageous, since it reduces the need to transfer networks, it also creates problems for the companies. At this stage, it may be unclear whether the networks are used by the individuals concerned in the companies' best interest, or whether the net effect is instead that the companies are used by the individuals. The core question concerns whether the company is able to mobilize the infrastructural networks of the senior officials when required, or if they only have the company as a basis for their personal network. Still, there are obviously many highly competent senior officials, and it is essential to use their qualifications.

The usefulness of the networks can be illustrated by the somewhat surprising observation that the re-emergence of the European Communities after the adoption of the Single European Act in 1985 was not at all foreseen by the respondents in the empirical investigation reported here. For instance, one of the functional directors interviewed stated in 1984 that

> "the EEC contacts are no longer so important. The EEC is an old and powerless organization which cannot any more achieve any results." (Functional Director, Industrial Group)

Another respondent, a company chairman, claimed that

> "EFTA and EEC are of no importance nowadays".(Chairman, Industrial Group)

This attitude supports Hamilton's observation (1989, p. 40) that the EEC issue was virtually absent from public discussion in Sweden between 1973, when the Free Trade Agreement between EEC and EFTA was concluded, and 1987, when the process leading up to the internal market of 1992 was launched. Thus, the infrastructural networks do not seem to have provided any other information in this case to the persons involved than that of the prevalent general opinion in Sweden of the time.

Infrastructural networks are difficult to manage. However, this is not as problematic as it may appear at first. These networks should anyhow not be too rigidly managed, because this may destroy their effectiveness. Their usefulness is difficult to assess as regards actual gathering of advance information or "pulling strings". However, they are connected with much prestige, which can benefit both the companies and the individuals involved. When the infrastructural networks are treated as if they were important, they indeed become so inside and outside the company. They have a high symbolic value, which provides a motivational force for daily business life.

7

Managing by International Travelling
Björn Axelsson , Jan Johanson and Johan Sundberg

7.1. Why Travel in the Telecommunication Age?

Sitting in SAS business class from Copenhagen to Stockholm on a Friday evening one considers all the businessmen going to Sweden to spend the weekend at home. They come alone or in groups. Some of them look tired and worn out. One can easily imagine how they have spent days and nights negotiating with customers and are going home having lost or having gained a contract. Or perhaps they will start discussions with their own production and design departments on how to handle the demands of the foreign customer before returning to continue the negotiations.

Notwithstanding, huge sums are spent on these business travels. According to a Swedish study by American Express expenses on business travels by Swedish firms amount to 2-3 per cent of sales value (American Express, 1987). This is fifty per cent more than they spend on advertising. The costs of the travelling managers' is not included so the real cost of travelling is certainly around 5 per cent. In an age when almost everybody can be reached instantaneously through telephones, when reporting takes place on-line continuously, and when messages are exchanged by telefax and computers all over world it might seem unnecessary to spend huge sums, time and effort travelling around. In a way, the answer is obvious. Personal, face-to-face, contacts are important in business (Turnbull, 1979). It is important to get to know the persons with whom you do business. But this is only a general answer. More precisely, we may ask who are the businessmen having these personal foreign contacts. Whom do they meet abroad? What do they do when they meet and what gives rise to the meetings?

This is the background to a study of 260 Swedish businessmen returning from business trips abroad. Data were collected on sixteen SAS

93

flights on the Frankfurt-Stockholm, Paris-Stockholm, London-Stockholm, and Amsterdam-Stockholm routes. Structured questionnaires were distributed to those travelling in business class; 260 answered questionnaires were returned which corresponds to 65 per cent of the passengers on these flights.

7.2. Portraits of Four Business Travellers.

Portraits of some of the travellers can give a glimpse of the range of the travelling businessman.

7.2.1. The Purchaser Visits a German Supplier

Adam Andersson is purchaser in a Swedish automotive company. The company manufactures automotive components, is medium-sized and internationally oriented with ten subsidiaries abroad. It operates in markets with radical technical changes, strong international competition, and rapid expansion.

This trip went to Saarbrucken in Germany and took two days. Andersson, who has a commercial education, has been employed in the company for eight years, four of them in the present purchasing job with German business contacts. The purpose of this trip was to buy a new product; he was starting a purchasing project taking place in a long-term perspective. Andersson was not alone, he travelled together with the managing director and the head of his purchasing department as well as two persons from the agent in Sweden representing the German supplier. The German company was a completely new supplier and so are the contact persons in the company. Marketing people were the most important contact persons in the supplier company but general managers and production managers participated in the discussions.

The initiative for the trip was taken by Andersson himself who maintained that the principal aim was to establish personal contacts in the supplier company but it was also important to obtain information. Personnel, commercial, and technical matters were discussed. This was a typical business trip for Andersson who goes abroad 5-10 times per year on business. He considers them absolutely necessary in this type of purchasing situation and vital in his job in general. He has a feeling that the personal contacts are more important when doing business in Germany than in Sweden.

7.2.2. A Researcher Meets a Spanish Customer

Bertil Bengtsson has been working in a pharmaceutical company for one year. This is also an industry with sweeping technical changes, rapid expansion and strong international competition. The firm has slightly over 1,000 employees—10-20 per cent of them are abroad in some ten foreign subsidiaries. Bengtsson has a medical education from a university and is engaged in research and development.

He had been in Barcelona this time. The primary goal of the trip was to see a customer, but he also visited the subsidiary in Spain and attended a conference. At the customer's he met researchers, a medical advisor and marketing people. It was a new customer and so was the most important contact person. The iniative for the trip was taken in Spain. The purpose was an offer to test a new medicine. They planned to start a clinical test project. From another point of view the trip sought primarily to establish a new business relationship, secondly to obtain information, and thirdly to negotiate. The principal issues discussed were technical, but administrative and commercial matters were taken up as well. For such purposes Bengtsson maintained that personal contacts were essential. He also thinks that personal contacts are more important in Spain than at home in Sweden. His experience of Spain is only two months old.

He did not go alone, but travelled together with a medical consultant whose task was to co-ordinate the test programme and a biochemist responsible for documentation and information. It was a typical trip for Bengtsson who travels abroad 10-20 times per year on business.

7.2.3. A Marketing Manager Discusses Re-organization with a UK
Business Partner

Christer Carlsson, whose trip went to London, is marketing manager in a big, metal manufacturing Swedish company with ten foreign subsidiaries and less than 10 per cent of the employees abroad. He considers the company very internationally oriented. The industry is characterized by modest expansion, technical development and strong international competition. He has been with the company for four years, but has had English business contacts for eight years.

He visited an English business partner and met people from general management, marketing and control. He has known them for more than six years, i.e. before he joined his present company. The aim of the trip was primarily to exchange information about reorganization and contracts related to the reorganization; furthermore to tend the relationship with the partner. He had taken the initiative to the trip himself and it had been planned for some time. Commercial matters were in focus but legal issues were also handled. Carlsson stated that personal contacts are essential in situations like this. The trip was also very typical for Carlsson who goes abroad on business 5-10 times per year. This time he went alone. He considers personal contacts absolutely necessary for this type of issue, but they are always important in his job, in the UK as well as in Sweden.

7.2.4. The General Manager Tends a Relationship with a German Subsidiary

David Danielsson is general manager in an engineering company with some hundred employees, half of them abroad. They develop and manufacture equipment, are very internationally oriented, and have subsidiaries in six countries. The industry is characterized by some expansion and technical development and strong international competition.

He was abroad for two days this time visiting his company's subsidiary in Germany together with the technical director. It was a typical trip, one such as he makes more than twenty times per year. The initiative to the trip was his own. In the subsidiary he met general managers, marketing and design managers. He had known his contact persons for four years, i.e. as long as his company had had the subsidiary. The overriding purpose of the trip was to tend the relationship with the subsidiary. The trip has been planned for some time and concerned the introduction of a new product onto the market—a project which the accompanying technical director was responsible for. Technical, commercial and legal issues were discussed. Danielsson considers personal contacts essential for this type of issue and feels that they are still more important in Germany than at home in Sweden.

7.3. Who Travel to Meet Whom?

A first answer to the question why businessmen travel can perhaps be found by looking at who travel. In the small sample of businessmen going home to Sweden these days many different business functions were represented (Table 7.1).

TABLE 7.1: Business Function of the Travelling Manager.

Function	Respondents No.	%
General management	57	22
Marketing	61	23
Manufacturing	3	1
R&D	21	8
Design	5	2
Technical service	24	9
Purchasing	17	7
Data processing	8	3
Personnel	2	1
Controller/finance	14	5
Education	9	3
Others	21	8
No answer	18	7
Total	**260**	**100**

The Table shows that marketing — the introductory picture of the marketer returning from business negotiations with foreign customers is supported — is the single most frequent function among the travelling managers with general management in second place. Adding purchasing and controller/finance yields a group of commercial functions which accounts for almost 60 per cent of the travelling businessmen. Technical functions such as manufacturing, R&D, and technical service are important, but together constitute only 20 per cent of the total.

Although most of the businessmen perform commercial functions almost half of them — 45 per cent — have a technical education. Business education is also common — 35 per cent.

The majority have worked for a long time in their present companies and are experienced in their job positions. Approximately two thirds have served their company for more than five years and more than half of them have held their present position for more than three years. In general, they travel abroad fairly frequently. The average number of trips per year is 11 and more than 70 per cent of them travel abroad more than four times per year.

The businessman is usually also well informed about the country he or she is visiting. More than two thirds of them have had contacts in the country of destination for more than three years. In most cases the traveller is also well acquainted with the contact person abroad. In only 17 per cent of the cases has this person been known for less than a year and in more than half for more than five years.

The travelling businessmen are most often — 40 per cent — employed in the manufacturing industry, but several of them — 22 per cent — work in trading companies. The rest come from the construction industry, banking and insurance, consultancy, research, and public administration with just about equal frequency. The companies of the businessmen vary in size from firms with a handful of employees to large corporations with tens of thousands. Twenty per cent of the flight passengers work in companies with more than 10,000 employees, and eleven per cent in firms with less than 100.

Almost all companies operate internationally, although to different degrees. Three fourths of the businessmen characterize their company as "very internationally oriented" and only six per cent as "not internationally oriented". This picture of international orientation is emphasized by the number of countries in which their companies have foreign subsidiaries; 16 per cent of the companies have subsidiaries in more than 40 countries and half of them in more than 15. Furthermore, half of the companies have more than 10 per cent of their employees abroad. This group includes major Swedish multinationals, such as Volvo, SKF, Atlas Copco, Ericsson, etc.

This is a set of businessmen with considerable international experience, commercial as well as technical orientation working in companies with a strong international orientation. For what purposes do they travel abroad?

In a network perspective the obvious starting point for a discussion of what businessmen do is whom do they meet. The kinds of business or organization unit which they considered to be the main destination were first of all suppliers, second conferences, third subsidiaries, and fourth customers (Table 7.2).

TABLE 7.2: Unit of Destination of the Travelling Manager.

UNIT OF DESTINATION	All		VISITING BUSINESSMEN		
	No.	%	General manager %	Marketing manager %	R&D manager %
Subsidiary	37	14	19	16	13
Parent company	16	6	7	6	2
Sister company	9	3	0	4	5
Representative	12	5	5	7	9
Total Internal units	**74**	**28**	**31**	**33**	**29**
Customer	33	13	12	15	13
Supplier	52	20	19	18	7
Other partner	12	5	6	7	4
Competitor	6	2	2	1	2
Bank	-	-	0	0	0
Public authority	3	1	1	1	4
Total External units	**106**	**41**	**41**	**42**	**30**
Fair	20	8	6	11	2
Conference	48	18	18	11	35
Total Events	**68**	**26**	**23**	**22**	**37**
Others	10	4	4	3	4
No answer	2	1	-	-	-
Total	**260**	**100**	**100**	**100**	**100**

Given the network view it is natural to make a basic distinction between visits to specific counterparts and visits to more general events where the counterparts are less specific, perhaps even unknown to the traveller, for example fairs and conferences. Among all the travelling businessmen 26 per cent went to such events (Table 7.2). The others went to meet a specific business or public unit. The three most common specific destinations are subsidiaries, customers and suppliers. Almost no businessmen travelled to see competitors, banks or public authorities.

In general, in business studies, a basic distinction is made between those who belong to the same firm and those who work in other firms or organizations. In the former, it is assumed, close, hierarchical relations exist between persons, in the latter arms-length market relations predominate between firms and affect the relationships between individuals. From this point of view it is interesting to compare those travelling businessmen who went to see a unit or part of their own organization— subsidiaries, parent or sister companies and representatives—with those who went to visit a unit belonging to a different organization—customers, suppliers, other business partners, competitors, banks, and public authorities. The Table shows that visits to external units are more common than those to internal units, but the difference is not great—41 and 28 per cent.

Evidently, different managers can be expected to go to different destinations. Different business functions require contacts with different counterparts. For example, this Chapter's introductory image of the marketing manager returning from negotiations with foreign customers implies that marketing managers primarily meet external units. This is not supported by the Table. On the contrary, they go as frequently to internal units as do general and R&D managers. The only distinct, and expected, difference between the managers is that the R&D managers often go to conferences. But they too frequently visit both internal and external units. The overall conclusion from this comparison is similarity rather than difference.

7.4. What Kinds of Relationship Do They Have?

In the first Chapter of this book it is argued that business relationships tend to endure. This is one of the corner-stones of the network theory. Ford (1979, 1982) identifies fives stages in the development of business relationships. These are 1) the pre-relation stage, 2) the early stage, 3) the development stage, 4) the long-term stage, and 5) the final stage. Although he does not infer that there is any deterministic development he argues that a number of factors cause a gradual development over time. Obviously, any relationship can be interrupted at any moment for a variety of reasons by any of the parties, and any relationship can fall back into an earlier stage but basically it takes time to build a working business relationship. His discussion refers to business relationships between different firms but the argument can also be applied to relations between units in the same firm. It takes time to make such relationships work as much experience from mergers and company acquisitions shows.

In Table 7.3 the number of stages has been reduced to three, relationships which are less than one year old are considered as being in the early stage, relationships between one and five years belong to the development stage, and older relationships than five years to the long-term stage. The first column in the Table shows that almost four fifths of all the visits concerned relationships which have passed the early stage – they are more than one year old. Almost half of the relationships are older than five years – all these are in the long-term stage. The mean age of the relationships is close to five years – they are just moving from the development into the long-term stage. Nevertheless, the relationships probably represent a wide range of stages.

TABLE 7.3: Duration of the Relationship and the Unit of Destination.

AGE OF RELATIONSHIP	Total		DESTINATION UNITS Internal	External	Events
	No.	%	%	%	%
Less than 1 year	53	22	9	29	28
1-5 years	71	29	38	26	22
More than 5 years	112	47	52	43	49
No answer	5	2	1	3	2
Sum	**241**	**100**	**100**	**100**	**100**

But there are differences depending on the units of destination. The relationships with internal units are seldom in the early stage, whereas almost one third of the external relationships are. Nevertheless a considerable proportion of the visits to external units are devoted to managing relationships in the development and long-term stages. Visits to events often concern completely new relations, thus seem to fill a contacting function.

A comparison between different managers, which is not shown here, reveals very small differences between general, marketing and R&D managers – the latter group seems to go slightly more often to relatively young relationships, which is probably related to their more frequent visits to events. Thus, the similarity between different managers appears again.

In a network perspective the next step is to see which persons the managers meet when they travel. According to the dominant pattern they most often go to see general managers (32 per cent), marketing managers (23 per cent), and R&D managers (16 per cent) and general managers most frequently meet general managers, marketing managers meet marketing managers, and R&D managers meet R&D managers, i.e. managers meet their colleagues when they go abroad.

Establishing and tending personal relations can be seen as a basic element in managing business relationships and networks. Evidently, then, stable personal relations may also be important ingredients in international business. This is supported by Table 7.4.

TABLE 7.4: Age of the Relationship to the Contact Person.

AGE OF			DESTINATION UNITS		
RELATIONSHIP	Total		Internal	External	Events
	No.	%	%	%	%
Less than 1 year	94	39	26	50	38
1-5 years	91	38	54	27	38
More than 5 years	43	18	19	18	16
No answer	11	5	1	5	8
Sum	**239**	**100**	**100**	**100**	**100**

Obviously, the personal relationships are generally younger than the business relations — almost 40 per cent are less than one year old and less than 20 per cent more than five years. The Table also shows a clear difference between the contacts with the three types of counterpart. The internal contacts are mostly between one and five years old whereas the external contacts most often are less than one year.

7.5. Action, Information or Network Cultivation Abroad?

A common stereotype of the international businessman in his mission abroad is that he goes to negotiate with business counterparts or to solve urgent business problems, i.e. his travelling is thought to be action oriented. A second stereotype is closely related to the textbook view of international business (Keegan, 1989; Toyne & Walters, 1989). There a basic distinction is usually made between those decisions which are taken at the headquarters — often labelled strategic — and those — tactical — taken in foreign subsidiaries. This view considers international business primarily as a matter of decision- making, and travelling is required to gather the unstructured information necessary to supplement the more structured data transmitted in reports and accounts. This information-oriented stereotype can be seen as describing a structure lying below the surface of action.

A third stereotype can be associated with the network view. The international businessman travels around the world as a matter of routine primarily in order to develop his or his company's network. This network-oriented stereotype is still further away from action. It assumes that a network structure has to be kept alive so that it can be activated for the purposes of information or action purposes later on. This stereotype is a further step below. Travelling is, in this perspective, mainly a matter of confirming each others' existence.

Evidently, none of these stereotypes is entirely true or false. Each of them is probably more or less true in every international business situation. Every business trip can be expected to aim at action, information and network cultivation. Table 7.5 illustrates the orientation of the trips. The first two columns show how many trips are undertaken with action, information or network as the primary aim, and the following how often such aims were indicated as important.

TABLE 7.5: Aim Orientation of the Business Trips.

Aim Orientation	Primary Aim		One Important Aim	
	No.	%	No.	%
Action	100	38	144	55
Information	83	32	162	62
Network	70	27	143	55
No answer	7	3	...	...
Sum	**260**	**100**	...	...

Evidently, the three different aim orientations of business trips are considered almost equally important by the businessmen. Thirty-eight per cent of the trips are made primarily in order to take action, 32 per cent in order to exchange information, and 27 per cent to cultivate networks. Similarly, they are just as often mentioned as important by the businessmen. So, on average, there seems to be no difference between the three kinds of aim orientation.

Action orientation was measured in two ways; negotiations and problem solving. Problem solving was the principal objective of 60 trips, that is almost one quarter of the cases. Negotiations constituted the primary purpose of 40 trips, or 16 per cent. The information orientation was slightly less frequent than action, but gathering information was the single aim most frequently mentioned as most important, 67 trips or more than a quarter. Very few trips, however, were made in order to inform others.

Network cultivation is composed of, on the one hand, a distinction between personal and company relationships, and on the other a distinction between establishment and maintenance of relationships. Establishment of personal relationships and maintenance of company relationships are most frequently mentioned as the primary purpose of the trip.

Although the three orientations are equally common on average, different trips have different aims and it is worthwhile to explore some of these differences. Starting with the distinction made above between visits to internal and external units, versus events, the most striking is that the trips to events differ completely from the others insofar as the primary aim is predominantly information-oriented. Events such as fairs and conferences are attended by managers primarily in order to gather information (Table

7.6, col 3). This is not surprising. Nor is it surprising that action very seldom is the aim of such trips. But it is somewhat surprising that making contacts is not more important on such trips. Comparison between visits to internal and external units reveals that the internal trips are more action-oriented—53 per cent of the visits—than are external trips where action and network orientation are on a par—38 and 36 per cent.

TABLE 7.6: Aim Orientation of Visits to Different Units.

AIM ORIENTATION	VISITS					
	Primary Aim			One Important Aim		
	Internal	External	Events	Internal	External	Events
	%	%	%	%	%	%
Action	53	38	12	92	87	24
Information	24	21	62	78	68	97
Network	18	36	20	60	94	87
Others	5	5	6	...	...	...
Sum	**100**	**100**	**100**	...	...	...

Evidently, visits to different destinations are made for different reasons. This is illustrated by Table 7.6. It shows that action aims are almost always mentioned as important in the visits to both internal and external units but very seldom in visits to events. Information aims—i.e. gathering information—are always cited among those who go to events and very often in the other two groups too. Finally, network aims are almost always declared by those who go to external units and events. They are also adduced concerning most of the visits to internal units.

Although the pattern is diffuse it may be inferred that action is the most important aim when going to internal units, network cultivation is relatively most important when travelling to external units, and information in regard to trips to events. The difference between internal and external units is, however, rather small.

Ford's (1982) discussion of the development of relationships can be interpreted as implying that all three types of aim are most important in the early stages of relationships. Negotiations and problem solving are required more often in the early stages than later on when the exchange has become more routine. Information exchange is also more important in the beginning when the parties do not know each other very well. Later on information is probably less of a problem. Network cultivation is also a more urgent need at the outset. In a way, however, the network theory implies that network cultivation which involves building a basic structure is heavier in the beginning, followed by information which constitutes a secondary structure, on the top of which action forms a kind of surface. This view implies that network cultivation will be heavier in the early stage of relationships, later on information exchange will take over, and lastly action will dominate.

Table 7.7 gives tentative support to this view. Network cultivation is most frequently the primary aim in the early stage, i.e. during the first year of the relationship 44 per cent go abroad primarily to develop relationships. After that stage it is definitely less important than the others—23 and 24 per cent. Information is also primary in the early stage—35 per cent—but its relative importance decreases gradually, mainly in the long-term stage. Action, finally, is clearly less significant in the early stage and also obviously more important than the others in the following stages. The same pattern—increasing importance of action over time and decline of network cultivation—can also be seen when all aims mentioned as important are analysed (this is not in the Table).

TABLE 7.7:   Aim Orientation of Visits During Different Relationship Stages.

Primary Aim Orientation	Relationship Stage		
	Early %	Development %	Long-term %
Action	22	44	49
Information	35	33	27
Network cultivation	44	23	24
Sum	**100**	**100**	**100**

From a network point of view it seems reasonable to assume that business travelling is very much a matter of routine. The businessmen regularly go abroad to meet other businessmen in order to confirm to each other that they exist and are prepared to do business together. From another point of view they could be expected to go abroad when something happens, the trips are prompted by specific incidents or problems, which may be more or less sudden.

TABLE 7.8: Cues and Aim Orientation of Business Trips.

| | Action | Aim Orientation | | Sum |
| | | Information | Network | |
	%	%	%	No.
Sudden problem	23	11	13	41
Non-sudden probblem	52	36	39	108
No specific problem	25	53	49	103
Total	**100**	**100**	**100**	**252**

Sudden problems do not seem to play a major role in the business travels — only in 15 per cent of the cases. Thus, international business travelling seems to be a fairly stable, regular activity. When it is caused by problems these are rarely sudden.

Action as main aim is most frequently linked to specific but non-sudden problems or events, such as the launching of new products, symposia, exhibitions, purchasing negotiations, organization changes etc. Information and network building as main aims are seldom related to specific problems. This is not surprising.

Although not shown in the Table a comparison between the goals of the trips with regard to cue indicates that events differ from both internal and external units insofar as these trips are almost never prompted by a sudden problem and seldom by any problem at all. There is also some difference between internal and external unit visits. Internal visits are more often of a routine character than external visits, which are more often related to non-sudden problems.

The problem relation of the trips does not seem to be dependent on the stage of the relation. Sudden problems are unusual in all stages.

As a further step in the analysis of what the travelling businessmen do when they go abroad one may ask to what extent the trips concern specific projects. In general, much business action is related to specific projects;

some business action is also presented as projects mainly in order to increase its penetrative power. Table 7.9 shows how often the trips are related to specific projects; as can be expected information and network trips are less often related to projects than are action trips. Project related trips occur before, during and after project implementation.

TABLE 7.9: Project Relation and Aim Orientation of Business Trips.

Project Relation	Aim Orientation			
	Action	Information	Network	Sum
	%	%	%	No
No	37	53	52	103
Yes - planning	12	18	16	34
- start up	12	8	19	29
- implementation	23	10	10	34
- completion	11	1	11	
- review	6	10	3	14
sum	63	47	48	121
Sum	**100**	**100**	**100**	**224**

The visits to events are less often related to projects than are visits to both internal and external units which are almost identical with regard to project relation in general as well as in specific stages. There does not seem to be any difference between relationship stages with respect to the frequency of project trips.

7.6. Summary

The study of the Swedish businessmen travelling abroad gives a picture of an experienced, competent businessman with a college education, most often technical or commercial. He—there seem to be no shes—is predominantly marketing, general or R&D manager and goes abroad very often to visit functional colleagues in the same company or in a different company with about the same frequency. He often goes to general events such as fairs or conferences. He works in industrial or trade companies which are highly international. Both he and his company have often well established personal and company relationships with the counterparts abroad.

The purpose of his trips is usually some kind of action, but such action almost equally often pertains to information or network cultivation. Network cultivation seems to be the most important aim in the early stage of relationships and action in the late stage, supporting a view of network cultivation as most basic, information as based on networks, and action as based on both networks and information.

Overall the study conveys a picture of international business travelling as a regular, stable activity which is relatively independent of the function of the businessman and of the counterpart with whom he is doing business. It is a continuous activity, building the foundation for future business. The introductory picture of the businessman returning home from international business negotiation is only part of the truth — and not even the main part.

Developing Countertrade Networks
Hedvig Brorsson

8.1. What is Countertrade?

More and more developing countries are posing requirements of countertrade. The reasons vary, e.g. shortage of foreign currencies and other financial problems, trade barriers of industrialized countries, difficulties in expansion of new markets and a need to involve exporters in development projects.

In all probability countertrade is here to stay for the foreseeable future. In situations with keen rivalry among companies from industrialized countries, those willing to accept and realize countertrade will gain a competitive advantage.

Due to the countertrade, complex networks of connected relationships are created. In order to be able to develop their positions in those networks, Western companies have to understand them, e.g. how to perform necessary activities in connection with countertrade.

This Chapter examines the development of relationships among companies engaged in countertrade transactions. The description is based on a case study of a countertrade network which emerged from Indonesia.

The term countertrade denotes transaction activities of various types in relation to international trade. One basic feature is the establishment of more connections between relationships which probably would not have occurred without the application of countertrade. This concerns above all the connection of import and export activities. In other words, the element of reciprocity can be assumed to be more pronounced in countertrade transactions than in conventional ones.

In general, countertrade means international transactions in which a seller provides a buyer with deliveries and contractually agrees to purchase goods from the latter to an agreed percentage of the value of his sales contract. The main difference with respect to other types of trade is thus the contractual connections created between the deals.

In this Chapter the classification of countertrade types is fairly generalized, using the four most common terms. They are all defined as being connected in one way or another. The division into categories is made in terms of the agreements:

I: Barter: Barter is a pure exchange of goods on a single occasion. Each contracting party agrees to receive certain specified goods instead of convertible currency. Generally the goods which flow in each direction are defined by the trading partners as being equal in value. Undertakings are settled in one agreement.

II: Compensation transaction: The foreign supplier receives a certain percentage payment in products, the rest in money. One agreement is established.

III: Counterpurchase (parallel transactions): Two ordinary transactions with separate agreements are inter-connected. The foreign supplier undertakes to buy counterpurchase products to a certain value of his own sales.

IV: Buy-back: A foreign company selling e.g. technology, production plants or equipment, agrees to buy back the resultant products, e.g. products that are produced with the bought equipment. In another example payment is made in the form of licenced products instead of royalties.

The network approach is based on the assumption of inter-connected relationships, developed through exchange and adaptation processes between organizations. The connectivity feature makes the network approach suitable for the study of countertrade. Furthermore, in countertrade economic, social, cultural and political bonds are developed between the organizations, on both the macro and micro levels. The network approach makes it possible to study connected relationships at different levels.

In countertrade, the contracts of import and export transactions are connected to each other. Several activities have to be adapted to these circumstances, which means that the mutual processes within the relationships between organizations will be affected. For example, the process of negotiation will probably become more complicated and time-consuming than in conventional trade. It is even more difficult when a company has to deal with activities which they have never considered before. One recourse then is to learn from, or co-operate with, other organizations. Whether they do so or not, the capability of the companies to adapt to each others' values and needs, based on different cultural and social backgrounds, becomes crucial. For example, the imports to Indonesia are to be valued for payment in goods, which in turn depends on how the parties can agree on the value of these goods.

8.2. Countertrade Networks in Indonesia

Most Western companies facing countertrade requirements when selling to Indonesia, are private ones without co-operation with their governments. As concerns Indonesia, the government holds a central position in the countertrade network, having formed the rules to increase its control over the foreign trade. The countertrade unit within the government is the co-ordinating body for the countertrade. The countertrade policy is related to imports made by Indonesian public sector enterprises. The government is the first agent encountered by industrialized companies when selling their products there. However, this formally central position does not necessarily mean that the government has most real power in the network. Several private companies, which have negotiated directly or indirectly with the government about the countertrade requirements, have succeeded in reducing it. This indicates that at least some companies have reached a good position in the countertrade network. It remains to investigate the ways to reach such a position.

Once a countertrade deal is signed and it is a matter of exporting countertrade products from Indonesia, connections are made to Indonesian private sector exporters. It is important to identify such organizations in this sector, as they are in a position to direct the countertrade activities in desired directions. However, it should be remembered that also semi- or fully public Indonesian organizations have to be taken into consideration when reaching agreements.

Both foreign and national trading companies undertake the responsibility for countertrade, and often co-operate with each other. The Indonesian government has tried to improve its position in relation to companies from industrialized countries by supporting and advocating the use of national trading firms, some of which have specialized in countertrade. It is, however, questionable whether such measures have any positive development effect for the local Indonesian producers. They are found at the lowest level in the countertrade network, and it is from them that the Western companies, or engaged traders, will buy their products for the countertrade deliveries.

Most countertrade transactions in Indonesia have been of the counterpurchase (parallel)-type, i.e. regulated in the policy. Officially the transactions in both directions have to be equal in value. According to the countertrade unit within the government, the other types of countertrade, apart from barter, have also been executed in Indonesia. The products countertraded have, often through the engagement of a third party, been sold in the world market at pressed prices. This is due to the large quantities of, usually standardized, goods involved.

According to the countertrade regulations, the foreign companies are responsible for the realization of the countertrade deliveries. This means that the Indonesian companies do not actively contribute to them, so that their expected development in e.g. marketing and technological respects is disregarded.

When forming future countertrade policies, Indonesia has to an increasing extent started to take more long-term considerations. This is seen *inter alia* in the plans to introduce a buy-back policy. If the countertrade policy also comprised requirements of e.g. foreign investments, transfer of technology, know-how and the like, the possibilities to tying the companies together in more long-term development generating co-operations would increase. Both domestic and foreign companies would play a more active role in the activities connected to the countertrade deliveries. More repeated business within the framework of the same co-operative relationships could result.

8.3. The Countertrade Network of an Indonesian Focal Company

Through a case-study, the preconditions for, and creation of long-term co-operation in the Indonesian network will be discussed. Most of the connected relationships within the network studied originate in Indonesia, but there are also some parties in Singapore. The study is based on interviews with organizations in those countries, as well as on secondary sources. The interviews were held anonymously in order to promote candour. The questions discussed were: What factors give the network a long-term character? What possibilities do the companies from Western countries have to participate in interaction processes in the Indonesian countertrade network?

The purpose is to describe the relationships which the organizations mutually establish to handle countertrade in Indonesia. One important aspect consists in the preconditions for the long-term development of these relationships, i.e. the development of the companies' positions in the network. According to the network approach, this development occurs through continuous changes in the content of the relationships, so-called bonds, and of the connections between them. These bonds may be cultural, social, financial or political. It is important to note that such changes are caused by adaptation processes among the parties. The mode of connection of a certain relationship to others depends on its importance in the network.

The case study focuses on the activities related to the counter-deliveries from Indonesia and the degree to which Indonesian organizations take an active part in their realization. The analysis deals with interorganizational relations. Internal relations within the organizations are not dealt with. When using an interorganizational perspective, it is important to limit the period for the study. In this case, the starting point is 1982, when the policy was introduced, and up to late 1988. It should be kept in mind, however, that the network is continuously developing, also after this period.

The network will be described as originating from a focal Indonesian company, here called PT Focal. This is one of the few Indonesian countertrade companies. Most countertrade transactions in Indonesia are handled by foreign traders. The relationships described will form a so called organization set (Aldrich & Whetten, 1981). An organization set consists of those organizations in a certain network, with which a focal organization has direct or indirect links. Concerning indirect links, it should be specified how many steps separate a certain organization from the focal one. In this case, first organizations at most two steps from PT Focal will be described. In a second stage, also organizations three steps away from PT Focal are included. The relationships contain not only exchanges of products and payment, but also, e.g. social and cultural phenomena which form the bonds developed between the organizations. The selection of types of relationship (see the six types below) seeks to convey an understanding of how important activities are performed within the countertrade network. The connections within the network studied are illustrated in Figure 8.1. below.

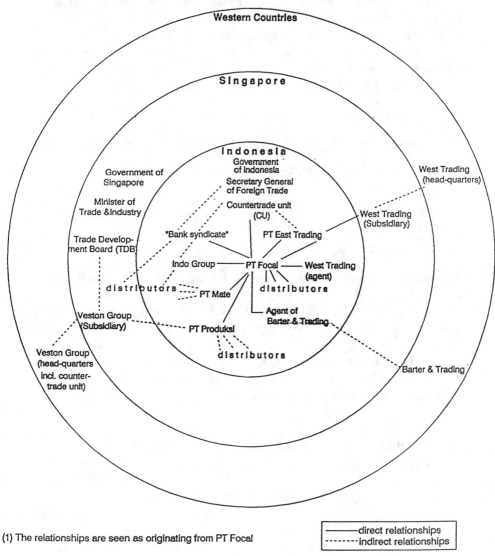

(1) The relationships are seen as originating from PT Focal

———— direct relationships
-------- indirect relationships

FIGURE 8.1:   Illustration of the Connections within the Indonesian Countertrade Network of the Case Study(1)

The case is reported in terms of the development of relationships, connected through exchange processes due to countertrade, and focuses on how the bonds, i.e. the content of the relationships, have developed through adaptation processes between the organizations. This also leads to a description of how the companies, through adaptation processes, become increasingly dependent on each other.

For all Indonesian companies, the term PT is used to enable their differentiation from the Western firms. PT (Perseroan Terbatas) is the Indonesian term for Co. Ltd.

The different types of relationship included in the study are:

1. Developing country trading house – Owners

2. Developing country trading house – Developing country producer

3. Developing country trading house – Developing country, own government.

4. Developing country trading house – Developing country, foreign government.

5. Developing country trading house – Developing country trading house

6. Developing country trading house – Industrialized country trading house.

The last type of relationship, no. 6, in this case the foreign companies have trading capabilities, so that the relationship Developing country – Industrialized country producer is not included. The activities are performed in the Indonesian market, and the different Western actors all, belong to the last type of relationship. This explains the large number of relationship types with only developing country parties involved.

8.4. Development of Countertrade – Based Exchange Relationships

PT Focal was officially established as a trading house in 1986. It is semi-privately owned, and belongs to a group of companies, here called the Indo group. PT Focal functions as a trading arm to this group. PT Focal is also owned by a state company, here called PT East Trading, which is an international trading company with interests in countertrading. It was thought that these interests could be activated by strengthening above all the social bonds to PT Focal, and increasing the latter's dependence thereon.

PT Focal is also supported by a domestic bank syndicate, having international contacts, which are expected to increase its financial reliability.

PT Focal has a collaboration agreement with a Western trading company, here called West Trading. When West Trading entered the countertrade business, it was in a good position to help other companies to fulfil their countertrade obligations. The government required that the countertrade deliveries be in addition to their traditional exports, a hard requirement for many foreign companies. However, West Trading had excess export capacity in Indonesia, i.e. effected more exports than required, which other companies could utilize for their countertrade obligations.

PT Focal and West Trading had co-operated long before 1986, when the former was established; i.e. PT Focal once went bankrupt, after which the name of the company was changed. Thanks to the strong, above all social, bonds developed in the relationships between the two, West Trading started to teach PT Focal how to perform necessary trading and marketing activities, and "the new" PT Focal was partly formed on this knowledge. They learned *inter alia* how to carry on countertrade with Comecon countries during that period.

Today, PT Focal's main activities are conventional trading, participating in government tenders, countertrading with various countries as well as third and fourth country re-export business. Being a member of ASEAN, PT Focal emphasizes the strength it has acquired, compared with foreign trading houses, through its connection with the preferential tariff system among the member countries.

In order to increase its marketing and sourcing assets, PT Focal has found it necessary to continue a very close relationship to West Trading. West Trading indirectly provides PT Focal with a world-wide network of sales-markets. An expert on trading matters is stationed at PT Focal's headoffice in Djakarta.

However, a conflict recently occurred between the two companies, which threatens to interrupt some or all of the bonds between them. PT Focal in particular is eager to bring the co-operation to an end; they are dissatisfied with the results produced by the expert, so they will "tell him to leave". The wish to interrupt the relationship is mutual, as West Trading has also expressed such intentions. According to a third source, the companies explain this intended breach by saying that "Eastern countries do not accept to do countertrade with an Indonesian company co-operating with a western one". However, it has proved more difficult than expected to terminate the relationships, due to established dependences. For example PT Focal mainly offers services as a trading firm, which means that the company must be prepared to take the risk of facing unexpected problems in connection with a certain deal. Then the support from West Trading is needed.

Furthermore, West Trading has a subsidiary in Singapore and in 1986 obtained "Pioneer-Status" for countertrade from the Singaporian government. This means that PT Focal is indirectly connected to the scheme. The scheme is administered by the Trade Development Board (TDB) in Singapore, which is subordinated to the Minister of Trade & Industry of Singapore. Some ten companies have obtained the status, which gives them *inter alia* tax incentives if countertrade transactions are done through Singapore. The Singaporian criterion for granting the status is that the company has a certain international strength in terms of worldwide connections. Doing countertrade with just one country is not sufficient. PT Focal is establishing some of its accounts in Singapore. They wish to carry on all necessary such activities through that country, as the connections created through Singapore are regarded as extremely valuable.

PT Focal also co-operates closely with another Indonesian trading company, here called PT Mate, which is very important to the former's performance in terms of carrying through business deals. For example, they often make offers on countertrade together, in the name of either or both parties. PT Mate, too, also entered into countertrade business on the initiative of the Indonesian government, albeit one year later than PT Focal.

PT Focal's relationship with the government is of great importance. This relationship involves serious disputes, i.e. during the negotiations between PT Focal and the countertrade unit (CU) within the government concerning which supplier to choose or what products should be allowed for the countertrade deliveries. But there are also very strong elements of dependence and co-operation within the relationships, i.e. through the above-mentioned state-ownership: PT East Trading has some very powerful government officials on its board of directors, in terms of business and social influence. Consequently, by definition, the relationship between PT Focal and the government is a very strong one, due to the bonds developed through conflict and co-operation.

One example concerns how the government forced PT Focal to enter into countertrade business. If they had refused, they would not have been recommended as a capable trading company. This shows how PT Focal is very dependent upon the government for its survival and indicates the relative power within the relationship. In this description, the relationship between PT Focal and the government is focused on the link with the countertrade unit (CU) at the Directorate General for Foreign Trade, Department of Trade. Officially, the government does not want to interfere in the execution of the counter-deliveries. In reality, however, PT Focal finds the government involvement prominent through the administrative procedures and e.g. during the negotiations.

The government wishes to increase its control over the foreign trade through the countertrade policy. But, the countertrade is not considered as being against free trade as it is an option for all countries. Indonesia uses its position in the "buyers' market" to implement the policy, i.e. when there is keen competition among foreign suppliers. The government intends to continue its countertrade policy, and hopes that the Indonesian exporters and producers will take this opportunity to increase their trade. As seen in its relationship with PT Focal, this is sometimes enforced.

Indonesia has established lists of products which are regarded as suitable for countertrade. The foreign suppliers are officially free to choose any of these. There are also lists of Indonesian exporters. In practice, Western companies often have problems in that the listed products are not available. Then it is important to know where to turn. PT Focal together with PT Mate and West Trading hope to be able to contribute with their knowledge in such situations.

In 1987, PT Focal initiated an exchange process with a Western countertrade company, here called Barter & Trading, which is owned by a group of Western companies. Barter & Trading has not done any countertrade business in Indonesia before. The relationship started when PT Focal, together with a Ministerial delegation from Indonesia, made an official trade visit to Barter & Trading's home-country. There they met representatives from Barter & Trading. Back in Indonesia, PT Focal sent a letter of proposal to Barter & Trading. However, according to PT Focal, the two companies have so far reached agreement only until "deal-level", and there has been a delay in exchanges of different types of information between them. The reasons are unclear, but it seems that Barter & Trading needs more authority from the management of the group, to combine countertrade activities with pure trading. Their present policy is to perform only countertrade, apart from some direct exporting activities.

Barter & Trading has an agent in Singapore, and now plans to establish a subsidiary there. Its activities in the region are rather newly developed and planned. Moreover these plans are to some extent dependent on whether the Asian division of Barter & Trading prevails upon the management of the group to accept the said plans concerning trade activities.

PT Focal also has direct relationships to Indonesian producers, both with and without owning them. In this study, one manufacturer has been included to illustrate the relationships between PT Focal and the producers, providing goods for the countertrade deliveries, sometimes even without knowing it. This producer will be called PT Produksi. The government has given PT Produksi the sole right to import all products of one of the types needed for its production. This means that other companies will have to pay PT Produksi a certain fee if they need to buy this imported product. PT Produksi is an example of a producer with strong bonds to the government, e.g. it is privileged as described above. This is not the case with the majority of producers, at least the smaller ones.

According to PT Focal, the social bonds between them and PT Produksi are very strong; "Instead of being based on money our relationship is based on mutual trust" (PT Produksi was less willing to talk about this relationship). On the basis of this trust they make special arrangements for the sales. If, for instance, PT Produksi is able to sell its products for USD 10 million "on the market", they could instead agree to sell them to PT Focal for USD 8 million. PT Focal, in its turn, has more developed contacts on the marketing side, and succeeds in selling the products for USD 12 million. Then the two companies divide the USD 4 million profit between them. PT Focal has been able to offer high-quality products for its countertrade deliveries. But what about PT Produksi? Apparently, PT Produksi finishes with the same profits as it would have obtained without the above arrangements, i.e. USD 10 million, which means that in strict economic terms the agreement is of no use. According to the companies, the profit comprises the close connection which PT Produksi thereby establishes to PT Focal, which serves *inter alia* as a guarantee, since PT Focal has certain important connections, both to the government and to foreign companies.

The relationship is beneficial also to PT Focal. Through PT Produksi, PT Focal is indirectly connected to the distribution network of PT Produksi, which is extensive. They both own a part of this network, but their shares only partly overlap.

There were some intentions from a Western trading company, here called the Veston Group, to enter a relationship with PT Focal. The Veston Group would have provided them with *inter alia* financial support. The Veston Group could thereby have channelled some of its excess products from Eastern Europe. One specialist activity of the Veston Group is to sell Eastern Bloc products in the Asian market. However, these plans were abandoned.

The Veston Group has a counter-trade unit, Veston Counter, in its home country, and a subsidiary in Singapore. Both operative and strategic decisions are made at this subsidiary, but they have to be approved by Veston Counter. The subsidiary is relatively independent, "as it has the local knowledge".

The Veston Group has entered into a relationship with PT Produksi. They have discussed plans for a buy-back arrangement (according to a third source the Veston Group has already completed a buy-back deal with them). PT Focal is indirectly connected to this relationship. However, the Veston Group found that PT Produksi did not keep its terms of the agreement. For example, according to the Veston Group, there have been deliveries containing other goods than those agreed upon. The conflicts which ensued prompted both parties to agree that the agreement should slowly "vanish". All the connections within the organization set are illustrated in Figure 8.1.

8.5. Bonds, Power and Change in the Countertrade Network

The countertrade network described has grown out of the complex relationships which became inter-connected through the occurrence of countertrade in Indonesia. Some connections, e.g. those between PT and

Barter & Trading, the Veston Group, and the Countertrade Unit within the Indonesian government, were clearly established due to the countertrade, and thus show how this type of trade contributes to new links. However, the connections within the organization set, even that with West Trading, may all have emerged also without the policy. The difference is the content of the relationships, which now includes elements pertaining to the countertrade. In other words, new or more extensive types of bond between the companies are created. These bonds, related to countertrade, have to do with the capability to connect import and export activities, which is the basic feature of countertrade. The technical, planning, cognitive, socio-economic, and legal bonds are therefore, through processes of adaptation between the companies, developed to co-ordinate such activities.

The countertrade compels the companies to co-ordinate more activities at the same time which requires availability of more resources, either through the company itself or through co-operation with others such as trading firms. In the case study, this is seen in the relationships between PT Focal and West Trading, PT Mate and the owners, which provide PT Focal with resources such as connections to the government, to an international marketing network and the like. PT Focal clearly gives its customers, the foreign suppliers, information on these co-operation partners since this is their strength. The customers will probably engage the third party which is considered most capable of carrying through countertrade deliveries. The Indonesian government will probably give the import contract to the industrialized country company which has the greatest possibilities to sell countertrade products.

It is important that the organizations within the network be capable of coordinating the activities which are considered to be the "right" ones by the majority of the organizations, especially by those with relatively more power. Therefore, it can be assumed that the more "right" the knowledge of activities in the countertrade network is, the more power an organization may obtain in a certain position there. The organizations are only able to obtain new knowledge within reach of their earlier experiences, which means that their learning process is performed gradually (Lindblom, 1959). The Indonesian government has a central position formally, but little practical experience of carrying through the actual countertrade-transactions, which enables Western companies to develop their positions towards it. This also depends on how they learn to handle other interests and activities there.

For example, if there is keen competition among the foreign companies, the bargaining power of the Indonesian government and/or state-owned company which handle the imports and initially award the contracts, becomes relatively strong. A foreign company, such as West Trading or Barter & Trading, would occupy a better position during the negotiations if they co-operated with a company like PT Focal which has good connections to the government and to other actors of importance, either for realizing the countertrade deals or for evading the requirements. In the case study, West Trading has established such a co-operation with PT Focal. Their joint capability to offer services in connection with countertrade increases.

To be able to choose PT Focal, a Western company then has to know more about the network in which PT Focal operates and the relationships on which its activities are based. In a complex environment like the Indonesian, it is also important to learn the processes which occur within the relationships, i.e. how the bonds develop. Such knowledge can be obtained through mutual adaptation through participating in interaction processes with local companies.

The case deals with some bonds within the relationships in the countertrade network. For example, bonds of knowledge are developed between the Indogroup and PT Focal. Furthermore, PT Focal has important financial bonds primarily to the "bank syndicate", but also to PT East Trading and West Trading.

From the case it can be seen that social bonds are very important in the Indonesian countertrade network. The connection between PT Focal and PT Mate is based on relationships containing strong social bonds. The two companies have to a large extent established the same types of relationships to e.g. the government and coordinate complementary activities so as to divide the work between them.

The relationship between PT Focal and PT Produksi also has strong social bonds. As a matter of fact, the social bonds in this relationship are considered more important than e.g. financial and technological links. The profits on the investments made in this relationship are not measured in economic, but in social terms.

The relationships with West Trading, and with the government, also indicate how conflicts actually reinforce the links. In the process of solving the conflicts it seems that the social bonds may be affected so that the dependencies between the organizations increase. This could hinge on the way conflicts are solved. This shows that one criterion for selecting relationships which could be stable in the long run should be the ability to solve conflicts. Such a capability is dependent on the social bonds developed. When the bonds evolve in the "right" way (i.e. considered to be so by the majority, Lindblom 1959), the positions will be developed as desired.

The case study of the countertrade network shows how different interests push the processes of adaptation of e.g. activities in certain directions, which make the development of the network a dynamic one, taking certain, but uncontrollable, directions.

Concerning the relationships with the Veston Group and Barter & Trading, the exchange is becoming less frequent. However, this does not signify that they are terminated; they could during a period even become more or less dormant. The exchange process implies that the parties test how well they fit each other. The same concerns the relationship between the Veston Group and PT Produksi.

It would seem that West Trading has an advantage in developing its position in the countertrade network since they have had relationships with PT Focal in Indonesia for a long time. West Trading also has an advantage in the position it has developed in Singapore, which is an attractive resource to PT Focal. Barter & Trading and the Veston Group also have problems with decision making on matters regarding Indonesia and Singapore; should they be taken locally or at the headquarters in the home country?

The buy-back plans show how the organizations in the countertrade network try to use countertrade as a development strategy. As the developing country markets become increasingly important to the Western companies, they will have to play more active roles in countertrade activities in co-operation with local firms. The Veston Group initiated some buy-back plans with PT Produksi. Many questions arise when considering buy-back, e.g. whether the technology should be transferred, or whether it should be developed locally. In the buy-back plans between the two companies it was difficult to reach an agreement on such issues.

It is important to foreign companies, when planning how to organize their countertrade activities, to remember that opportunities for such trade may arise suddenly, which requires unconventional solutions. It is possible that as a result of countertrade companies will start to buy from each other to a greater extent, the number of trading firms will increase or companies will diversify more. It becomes crucial to learn how to handle countertrade networks.

Experiential Network Knowledge in International Consultancy
D. Deo Sharma

9.1. Objectivity in International Technical Consultancy

During recent decades the governments in various parts of the world have invested heavily to speed up the industrialization of their respective countries. Huge resources have been poured in the industrial sector for its development and improvement. However, the planning of industrialization and the implementation of industrial and infrastructural projects demand specialized skills which are time consuming to acquire. Few firms possess these resources. In the previous decades a number of firms have developed to offer specialized skills to the market. These firms render assistance in a number of fields, namely they detect business opportunities, plan projects to avoid cost overrun and snags, search suppliers for equipment etc. Technical consultancy firms (TCFs) are one kind among these.

TCFs render a variety of different services to the clients. A fundamental strength of these firms is said to be (or should be) their objectivity. It is stated that TCFs (should) offer objective technical counsel to their clients (UN, 1972, ch. 1). The term 'objective' denotes that the advice rendered by the TCFs is free from external influences, is the 'best' for the clients. It is implied that their advice is based on the objective evaluation and comparison of the alternatives. The TCFs, on the basis of their superior knowledge and experience of technology, select the most rational solution to a problem. An underlying assumption in this discussion is the very nature of the technical knowledge, namely, such knowledge is deterministic, irrespective of the nationality or culture of the TCF.

The purpose of this Chapter is to discuss the nature of the knowledge possessed and the solutions offered by the TCFs. It is argued that no technical knowledge, including that of TCFs, is objective, free from external influences. Technical knowledge is associated with, and derived from the network of relationships in which a firm is engaged and, thereby, not absolutely objective. It is influenced by and an outcome of the network of relationships in which a TCF participates. It is, consequently, unreasonable to perceive technical counsel by TCFs as wholly objective and rational. The recommendations offered by the TCFs, the alternative(s) selected to resolve a problem etc are determined by the nature of the network of their relationships. To expect a fully rational decision (i. e., 'the best alternative', 'the best solution to solve a problem' etc) is difficult. In other words, there is always a 'bias' in the technical solutions and recommendations which TCFs suggest and the nature of this bias is decided by the network of relationships in which TCFs are involved.

The above argument is illustrated with the help of a discussion of TCFs and their impact on domestic exports (in the rest of this chapter the term 'domestic' implies the country from which a TCF originates).

In the following section TCFs are briefly introduced. Then follows a discussion of the knowledge possessed by the TCFs. A distinction is made between objective and experiential knowledge. This Chapter is completed with a discussion of the influence of experiential knowledge on TCFs export behaviour. The discussion is based on and illustrated by data about Swedish technical consultants' foreign operations..

9.2. Technical Consultancy Firms — Services and Relationships

While there are thousands of TCFs in Sweden, most of them are small firms. These are founded on skills and knowledge and the overwhelming majority of their employees possess years of formal education and training.

TCFs can be classified on a number of principles, namely, consultancy vs. contracting, large vs. small, autonomous vs. dependent etc. Perichitch (1976, p. 7) produced the following classification, 1. Independent TCFs, 2. TCFs and contractors combined within the same organization, and 3. TCFs as part or a department of a manufacturing firm. TCFs render technical services and counselling to their clients in such diverse fields as infrastructure development and improvement, industrial development and planning at national, regional, or local levels, industrial restructuring, development of energy resources, transportation (road, rail, river basin etc.), telecommunications, geological and geophysical surveys, industrial manpower planning etc.

Not all the TCFs provide all the above-mentioned services. Indeed, the majority of the Swedish TCFs are specialized and render services in a limited field. The TCFs may specialize in either of two fields, infrastructure or installation (Sharma & Johanson, 1983). The former include technical consultancy on buildings, roads, town planning, airport planning etc. The latter includes such fields as process technology, electrical or mechanical issues etc. In general in industrial projects installation specialists predominate. In the infrastructure projects the structural TCFs are predominant. Moreover, some TCFs execute a variety of tasks whereas the others are nisch-oriented.

TCFs are hired as experts to counsel their clients for two main reasons. Firstly, occasionally clients do not master a specific expertise. Alternatively, TCFs are engaged to bridge a temporary gap within the client's organization (Gårdeborn & Rhenman, 1974). This is the case when the client firm is endowed with experts but these are engaged elsewhere. The counselling may concern a specific aspect of a project or the whole project (Sharma & Johanson, 1984).

Sharma and Johanson (1984) and Sharma (1985) identified seven different phases in the working process of TCFs, namely, masterplan, pre-feasibility and feasibility study, basic design, detailed design and tender document preparation, negotiations and purchasing, control, start and operations. The task executed and the network of relationships varies from phase to phase. In the masterplan phase a general picture of the viability of an industry in an area (country, region etc) is analysed. This requires skill and the network of relationships includes universities, research institutions etc. In the prefeasibility and feasibility design phase technical consultancy on a particular project starts. The general concept of the project is analysed and the economic viability investigated. Only a limited number of experts are engaged. In the basic design phase the technical concept of the project is finalized. At this stage relationships with the industrial firms, research and technical institutions, and the other TCFs are required. In the detail design and tender document phase the work initiated in the basic design phase continues and the minor details are defined. Tender documents are prepared and dispatched to the manufacturing firms and the other suppliers. The shape of the relationships is the same as in the previous phase. In the next phase negotiations are undertaken to procure goods and services for the project. In this phase TCFs help the clients through interpretation and evaluation of the competing bids. Criteria to evaluate the competing bids are specified and applied. TCFs are (primarily) engaged in the technical aspects of the evaluation. Relationships with the equipment producing firms are required. In the control phase TCFs are responsible for exercising control over the task executed by the construction and civil engineering firms. The purpose is to ascertain that their performance conforms to the technical specifications. Probably the most important relationships required are those with the construction and the other civil engineering firms. Lastly, in the start and operations phase TCFs help optimize the production process. In this stage relationships with the manufacturing firms, equipment and system supplying firms are required. It is important to point out that not all the TCFs execute all the phases in all the projects. Frequently, TCFs specialize in only a few of the phases. For the purpose of this paper the last two phases are unimportant.

9.3. Experiential Knowledge in Technical Consultancy Networks

TCFs are knowledge-intensive firms. Investment in fixed assets is limited and the most significant asset possessed by these companies comprises their technical skills and knowledge. The overwhelming number of those working in TCFs are skilled and as a rule around 90% of the employees are technicians with years of formal education and training. Before a person is recruited as a technical consultant he will go through years of formal training. The remaining staff are science graduates, economists etc. also with years of formal education. The major portion of the TCF's knowledge is, however, experience.

As discussed previously, TCFs are hired as experts to counsel clients for two main reasons, namely because clients lack a specific expertise, or to bridge a temporary gap within the client's organization due to engagement elsewhere. Consequently, it is appropriate to analyse TCFs in terms of their knowledge and skills.

9.3.1. The Nature of Experiential Knowledge

Following Penrose, I shall distinguish between objective and experiential knowledge (1966, p. 53). The former accrues through other people, is transmitted through written media, is more objective in content and may concern the market situation, competition etc. In a sense it is a public good available to any interested actor.

The experiential knowledge is more subtle and particularistic and accumulated by those who participate in an action. Indeed, to a limited extent experience can be generalized and passed over to the other people i. e., experiential knowledge is, in some measure, transformed into objective knowledge. The generalization is, however, difficult as experiential knowledge is acquired by the people who participate in a particular act and interaction. Experiential knowledge is a cause of change, sureness and confidence.

Experiential knowledge impinges upon a person in two different ways, namely, changes in the knowledge acquired and changes in the ability to use knowledge. As we shall observe gradually the latter component is of particular interest.

As mentioned in the introductory Chapter of this volume, the members or the actors in the inner circles of a network are interconnected through strong ties. This implies existence of considerable experiential knowledge. It is through experience that actors in a network approach each other and strong ties evolve. A pre-condition is, however, that in business networks—and TCFs are a part of the business network—the experiential knowledge is positive and rewarding for the interacting parties. Rewards may or may not be pecuniary, and may accrue in the short, medium, or long term. Moreover, each isolated interaction need not be financially profitable. It is sufficient that it is rewarding. Negative experience, for instance, due to the failure to meet commitments or to live up to expectations, will produce a reverse effect. Failures jeopardize and complicate the task of developing and nurturing strong ties.

Experiential knowledge, in other words, contains information and clues to the network, its members, their respective centrality, the rules of the game and the code of conduct, and the division of labour within the network. The above pieces of information are soft and belong to those who participate in a network. Moreover, they are unwritten, evolve and change over time. As members of a network gain additional experiential knowledge the level of knowledge and interaction within the network alter.

TCFs may obtain experiential knowledge through a number of mechanisms. One is evidently participation by the members in a particular act. Alternatively, members with appropriate experiential knowledge can be hired from outside. This allows TCFs to acquire experiential knowledge of other networks with a different set of members, norms, code of conduct etc. For example, occasionally TCFs interested in international operations hire individuals with experience of international markets in the belief that this will help their firm to reach international clients.

9.3.2. Experiential Network Knowledge

TCFs have both objective and experiential knowledge. They possess general knowledge of the problems, solutions etc. in their respective areas of expertise, inculcated through years of formal education and training. Through formal education consultants grasp the general scientific and technical principles and their applicability. The knowledge is objective, unrestricted, and gained through 'book' reading. Although such knowledge is important for TCFs their actual work, i.e. the advice they offer and the recommendations they furnish, is seldom determined by this type of knowledge. This does not imply that formal education is unimportant. This is essential to gain legitimacy and a foothold in the profession. It is the experiential knowledge, however, that really matters.

TCFs gain experiential knowledge from the members of the network, specifically from those with whom they have strong ties. The experiential knowledge enables TCFs to investigate, understand, estimate and appreciate the capabilities and constraints of the other members of the network. This also allows TCFs to estimate and evaluate the applicability of a particular way of observing and analysing a problem and its suitability. The very existence of strong ties is, indeed, a sign that the members have worked together for a long time, that they enjoy each other's trust, the experience is positive and rewarding. Or strong ties fail to evolve. The experiential knowledge is the outcome of a process of selective perception, distortion, omission and can be separated into two components, namely, experience of particular companies, and experience of a particular technology. Experience of particular companies is a source of knowledge of decision-making, structure, administrative and information routines, etc. Experiential knowledge of a technology is important to assess its strength or weakness respectively, and applicability. Either type of experiential knowledge is important to manage network relationships and minimize uncertainty.

The existing network is not merely a source of experiential knowledge to TCFs but also restricts their sources of alternative experiential knowledge. The membership of one network implies non-membership of the competing networks. Consequently, TCFs develop ties with a limited number of partners. The process whereby this takes place is unconscious and subtle. A particular TCF may disregard of it and no formal decisions may be involved. But it is present. As discussed earlier the experiential knowledge of TCFs is restricted by the manufacturing firms, R&D organizations etc. with which they interact. As a result TCFs with a wide network of relationships receive more divergent and frequently a deeper knowledge than those with a narrow set of relationships.

The experiential knowledge limits the freedom of action and guides the operation of TCFs. This happens at several stages and exerts several influences. Firstly, the experiential knowledge of a TCF will influence the manner in which problems, opportunities and the underlying causal relationships are uncovered. Secondly, it will affect the solution offered to remedy a problem. TCFs hesitate to submit 'completely' novel solutions to a problem. Their solutions are determined by their experiential knowledge, which in turn is guided by their network of relationships. In this respect each relationship in the network is unique and a source as well as an outcome of unique experiential knowledge. The experiential knowledge in the network is, however, mutual. TCFs gain knowledge of the other members of the network and vice-versa.

The above argument is illustrated with the help of TCFs' assistance to domestic exports. The research by the author shows that the network of relationships of the Swedish TCFs is overwhelmingly Swedish and that these firms lend support to domestic exports.

9.4. Network Internationalization of Swedish TCFs

That TCFs exert a positive influence on exports is highlighted by their response to a survey executed by the author. The survey was preceded by data collection through face-to-face interviews with representatives of over 25 TCFs. More or less all the Swedish TCFs with foreign operations participated in the survey. The questionnaire was dispatched to 210 TCFs and 92 answers were received. Slightly less than 70 of these were engaged in foreign operations.

9.4.1. Experiential Knowledge and Exports

The TCFs mentioned six main mechanisms to support domestic exports. For example, 37 out of 56 respondents (approximately 65 per cent) indicated that they support exports through propagation of knowledge and information on domestic goods and services in the international market. In addition, the respondents specified that they support exports through other mechanisms, namely, through recommendations to international clients to use domestic goods and services, or through a favourable interpretation of the tender documents submitted by the Swedish suppliers etc.

At the beginning of this Chapter the working process of the TCFs was described and seven phases were identified. In each of these seven phases a different set of tasks is performed and counsel offered. The experiential knowledge is important at each of the phases. Firstly, experiential knowledge exerts decisive influence on the functional solutions offered by a TCF. In order to serve the interests of the client TCFs specify the desirable functional solution to the problem and the opportunities. Experiential knowledge is important as for every problem a number of functional solutions are suitable. TCFs with different experiential knowledge may suggest different functional solutions in the same project. Moreover, a number of different suppliers with their respective pieces of equipment are in a position to achieve the desired functional solution (or they claim so). The system concept finalized and the design produced is, consequently, significant.

In the survey conducted by the author this was found to have an essential bearing on export opportunities for the domestic corporations. As many as 21 of the 55 respondents specified this mechanism as either very important or important as a means to further domestic exports. Since the major part of the network of the TCFs is domestic the functional solutions offered and the design these firms produce in international projects are determined by the domestic experiential knowledge. This happens partly at the prefeasibility and feasibility phase but primarily at the basic design phase.

In the detailed design and tender document preparation phase, as stated earlier, TCFs render a number of services to their clients. Tender documents and vendor lists are prepared. Procurement decisions are thereby influenced in a number of ways, namely, through recommendations as to prospective suppliers, through propagation and supply of information on domestic suppliers of goods and services, and recommendations to use a particular piece of equipment in the project. For example TCFs include in the vendor list 'only' those suppliers of whom they have positive experience and whom they trust. Indeed, at this stage the objective knowledge of TCFs concerning a branch, suppliers etc. is also important. To create competition in the project, and to maintain neutrality and objectivity a number of potential suppliers are included in the vendor list. Equipment suppliers with whom TCFs are engaged in strong relationships are included in the vendor list and, thereby, qualify to participate in projects. In our survey, as stated earlier, as many as 37 of the 56 respondents mentioned that they help domestic exporters through this mechanism. Moreover, 22 stated that they support domestic exports through recommendations to the international clients to use domestic goods and services.

In the following phase, the negotiations phase, the project owner negotiates with the suppliers. TCFs participate during this phase together with clients to reach a final decision through use of 'objective' criteria and judgement to evaluate and select among the competing suppliers. Experiential knowledge is vital. Positive experiential knowledge of an equipment and its source is evaluated highly and positively. Indeed, the very criteria used by the TCFs to evaluate and rank the competing bids and the suppliers are the outcome of the TCFs experience of the equipment and the suppliers. Positive experiential knowledge leads to repetition and the use of the same criteria for evaluating and comparing the suppliers. Consequently, the members of the network who enjoy strong relationships with TCFs are rewarded at each of these stages. This is significant as in industrial sectors the range of available technology as well as equipment is wide, indeed much wider than generally realized (ILO, 1984, ch. 1). In more or less all industrial fields a range of technologies exist which vary along the different dimensions, namely, labour vs. capital intensity, complex vs. standard, old vs. new, etc.

In this phase TCFs influence the procurement decision in three different ways, namely, they can recommend the use of domestic equipment in a project; interpret tenders objectively so that the domestic equipment suppliers compete in the project on a fair basis, and lastly, actually favour domestic sources of supply. The response of the firms on the first issue was discussed earlier. In the survey 19 out of 54 TCFs stated that they help domestic exports through objective interpretation of tenders. Surprisingly, around one fifth of the respondents reported that they help domestic exports by an outright favourable interpretation of the domestic compared with the foreign tenders. This is contrary to the expectations as independent TCFs are hired to offer objective advice.

In addition TCFs also help domestic exporters through their supply of international project-related information. This flow of information may take place in a number of ways but the process is seldom formalized. The process is informal, as TCFs meet members of the domestic network and discuss issues, including opportunities abroad. These discussions may take place at the different project sites where the TCFs are working together with the equipment suppliers. Thereby, information on foreign projects as well as export opportunities abroad is passed on. In our survey 18 out of 54 TCFs ranked this alternative as either a very important or an important means to support exports.

9.4.2. Internationalization of the TCF Network

The network of a TCF is to varying degrees domestic or international, and consequently so is the experiential knowledge. The more domestic the network the more domestic the relationships with the suppliers of technology, goods and services, the more domestic the approach to problems and opportunities, the more domestic the criteria used to evaluate and compare the sources of supply. Conversely, the more international the network of relationships the more international is the experiential knowledge. The TCFs with an overwhelmingly domestic network of relationships and experiential knowledge observe problems from a 'domestic' angle, suggest domestic-based solutions, include domestic sources of supply in the vendor list, and utilize domestic-based criteria to evaluate the competitive bids. These TCFs 'favour', openly or tacitly, consciously or unconsciously, domestic sources of supply in international projects. However, as the operations of the TCF or network of relationships are internationalized the characteristics of the experiential knowledge alter and become more internationalized. In this process TCFs also learn to utilize the experiential knowledge in a different manner. Evidently, international operations result in interaction with a number of legal and social systems, technical norms, and buyers. Internationalization leads to improved interaction with the overseas economies, culture, and source of procurement. The experiential knowledge as well as the ability to use it is altered.

Swedish TCFs as a rule started their operations with the idea of serving the domestic market and the overwhelming proportion of these firms continue to do so. Only a limited number of TCFs have undertaken international operations. Over 90 per cent of the Swedish TCFs have no or insignificant foreign operations (Svenska konsultföreningen, 1982). Their experiential knowledge is Swedish based. As these TCFs execute international projects they observe the problems and opportunities in Swedish terms, use Swedish criteria to evaluate the various alternatives based on their Swedish experiential knowledge and recommend Swedish solutions. Indeed, occasionally it happens that they are hired primarily for the reason that they offer Swedish solutions. Clients are impressed by the Swedish way of solving a problem and prefer a similar solution in their own country or project.

9.5. Concluding Remarks

In this Chapter the issue of 'the objectiveness' of technical consultancy is discussed. In contrast to the frequently stated view that TCFs offer objective counselling, it is argued that the advice and the services rendered by TCFs are based on and influenced by the network of relationships to which they belong. TCFs are guided by their own experiential knowledge which is domestic oriented. Moreover, this has to be so if TCFs are to function and remain viable as commercial organizations. Achieving absolute rationality in the classical sense is an impossibility even in professional firms like TCFs. The appropriateness of a TCF for a project should be evaluated on its network of relationships rather than the firm alone. The elements of 'irrationality' which penetrate its counselling will not necessarily be inimical to the interest of the buyer, unless indeed, the network of the TCF is too narrow. Lastly, in the international market appropriate technical counselling can be supplied even by the TCFs engaged in national networks but with international relationships.

10

Managing International Package Deal Projects
Amjad Hadjikhani

10.1. Package Deal Projects in Business Networks

During recent decades international package deal projects have become increasingly significant in the international business arena. In projects a contractor is responsible for setting up a new plant including both hardware and software for a buyer. The contractor signs a contract with the buyer and undertakes the management of the project. The fundamental issue in these organizations is the management of the resources. The contractor establishes a project group which pools resources from various sources. Since resource acquisition varies, the project group necessarily turns to different external sources. Therefore the project group signs contracts with specialised sub-contractors for the parts which are not available within the firm. The collaboration between firms for the accomplishment of a project results in the emergence of an organization containing members from different organizations. This organization focuses on a clear, specific goal and passes the stages of planning and negotiation, production, installation and operation. When the goal is achieved, at the operation stage, the exchange of resources ceases, the contractor receives the fee and the buyer undertakes the operation of the plant (Hadjikhani, 1985, pp. 21-23). This indicates that the package deal organization is temporary, in the sense that it is born when one entity in the planning stage draws up a contract for the entire plant with another entity, and it is dissolved at the end of the operation phase when the transaction is completed (Hayden, 1976, p. 3).

The management of relationships for the exchange of resources in the project organizations has been the subject of earlier studies. The theoretical tools from the temporary organizations are employed for analysis of the relationships. Accordingly, the project organizations have been defined as coalitions of members who temporarily pool their resources for a project with no expectation of any further cooperation after project termination;

138

management's task is to orient the members' activities towards the project's specific and clear goal. The members' resource contribution is temporary and management of the coalition is assumed to terminate when the goal is achieved. In other words, the organization and managerial tasks evolve for a project and dissolve after project termination.

The business network model conveys, however, a somewhat different picture. It suggests that the contracting parties may be engaged in, to some extent, overlapping networks connecting a number of suppliers, competitors, customers, consultants, public agencies and other units. It suggests also that the supplier may be involved in more or less lasting and close relationships with a set of sub-suppliers and that these relationships are activated when the package deal project is organized. Thus it can be expected that the supplier's network is an important resource enabling him to carry out the project and that he has an interest in developing this network during the project. Against this background this chapter describes and analyses an international package deal in which the Swedish ASEA Relays supplied electrical equipment to a Brazilian project.

10.2. A Swedish-Brazilian Package Deal Project

In 1982 ASEA Relays started negotiation about a package deal project concerned with the supply of relay, control and communications system for transformer stations in the Santa-Catarina state in Brazil. Beside ASEA Relays, a German and a Japanese firm were invited to tender. But ASEA Relays was elected by the buyer, Electrosul (ES). ES is a state-owned organization, responsible for production and distribution of electricity in southern Brazil. The project included transfer of both software and hardware. The hardware covered 10 relay, control and communications systems for power lines with 525-750 kV. The software concerned the engineering knowledge required for adaptation of the relays and control systems' standard technology to ES's specific technological application. The total cost of the project was 20 MSEK of which 15 per cent was devoted to software. The project was complex and unusual since it required more than 20 thousand technical adaptations.

In 1982 a project leader from the project unit of the ASEA Relays assumed responsibility for the management of the project and the project organization evolved and became active. ASEA Relays' formal organizational structure is illustrated in Figure 10.1 below.

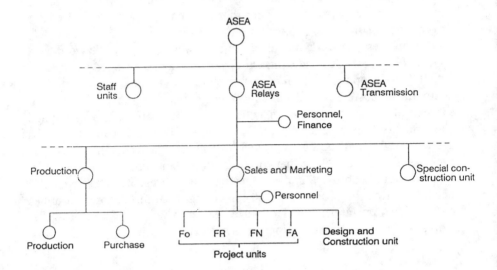

FIGURE 10.1: The Formal Organization Structure of ASEA Relays

FO = Latin America and Asia FR = Sweden FN = North America,U.K., Nordic Countries, East Europe FA = Australia, New Zealand and Continental Europe

Source: ASEA Organization, Public Prints.

The project unit together with the design and construction units involve more than 30 engineers. These engineers established different project groups on the bases of their technological and geographical specializations. For this project the project leader from FO engaged four engineers from the design unit for the technical adaptations and two technicians from ASEA's subsidiary in São Paulo. Together they constituted a project group which started to mobilize resources in 1982. This resulted in the emergence of a project organization comprising units from ASEA and external sub-contractors.

The project organization included two draughtsmen and one contact man from ASEA Relays'construction unit. The contact man's duties were to liaise between the organization and the purchasing unit and staff units from ASEA. The staff units included legal and printing units. These units were involved for a short period at the planning stage of the project. The project leader, the engineers and the technicians were active from the stage when the project organization was established. When the sets of drawing were completed, ASEA Relays' production unit in Sweden, which also manufactured all the technical components, became involved for some months. Besides these members, the project leader engaged the purchasing unit in buying standardised components.

The project organization also included several sub-contractors. Some of these came from the ASEA group. But for specific, complex components, 15 external sub-contractors from Sweden, Germany, Brazil and USA were engaged. All these sub-contractors were participating in the project organization during the assembly and erection phases. The length of the sub-contractors involvement in the organization varied, mainly depending upon the complexity of the components' technologies. ASEA Relays engaged an American sub-contractor for production and installation of the whole communication system. The measuring instruments and instruments in the relay and control system were supplied by a German and a Swedish sub-contractor. The signal system was provided by a sub-contractor from Brazil. These sub-contractors were involved until the operation phase.

The operation phase started at the end of 1987 and in April 1988 all the stations were handed over to ES. After completion, the technicians from São Paulo returned to their duties in ASEA's Brazilian subsidiary, the project leader and engineers were transferred to another project and the project organization was dissolved.

10.3. Mobilizing a Pre-Project Network

The earlier presentation of the Brazilian project focused on the temporariness of the relationships between the involved parties. According to this account the exchange of resources started in 1982 and terminated in 1987-1988. Since it was assumed that the project was unique, the time and cost were limited the project had a life cycle, and the management task was temporary. In this context some interesting questions can be raised. For example, what were the project group's relationships with other involved parties before the project and accordingly, how did the project group mobilise the resources? The following section focuses on the situation existing before the planning stage of the Brazilian project.

If we observe the project group's net of relationships prior to completion we find two types of relationship, namely active and inactive or sleeping. This categorization can also be related to the types of technology, standardized (semi standardized is included), and complex or specific, of the component parts. This project required hundreds of standardized components. The requirements were similar to those imposed in earlier projects managed by the project leader and others from the project unit. The purchasing unit already had relationships with thousands of sub-contractors. In this project the project leader could simply activate sleeping standardized relationships of the purchasing unit. This unit purchased components for both the production unit and the project unit. Out of ASEA Relays' total sales of 500 MSEK per year, only 50 MSEK belonged to the project unit. So, there was already a regular flow of standardized components from these sub-contractors to the purchasing unit and thence to the production unit. This had resulted in the emergence of standardized rules between the sub-contractors and the purchasing unit. The project leader avoided new relationships. There was also a general policy in the project unit that project leaders were to activate already established relationships as far as possible, since these were standardized and consequently the costs in time and money needed for the operation were reduced.

For the second type of technology, the complex or specific, because of the components' costs and technologies, the project leader and sub-contractors in this project had direct contacts. But these contacts also had a history. For the power line career system (for communication), e.g. an American firm was involved. In 1981 ASEA Relays' production unit had its first technological co-operation with this firm. The project group was connected to this firm since the engineers from the group undertook the technological adaptation of some components. The connection, together with the price and quality, prompted the project leader to select the firm. There were 20 firms in the world producing the same components. Four of these, General Electric, Siemens, Electro Bureau, and a Japanese firm had previous relationships with the project unit for other projects. One of the four firms had a fifty percent lower price than the international price. But this relationship was not activated since the product quality was very low.

There were more than 100 sub-contractors in the world producing the instruments needed in the project. The purchasing unit had stable relationships with only seven of these. The project leader had also previous direct relationships with these sub-contractors. In this project the price, the quality and the service impelled the project leader to activate one of the relationships. Even for these components the purchasing unit always turned to these seven sub-contractors and therefore undertook the maintenance of the relationships.

Prior to this project, there was a connection between the project group and ES. It was well known in Brazil that ASEA's products contained a high level of technology and the firm had a leading position in several industrial products. Before this project ASEA Transmission was already involved in several transformer stations projects, and ASEA Transmission purchased relay components from ASEA Relays. But ASEA Relays in Sweden had not been involved in any package deal project with ES. In two cases ES had purchased relay components for 300 TSEK. For these standardized products ASEA's subsidiary received the orders then sent them to the relays production unit in Sweden. There was also a permanent contact between the subsidiary's technicians and ES. In 1982, the technicians from ASEA's subsidiary in Sao Paolo informed about the project and the connection between ES and ASEA Relays was thereby activated. The emphasis of the project leader on the technicians' relationships was one of the main reasons why the Japanese lost the contract and ASEA Relays was chosen.

However, parallel to this positive contact there also existed a general mistrust toward ASEA Relays. This derived from the ES and other Brazilian firms' opinions about the economic development resulting from MNCs' operations in Brazil. The mistrust became stronger when another project, which was carried out by a German firm, was completed. A few years before entering into negotiations for this project the German firm had signed a contract with ES for installation of relay and control systems. In the early stage of the completion conflicts arose between ES and the German firm. The project completion continued but neither side made a real effort to resolve the conflicts. When the project was terminated, the mistrust in their relationships was aggravated since ES, when taking over the systems, evaluated the results as unsatisfactory. In consequence ES's mistrust of foreign firms, among t hem ASEA Relays, became stronger. It was also because of this situation that, when negotiating for the present project, the German firm increased the project cost by more than 20 per cent in order to lose the competition but keep its reputation.

The relationships explained above are illustrated in Figure 10.2 below.

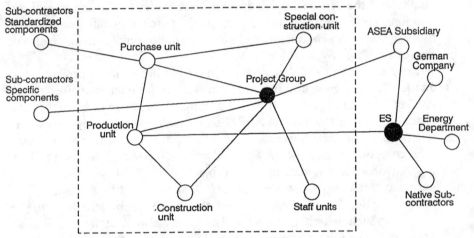

FIGURE 10.2: Pre Project Network
Source: Interviews

10.4. Post-Project Network for Future Use

The earlier discussion illustrated the existence of relationships and connections between some of the involved parties before they entered into the Brazilian project. The relationships did not evolve from scratch. The fundamental management task of the project group was to utilize, as far as possible, the already existing network in mobilizing the resources. But how did the network appear after the project completion and how was the maintenance of the network undertaken? The following section focuses on the network after project termination.

The main goal of the project group's involvement in such project was not only the project itself. It was rather the future possibilities in the country of participation in new projects from ES or other buyers. The project group sought to build a stable relationship with ES and its networks.

When the project group from ES took over the systems and observed the appropriate functioning of the machinery, its mistrust in the early stages successively waned. Achievement of such a result had not been an easy task. It required the elimination of conflicts through an intensive technical and social co-operation in the project completion. In one example, the conflicts concerned the matter of technological adaptations. The technology in the transformer stations required some changes in the technological adaptations undertaken in the original agreement. In cases of minor changes, the technicians succeeded in receiving approvals. For other changes the approval of the Engineering Department in Brazil must be obtained, because the project was financed by the World Bank and the Engineering Department had control over the project's cost. More than 15 personal meetings were arranged. But in spite of these efforts no progress was made. As a result the project leader used his ultimate power and declared that ASEA Relays intended to withraw from the project. After a short period the adaptation changes were approved by both the Engineering Department and ES. Conflict also arose when ES shortly after signing of the contract asked for the sets of drawings. After hard negotiation, the project leader convinced ES that 20,000 technical adaptations illustrated in 2,500 technical drawings could not be delivered in a very short time.

However, the intensive interactions in reducing the mistrust and conflicts had positive results. The members of both sides became familiar with each other's modes of behaviour and values. In the earlier stage of the project the project leader emphasized the strengthening of the connection (via technicians) since they were familiar with the ES's social values. But now the technicians had lost their former positions in the network. The intensive social and technical activities had brought ES and the project group in Sweden closer to each other. In this context, the project leader explained that:

> if there arises a request for another project, I am going to contact the ES project-leader personally. Even if the ES project-leader leaves the ES, we know a dozen people in ES.

There were also technical interdependences which activated some relationships after the termination of the project. In general, after completion of such a project, the technical activities concern, a) purchases of spare parts and b) buying of new systems to increase the capacity of the system. For the spare parts, the ES project-group employed an unusual policy. At the negotiation stage, one demand raised was to include the spare parts in the tender. This policy sought not to reduce technological interdependence but to avoid the complex Brazilian bureaucratic rules for import of spare parts. After completion there have been several occasions when parts were not available in ES which means that the relationships between ES and ASEA Relays were kept active.

The relationships with the suppliers of standardized components were inactive for a short period until the project group became involved in a Chinese project. During this inactive period, as in the period of pre-project interaction, the purchasing unit maintained the network since there was a constant flow of these components from the sub-contractors to the production unit. The activation of the relationships involving specific components depended on the outcome of the relationships from the Brazilian project. In this context the project leader explained that:

> After the Brazilian project when I was looking for sub-contractors for the China project, I had in my mind which sub-contractors could really fulfil our demands.

For the instrument components in the Brazilian project, for example, the project group was connected to a sub-contractor in Germany. A Swedish sub-contractor purchased the components from the German sub-contractor and sold them with no technological change to the project organization. On the completion of the Brazilian project the German sub-contractor sent an engineer to ASEA Relays for the purpose of the technological assistance. The project leader stated that:

> such an assistance naturally influenced the choice of the sub-contractor for the China project.

In other words, because of the Brazilian project some relationships became stronger. But, having positive relations with the sub-contractor does not guarantee the activation of the network in the next project. The American firm's relations with the project group were positive. But when the project group entered into the next project, they selected another sub-contractor (from the ABB group) notwithstanding that the project group and the chosen sub-contractor had no earlier relationship and the price they offered was a little higher than those of other competitors. The main reason was that the merger between ASEA and BBC (called ABB) in 1986 caused the emergence of a relationship within the ABB group which was stronger than the ABB Relays project group's relationship with the American firm. Of course the offered price had some influence. In the Brazilian project despite the fact that the Electric Bureau belonged to the ABB group it did not become involved because the firm stated a price for the power line career component which was much higher than that set by the American firm.

So far, as discussed above, all the relationships used in the project were older than the project organization. But there were two factors which caused the development of new relationships with sub-contractors, a) ES's specific technological applications for standard components, b) ES's specific demand for involvement of a domestic sub-contractor. These two factors together with the required engineering knowledge for adaptation of the technology made this project unique. ES used ten components which are usually categorised as standard. For these products five sub-contractors were involved, two being completely new. In one case, the signal system, the project group accepted ES's demand for involvement of a Brazilian sub-contractor for two main reasons; viz. pressure from the government and the ES personnel's familiarity with the native technical systems. The project leader received information from the subsidiary that the quality, particularly the soldering, carried out by the domestic sub-contractor, was not satisfactory. The project leader still accepted the deal, but only because he intended to build a positive relationship with ES with a view to future co-operation. However, the results of co-operation with the Brazilian sub-contractor were unsatisfactory and the project leader considered it difficult to have any relationships with that firm in the future. A reactivation may only take place if a buyer absolutely requires that components be delivered from this particular sub-contractor.

For the component called terminals, the project leader established relationships with a small Swedish sub-contractor who had no earlier direct relation or connection with the project group or purchasing unit. In the other three cases, the project group had formerly been connected with the sub-contractors via the purchasing unit. But in this project the specific demands of ES applied for direct contact.

The net of relationships after the project completion is illustrated in Figure 10.3 below.

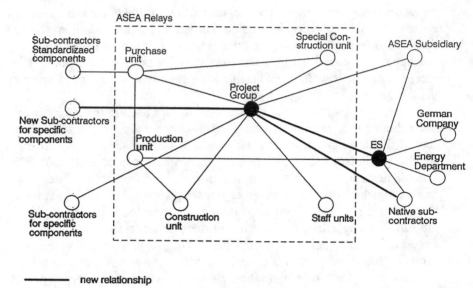

new relationship

old relationship

FIGURE 10.3: Post Project Network

Source: Interviews.

The project is terminated but as Figure 10.3 demonstrates the net of relationships still exists. Some are involved in the Chinese project while others are inactive. Because of this project some new relationships have emerged.

10.5. Conclusions

Earlier studies on package deals projects deal with the temporary nature of the resource exchanges. The organization is recognized as a short-lived coalition and the managers orient the activities toward a specific goal. The activities in the resource contribution are temporary and the management of the coalition is assumed to terminate when the goal is achieved. The organization is regarded as having a life-cycle, which starts with the project and dissolves after the project's termination (See Aldrich, 1979, pp. 317-319; Foord, 1987, pp. 120-124; Goodman, 1981). In this perspective the structure is the foundation. In a sense the members, when contributing resources for a project, separate from an already established structure. When the project is completed the members return to their earlier structural positions. Members come from a formal structure and return to a formal structure. The project organization concentrates only on the period in between and therefore the temporariness of the management is in focus. Since the organization is viewed as temporary with no relationships before and after, the newness of all the relationships is implicitly in the assumptions. Therefore, in every project the management is assumed to undertake mutual adjustment to co-ordinate the relationships (see Dilworth, 1985).

The use of network theory (see Johanson, 1989) to study the project organizations placed in question the matters of temporariness and newness in the relationships. The point of departure in the presentation of the Brazilian project was the temporariness of the organization. But when the study changed the point of departure new facts and conclusions about the management of the relationships were disclosed.

As the case above illustrates there are relationships in both the pre and the post stages. Further, these relationships influence the project completion. In the pre-project stage, it is first incumbent on the managers to activate old relationships and connections. In other words, their fundamental task is to mobilize the already established network. So the net of relationships is older than the project's life-cycle. Therefore, for some components standardized roles can be employed in the management. If all the relationships for a project are new, a need arises for a great deal of technical co-operation. This may be true only for a seller involved in a project with new technological requirements.

Studies dealing with the relationship between buyers and sellers produce similar results. Relationships are stable since buyers and sellers are acquainted with each others' social and technical abilities. Therefore, the interdependence can simply be managed through standardized rules.

The project manager's strategy is to utilize earlier relationships as far as possible and avoid new relationships. Establishment of new relationships would increase the cost, the time and the uncertainty. In other words, the relationships have much longer lifetime than the project itself (Håkansson, 1986, pp. 6-8). It is true that the relationships are project oriented but the seller sees them as a continuous interaction (Mattsson, 1979, pp. 160-163).

Evidently the network in the post project stage is not identical with the network in the pre project stage because of the uniqueness of each project. Every project requires some components with a specific technology which calls for intensive technical co-operation. In every project this leads to the development of, a) some completely new relationships, b) some relationships which become stronger, c) some relationships which are replaced by other relationships and finally, d) some relationships which become weaker than before. The establishment of new relationships or the strengthening of old ones with sub-contractors mainly depends upon the sub-contractors' technical and social interactions with the contractor. But the outcome of the relationships in the post stage depends mainly on the project manager's efforts during project completion. In the case above the project leader's aim was to replace the mistrust existing in the pre stage with positive relationships in the post stage. The project group therefore accepted new relationships dictated by buyers, notwithstanding that these relationships had some negative effects on the efficiency of the project.

A crucial area in the management is the maintenance of the inactive relationships in the pre and post stages. A long period of inactivity increases the uncertainty in the establishment of standardized rules. Via social and technological information the leader necessarily activates the network now and then for future needs. The connections via units having continuous relationships with the buyer and sub-contractors facilitate the management procedures. These units maintain the network and when necessary hand over the standard procedure to the leaders. This avoids the reactivation of network through intensive technical co-operation which otherwise would have been needed for completion of a project.

PART III
Understanding Network Change Processes in
International Business
Mats Forsgren and Jan Johanson

The third part of the book treats in different ways how changes in specific networks can be seen as outcomes of the properties of these networks. Two of the chapters deal with the financial markets. In Chapter Eleven Henrik Didner remarks that the ownership of Swedish international firms up to the 1980s was concentrated to Swedish investors even though their internationalization has been in progress for a very long time. By looking into the process of ownership internationalization through a case study, and analysing the actors in the financial market and the relationships between them, he finds other reasons for this time lag than are usually reported in international portfolio theory. One main conclusion is that well established foreign operations seem to be more or less prerequisites for maintaining a foreign ownership interest because of the long-lasting relationships between the firm, investors, brokers and investment banks that such operations must create.

In Chapter Twelve Lars Engwall discusses the internationalization of Swedish banks. He shows that a bank wanting to internationalize will encounter certain barriers, some which are connected to rules and regulations of the home country and some which are dependent on the relationships within the existing network of providers of international capital and customers. He concludes that the development in computer & communication technology is based on a lower degree of person to person contact which in the future will decrease the bank's traditional actor oriented view on financial networks towards one more activity oriented. The inherent tendency to preserve the balance of power between actors in a network is the starting point for the analysis of the international rock drilling industry, carried out by Mats Forsgren and Ulf Olsson in Chapter Thirteen. A takeover within that industry prompted a series of moves and

151

countermoves by different actors in order to preserve the balance. Forsgren and Olsson claim that these types of actions are more likely the more committed the actors are, and also that in a network with a few deeply committed actors there is a tendency throughout the system to reduce the number of actors with shallow commitment.

The last two chapters of the book deal with another important issue within international business research; viz. the establishment and development of positions in an industrial network in other countries than the country of origin. In Chapter Fourteen Nils Kinch analyses the successful story of Volvo in the US market. He argues that the introduction of the Volvo car in that market and the following years' remarkable growth in sales was not the well planned and expected event reported in the official history of Volvo. Kinch also discusses possible reasons why a European company could establish a position in a market so heavily dominated by GM, Ford and Chrysler and with close relationships between manufacturers, dealers, service facilities and customers. He finds the answer in the way the network was structured.

The network structure also plays an important role in Chapter Fifteen in which Maria Bolte and Nazeem Seyed-Mohamed present the history of the Swedish firm Atlas Copco's attempts to introduce the firm's compressor product in the US market. This case illustrates the difficulties, faced even by a firm with large resources, in establishing a position in a moderately structured network other than by "buying its way in" through acquisition of an actor already on the inside. But the authors also argue that in a network characterized by person-oriented rather than activity-oriented relationships this action, though perhaps necessary, is not enough. Further investments in relationships are required in order to reach a position in such a network.

11

Managing Ownership Internationalization
Henrik Didner

11.1. Foreign Ownership in Swedish Multinationals

"AB Fortia, the Swedish biotechnology and pharmaceutical company, filed with the Securities and Exchange Commission for the proposal of sale of 2.5 million American Depository Receipts, representing 2.5 million of the company's non-restricted Class B shares" (Wall Street Journal, 26/10 1981).

A few weeks later Fortia, later on named Pharmacia, through the American Investment bank Morgan Stanley, issued three million shares to American investors. This raised a staggering $ 47m. (280 MSEK) for Pharmacia — equivalent to the three previous years spending on research and development. Pharmacia's only previous share issue, a rights issue in 1977, raised 50 MSEK.

Pharmacia was the first Swedish firm in modern times to raise equity abroad. How could a rather small firm like Pharmacia at that time probably unknown to foreign investors do this?

The ownership of the Swedish multinationals (MNE:s) has up to the 1980s, been confined chiefly to Swedish investors. The ownership has not been internationalized to the same degree as the operations. In the 1970s the tendency was actually the opposite, foreign investors were net-sellers of Swedish shares although the absolute amount was small. During the 1970s a number of firms, e.g. Ericsson, AGA and Esselte, also tried to attract foreign ownership capital through the issue of convertible bonds in London. The experience from these issues pointed in just one direction: it was only a question of time before the converted bonds, i.e. shares, flowed back to Sweden. Although a number of Swedish MNE:s had their shares listed abroad, most commonly on the London Stock Exchange, the trade in these shares was very thin, reflecting poor foreign interest.

During the 1980s a new situation has emerged. Foreign investors have so far approximately doubled their holdings of listed Swedish shares; from

153

3−4 per cent to around 7 per cent of the total value of listed Swedish shares 1987 (SOU 1988:38 pp. 277, 280). The foreign investors' holdings are

TABLE 11.1: The 21 Swedish Listed Firms with the Highest Degree of Foreign Ownership Autum 1987. Percentage.

	1979	1987
Ericsson	11.8	36.7
Electrolux	10.4	25.4
Atlas Copco	3.9	24.4
SKF	10.7	22.3
Pharmacia	5.0[a]	19.7
Astra	3.4	16.6
ASEA	4.1	12.3
Volvo	5.9	12.2
PLM	13.4	11.6
AGA	3.2	11.2
Gambro	n.a.	9.4
Perstorp	6.1	8.2
Esselte	n.a.	7.8
Skåne-Gripen	n.a.	6.6
Sandvik	1.6	6.5
Skandia	n.a.	4.8
Bilspedition	n.a.	4.7
Alfa-Laval	4.6	3.5
Skanska	5.8	3.4
SCA	3.3	3.4
Stora	2.3	2.6
Average	6.0	12.0

[a]own estimate

Hennes & Mauritz, Boliden, Skandia International and Fermenta are excluded as no longer listed on the Stock Exchange, or for other special reasons.

Source: SOU 1988:38 p. 281.

concentrated to the big multinational firms. Table 11.1 below, which contains the 21 firms with the highest degree of foreign ownership, include all the large Swedish multinational firms except one, Saab-Scania.

The trade in Swedish shares abroad increased perhaps even more during the 1980s. London is now the trading place for shares in the large Swedish MNE:s (Affärsvärlden 1989/17, p. 13). But also in the USA, on the NASDAQ[1] list, a number of Swedish MNE:s have a liquid market for their shares.

Why has the internationalization of ownership lagged behind the internationalization of operations, and why and how did such a change occur during the 1980s? These are the main questions of this Chapter, to be discussed in the light of earlier research in Uppsala on the internationalization process.

Section two briefly presents earlier research on the international distribution of ownership. It concludes with an alternative answer to the above question, using a network oriented approach. Section three comprises a case study of the process of ownership internationalization in the Swedish firm Pharmacia. Section four discusses the case and the Chapter ends with conclusions in Part five.

11.2. International Portfolio Investments

International flows of equity can be labeled either portfolio investments or foreign direct investment. In the first case the investment is seen as a pure financial investment, whereas in the latter control is a central aspect.

The phenomenon international portfolio investments is chiefly discussed under the theoretical framework of portfolio theory. Foreign direct investments are mainly treated under the area of theories of the MNE.

Grubel (1968) made an early attempt to incorporate the international dimension into portfolio theory, which until then had considered primarily the American situation. Grubel sought (1) to specify the variables in a model which determines how the individual [portfolio] investor distributes

---

1   National Association of Security Dealers Automatic Quotations.

his assets internationally, and (2) to show what welfare gains investors could attain through international diversification.

Regarding the first purpose, the model, Grubel concluded that interest rate differentials are only one of several reasons for the international flows of equity. Other factors in his model are the growth and stocks of wealth, degree of correlation of returns on domestic and foreign assets, and differences in consumption patterns between nations. This leads to the possibility for equity to flow simultaneously in both directions between two countries.

Regarding the second goal Grubel found that there are great possibilities for investors to increase their welfare through international diversification. His analysis was based on stock market averages from 11 major countries.

A large number of articles followed. One group tried to construct more advanced models, and another supported the result concerning the welfare gains achieved through international diversification.

All these studies discuss differences between nations not between specific firms. The specific firm is of interest only with respect to the correlation of return to other shares. The degree of foreign ownership is only measured on an aggregated level and the foreign ownership of the specific firm is of less interest, as the unit of analysis is the investor. The investor is assumed to be rational, with the possibility of gathering as much information as any other investor. He is then free to make his choices without any contraints other than those incorporated in the model. The contraints are mainly institutional, such as regulations or unfavourable tax treatment, which are treated in the models as exogenous variables.

The third group of articles deals with the question of what role the shares of the multinational firms have for investors in the home country. This group of articles argues that investors can basically have two reasons to be specifically interested in multinational firms, i.e. to pay a premium for those shares. The first is that if the individual investor for some reason has to limit his horizon to his own country, then the multinational firm can give him international diversification. The second is the assumption that multinational firms have some kind of monopoly advantage. If so it is logical that investors are willing to pay a premium for those shares.

This third group of articles may, in the portfolio based framework, shed some light on the rationale for multinational firms' existence from a financial perspective. But this group of articles does not help us to explain the Swedish experience of increased interest from foreign portfolio investors during the 1980s.

11.3. Ownership Internationalization in a Network Perspective

This Chapter tries to answer the question about ownership internationalization by discussing how the increased foreign ownership of Swedish firms has come about. The basic belief is that the individual investor is not the autonomous rational actor he is seen to be in the portfolio theory. Here he is viewed as an individual actor in a network of relations. The center of the analysis must accordingly be such a network. His choice in selecting shares to buy, or sell, is constrained by the network in which he operates. For example, he has his broker, he lives somewhere, he has his contacts in different firms, he is familiar with certain information channels and probably has a special knowledge of a specific industry or group of firms. And for him to change his routines of investing may not be so easy. Of course there is a great variety of investors, from the "little" man to the professional who has both the resources to buy any information he wants and a vast contact network. But even the professional investor can be expected to be constrained by the relations he has in his network.

If the investor is seen in this perspective the question of why becomes more complex and portfolio models give a deceptive, simplified, explanation. Instead the question of how this internationalization process takes place becomes more interesting. It is important to understand why the degree of foreign ownership differs between firms. If such knowledge can be obtained the whole question about ownership internationalization can be better understood. The physical presence and size of a firm in a country becomes more significant. Extensive international activities give rise to relationships in which investors are involved in one way or another.

Brokers and investment banks increase in importance with this view. They have contacts with both investors and the firm, and must carefully balance the interests of different actors. Even if some of these financial firms are large, they can in no way gather information about all shares—they have to choose which ones to follow more closely. The complexity of the situation also increases as these financial firms consist of individuals with sometimes different interests. Some want to maximize commissions, others want to trade, and still others want to write well regarded analysts' reports.

The management of the Swedish firm has, of course, a role to play here. But they are just one of several actors on the scene. Moreover in the 1970s the management of some Swedish firms tried to interest foreign investors through convertible bonds issued mainly in London, but at that time it was not sufficient to extend the interest to retaining the securities as they were converted into shares. The interest in foreign investors may also change over time as the management learns how better to handle the investors' interest and the ways in which this interest can be used.

In this context time is important. What was regarded as wrong or impossible a year ago, may the next year be considered the right thing to do, as some important actors have altered their views. Time is also needed so that actors can learn and accumulate knowledge about each other.

In summary, investors are not seen here as rational, value maximizing, well-informed individuals. Instead their investment decisions depend far more on their personal relations. This implies that the internationalization process of ownership should not be analysed from a portfolio perspective, but on a level where important actors are identified and their relationships, roles and intentions considered. In this way a firm's size and degree of foreign activities become vital to attract foreign investors' interest.

Foreign investors' greater, and so far lasting, interest in shares of Swedish MNE:s are here seen to result from the latters' ever increasing presence in foreign markets. Employment in producing subsidiaries of Swedish MNE:s has increased considerably since 1978, especially in the US (Swedenborg, B. et al., pp.143-146). Another important aspect is that some foreign subsidiaries of Swedish MNE:s in the 1980s have emerged to become fairly self-sufficient units of considerable size (Forsgren, 1989). This means that the contacts these subsidiaries have with their external environment become more frequent and contain more vital information.

In several cases these foreign subsidiaries are a result of acquisitions by Swedish MNE:s. These acquisitions call for considerable local involvement, not least with banks, brokers and other actors in the financial market. The acquired companies are also sometimes old and well-known and bring with them a large contact net with local actors.

Foreign investors, it is argued in this chapter, are interested in Swedish firms because they are international, well-known and involved in many different kinds of activity outside Sweden. The foreign interest does not mainly come from the possibility that Swedish MNE:s may give investors a welfare gain in the portfolio sense. The greater interest from foreign investors is here seen as a gradual process where different actors over time learn more and more about each other and act according to their increased knowledge. The presence in major foreign markets is very important for long-lived foreign ownership interest. The emphasis on relations also implies that if foreign investors can be attracted to buy shares in a Swedish firm, e.g. through a stock issue or placement, the firm can use these new established relations to expand other activities abroad. If this can be achieved the possibility increases that the foreign ownership interest will persist.

If the degree of foreign ownership in the 20 firms[2] in Table 11.1 is correlated to the respective firms' proportion of employees abroad, number of employees abroad, proportion of sales abroad and finally amount of sales abroad the following results are summarised in Table 11.2 on page 160.

---

2   Skandia, an insurance company is excluded due to specific characteristics of the insurance industry.

TABLE 11.2: Degree of Foreign Ownership for 20 Swedish Firms Correlated with Proportion of Employees Abroad, Number of Employees Abroad, Proportion of Sales Abroad and Amount of Sales Abroad (1987).

Correlation Coefficients

	Degree of foreign ownership
Degree of employees abroad	0.40
Number of employees abroad	0.55
Degree of sales abroad	0.38
Amount of sales abroad	0.33

Sources: SOU 1988:38 p. 281, Annual Reports for the respective firms

These results do not contradict the hyphothesis that the degree of foreign ownership is connected to the firms' foreign activities. Employment abroad is probably a stronger indicator of foreign activities than just sales abroad. The number of employees has also the highest degree of correlation with the degree of foreign ownership.

The next section comprises a case study about the internationalization process of ownership in the multinational Swedish firm Pharmacia. The case is taken from Hörnell & Didner (1988).

11.4. Internationalization of Ownership in Pharmacia

Pharmacia, named Fortia until 1983, is basically a pharmaceutical firm. Its real expansion started in the 1940s when two pharmaceutical preparations were introduced to the market. Already in the early 1950s Pharmacia started to sell in the USA, which was one of the first foreign markets. Pharmacia expanded rapidly, not least in foreign markets. Until the 1980s the expansion resulted from products developed in the firm's laboratories, i.e. no companies were acquired. In the late 1950s equipment and products for research laboratories (for separation mainly) were developed, and in the 1960s diagnostic products. Until the 1980s research was completely concentrated to the Scandinavian countries. In the mid 1970s almost 80 per cent of revenues came from abroad, whereof nearly 25 per cent from the USA, which was, and still is, the largest foreign market.

During the 1970s the company's profits rose steadily. Encouraged by the good profit performance, Pharmacia undertook a large investmentin a research and development program in the beginning of the second half of the 1970s. But in 1979 and 1980 the profit expectations were not met.

At this time the president for the last 15 years resigned as he reached pensionable age. One of the first tasks for the new president, who was recruited outside the firm, was to ensure that funds were available in order to continue with the many promising developments which were under way.

At this early stage several alternatives were discussed. The more realistic included: another rights issue in Sweden, a division of the firm could be put up for sale, or specific research projects could be financed externally, e.g. through the American venture capital market. This last possibility arose after a trip to the USA in 1980 by the new president and one of his vice-presidents. The issue of shares to American investors was not considered as a realistic alternative at this time.

At about the same time the vice-president of finance happened to meet some American brokers. He then took the opportunity to ask them their opinion of the possibility of Pharmacia making a share issue for American investors. The reply was that it was completely unrealistic.

But things changed and just after 1980 mainly American and British investors became interested in foreign firms, even from "odd" countries such as Sweden. As the management understood that Pharmacia was an interesting company for investors, the idea of a share issue to foreign investors materialized. The Swedish stock market was still fairly quiet and regarded by management as too small to handle the amount sought by Pharmacia. The then dominant owner, the trade company Lundberg & Malmsten, were however willing to accept a share issue directed at foreign investors.

In spring 1981 management decided on a share issue for foreign investors, but the amount and place of issue were not determined. At this time the Pharmacia management was divided on the question of where to make the issue — London or New York. London was preferred by the vice-president of finance, but the president was determined to make the issue in New York.

In summer 1981 Pharmacia approached a number of American investment banks in order to obtain their views on how to proceed. The American bankers were now eager to take responsibility for a share issue.

The investment bank chosen was Morgan Stanley, New York. The choice was promoted by the management on the grounds that Pharmacia felt the working climate with Morgan Stanley to be highly positive, and this bank had a good reputation as analysts for pharmaceuticals. This last point was regarded by management as very important as Pharmacia was a comparatively unknown firm among investors in the USA.

Two years later, in 1983, the question of a second share issue in the USA arose. Management was divided on the question this time too. Some, among them the president, favoured a second issue. As the share price had risen so much it would be a good opportunity to raise more capital, it was argued, and also the liquidity would be stimulated as more shares came into the market. After a few problems during the autumn, the issue took place in the beginning of November, also this time with Morgan Stanley as lead manager.

Before 1980 Pharmacia had just effected one small acquisition outside Scandinavia. This was in 1977, in the USA, when a firm with 30 employees, a former supplier to Pharmacia was bought. But since 1980 Pharmacia have undertaken several acquisitions, also in the USA. The most active year was 1986 when two Swedish firms, quoted on the Stock Market, were bought, and a few American firms were acquired. At least one American acquisition was initiated by an American brokerage firm.

In 1984 there was a change of management in Pharmacia. A new president was appointed and the vice-president of finance was also replaced. American investors' ownership, at least measured through ADR:s, have decreased over the last few years, but the shares have so-far only in small amounts flowed back to Sweden. Instead London has become the major trading place for Pharmacia shares outside Sweden.

11.5. Critical Events

At the time of the first share issue in the USA, November 1981, Pharmacia was probably mainly known to individuals working in the fields where the firm had its strong market positions. In absolute terms the firm was small in the American market, but where it competed with its pharmaceutical products it had a strong position. The market positions of Pharmacia were also strong in the area of diagnostic products and laboratory equipment. But for investors it was probably only known to specialists in the areas mentioned.

These circumstances were of course recognized by the American investment banks. Just to place a share issue through their channels to investors would probably be possible, but if no liquid market could be established, i.e. new investors interested in the stock, there was a risk that the stock would soon lose the interest of investors. The responsibility of a lead manager towards the investors normally lasts a few months. During this period they usually support the share price, if necessary, and try to establish a liquid market for the shares. These considerations probably contributed to the limited interest of the American investment banks in 1980.

But in a fairly short time, around 1980, the circumstances on the Stock Markets in London and New York changed. One reason was increased interest in firms involved in biotechnology, or related fields. Another reason, coupled to the first, was the successful introduction on the New York Stock Exchange of the Danish biotechnological firm Novo. Novo is one of the leading producers of insulin and enzymes. During the years 1980–1981 Novo shares rose several hundred percent. The Novo case showed investment banks, investors and other foreign firms that it was possible to introduce foreign shares to the American Stock Market. In Europe too, mainly London, the interest in foreign shares increased.

Regarding shares listed in the Scandinavian markets the U.K. broker Grieveson Grant was often mentioned in the financial press as an "introducer" of these shares in London. This had the result that analysts and brokerage firms started to search for other interesting Scandinavian shares.

In 1980 foreign investors began to buy Pharmacia shares mainly through brokers in London. The interest was so great that a relatively large differential in price arose between the free and the restricted shares. One explanation of foreign investors' "discovery" of Pharmacia is that one analyst started to ask people at Novo questions about where they bought the equipment used to purify their products. The answer was Pharmacia.

Another event of interest was the launch of the new product Healon. In spring 1980 Pharmacia introduced Healon in the USA as the first market. Healon is a medical device used in eye operations. From the very beginning the product attracted great interest. At a conference on the American west coast in spring 1980 ophthalmic surgeons asked questions about how they could buy shares in Pharmacia. This is another explanation for the foreign interest in Pharmacia shares – American ophthalmic surgeons soon realized the potential for Healon and therefore bought the stock. As Pharmacia was the first company with this kind of product, and they still dominate the market, it could be priced to give good margins. As Healon proved to be a very successful product investors' interest in Pharmacia increased. The turnover of shares was high, and more and more analysts started to follow, and write positive reports about, Pharmacia. The shares issued in 1981 remained in American investors' possession. From time to time there was even a "shortage" of the stock as it was so popular.

At the time of the second issue of shares to American investors 1983 the share price started to falter. The explanation may in part be that the shares were previously pushed too hard by positive reports, but also that the whole biotechnology industry was devalued by investors. Analysts' reports of Pharmacia became more moderate, although sell recommendations were sparse, as they usually are in analysts' reports. The turnover of the shares was still high on the NASDAQ market and only a small number of shares had flowed back to Sweden.

It may have been a bold step by Pharmacia to go directly to the USA for equity, but several reasons for this can be found. The American investment banks definitely saw a growing area of business here – to introduce interesting European firms to American investors. This would not just earn them commissions through underwriting the issues, but also give them a strong position as market makers if trading in the shares could be established. Investors' interest in the biotechnology industry was high, and Pharmacia understood that they could position themselves as the "Biotech Swede". Pharmacia was, and definitely is, a very research-intensive firm, but a more suitable label may be "perhaps the leading supplier of equipment to the biotechnology industry, with a strong position in the area of diagnostics and a few good selling pharmaceutical products". But perhaps the strongest reason for the American alternative may have been Healon. As was mentioned earlier, USA was the first country where Healon was introduced. It was soon clear that this would be a good selling product. A problem, however, was to market it. Pharmacia had recently had some bad experience when marketing another product in America. Healon was however directed at a very specific and narrow group—ophthalmic surgeons, a well-educated group with high personal incomes. The move to make a share issue in America was probably related to the decision to market Healon by themselves, rather than through an American partner.

After 1981 Pharmacia expanded all their activities in the USA. The number of employees increased, several research co-operations were established, a research center was built on the West coast and several firms were acquired. There are good reasons to assume that their presence on the Stock Market helped Pharmacia in this expansion. Through the publicity Pharmacia obtained it became better known in the industry outside the areas where they were earlier recognized. Now they did not have to search for everything they needed, instead many came to Pharmacia and wanted or proposed co-operation in one way or another. Good contacts with the authorities are also very important to a firm like Pharmacia, as many of their products require formal permission to be sold.

These increased activities in the US are in this Chapter seen as very important when it comes to American investors' keeping their shares. This made it possible to attract new American investors to buy the Pharmacia shares when the investors who initially bought them sold for some reason. In this way the shares mainly remained in US instead of flowing back to Sweden. This case also shows how Pharmacia could take advantage of the publicity it obtained following its introduction on the American Stock Market. The success of Healon could be followed up by acquisitions to complement the product area of Healon. The firm could attract well educated people. To satisfy the American need for financial information, the position of investor relations was created and based in the USA.

The Pharmacia case also seems to show the complexity of the internationalization of ownership; no single factor determines what happens. Instead the internationalization process is shown to be much more erratic and subject to external circumstances as well as internal disagreements. The development after the issue is also seen as very important. Here Pharmacia's increased activities in especially the USA are seen as more or less a prerequisite for keeping the shares among foreign investors.

11.6. Summary

Until the 1980s foreign ownership of shares in Swedish MNE:s was on a low level. Only occasionally has there been an increased foreign ownership, e.g. after an issue of convertible bonds, but the shares have eventually been sold back to Sweden. But in the 1980s a different picture has emerged. Foreign investors' interest in Swedish shares has considerably increased and this interest has so far been lasting.

This Chapter emphasizes the importance of well established foreign operations in maintaining a foreign ownership interest. Foreign operations are performed within a network which *inter alia* entails investors, brokers, banks and other financial actors. A position within such a network is argued to be a necessary condition for a lasting foreign ownership.

Barriers in International Banking Networks
Lars Engwall

12.1. Banking Networks

In the Medieval trade fairs banking was performed at exchange tables, where money-changers facilitated payment for the traders. The basic principle for these bankers was that they went to places where prospective customers gathered. Already in the fifteenth and sixteenth centuries, however, great bankers like the Medici's and the Fugger's started to expand their activities geographically by opening up branches in various places (Walter, 1985, p. 14). With the passage of time this principle of branch building has gradually superseded the earlier ambulant mode of operation. Thus banks to-day run systems of branch offices, through which they collect and distribute financial resources (cf. Engwall & Johanson, 1988). This may be illustrated by the two largest Swedish commercial banks, Skandinaviska Enskilda Banken and Svenska Handelsbanken, both of which successively, but mainly in the 1920s and 1930s, expanded from the central cities of Sweden by acquiring local banks and thereby obtained a national system of offices (cf. Hildebrand, 1971 and Söderlund, 1964 and 1978)[1]. These two examples are not unique, however. Similar patterns can be observed in most countries. As regards the United States Cleveland & Huertas (1985) and Wilson (1986) thus provide similar evidence for Citibank and the Chase Manhattan Bank.

The said branch systems constitute vehicles for the collection and distribution of money as well as the provision of services. In this way branches enable the bank to establish relationships with various customers and providers, thereby linking to a larger business network. These links are of two kinds: actor-based and activity-based, the former resulting primarily

---

[1] It can be shown that there is a very high correlation between the number of offices and the amount of deposits. Jungerhem (1988) thus found correlation values above 0.9 between the two mentioned variables for the two Swedish regional banks Sundsvalls Enskilda Bank and Uplands Enskilda Bank in the period 1914-35.

from personal relationships between specific individuals, whereas the latter refer to impersonal transactions between organizations. In international banking actor- based relationships have earlier been particularly prevalent, since the obstacles to international penetration have been considerable for some time. The present Chapter will dwell on such obstacles by first discussing mobility barriers and then general barriers in banking. This analysis in toto will provide a basis for conclusions on movements from a dominance of actor-based banking networks to a greater emphasis on activity-based networks.

12.2. Mobility Barriers

Empirical studies in various contexts have indicated considerable inertia in economic and social systems. Mobility barriers thus constitute important general restrictions on business behavior (Engwall & Johanson, 1984). They include (1) barriers to entry, i.e. different obstacles preventing movements into a certain industry and (2) barriers to exit, i.e. impediments withdrawal from a certain area or activity. The former are often discussed in the industrial organization literature (cf. e.g. Bain, 1968, Ch. 8 and Scherer, 1970, pp. 129-234), whereas the latter have been introduced by Porter (1980). He defines them as "economic, strategic, and emotional factors that keep companies competing in business even though they may be earning low or even negative returns on investment" (*ibid.*, p. 20).[2]

The concept of mobility barriers basically belongs to the industrial organization tradition, which focuses on competitive conditions within defined industries. The concept may be useful, however, also when applying other approaches such as network analysis. In the latter context industrial networks are generally characterized as open and not controllable by any single actor (cf. e.g. Engwall & Johanson, 1988). It has to be acknowledged, however, that similar to other social systems, networks too are subject to barriers, i.e. that there are restrictions on possible relationships.

In terms of internationalization the earlier literature has primarily focused on distance-related barriers. First, the significance of physical

---

2   The major work introducing the concept of exit is Hirschman (1970). It elaborates on two means of dissatisfaction in an organization: voice and exit. In the former case dissatisfaction is expressed inside the organization, in the latter the dissatisfied member prefers to leave.

distance and its impact on transportation costs were stressed (cf. e.g. Beckerman, 1956). Later on Vahlne & Wiedersheim-Paul (1973) called attention to communication problems by introducing the concept of psychic (or cultural) distance. As regards manufacturing firms earlier research at Uppsala on the internationalization of business also underlined that the distance related barriers gave a gradual character to the process (cf. Johanson & Wiedersheim-Paul, 1975 and Johanson & Vahlne, 1977). This has been found pertinent to the geographical pattern of entries as well as to the entry mode. Consequently Swedish companies have exhibited an establishment pattern starting in culturally close countries with low commitments, then gradually moving to countries which are more alien with successively increasing commitments.

Another important type of barriers to internationalization are those which we will here denote as government-related barriers, i.e. restrictions imposed by governments on certain relationships (cf. Boddewyn, 1988). Here two basic types of barrier can be identified; First, emigration barriers, i.e. different obstacles imposed by governments in order to prevent domestic companies from developing relationships with actors in foreign countries. Second, immigration barriers, i.e. different restrictions on the entries of foreign firms. The main reason for *emigration barriers* is a desire for resource control, i.e. the wish of a government to keep scarce resources within national borders. In terms of physical resources these desires may result from shortages of certain materials and equipment or a wish to keep a competitive edge towards certain other countries. The former types of embargo have been particularly common in wars, whereas the latter have been imposed in peace time for advanced high-tech, especially defence-related, technology. Yet another important case is currency control, which has been, and still is, frequently used by different governments in order to handle the stability of exchange rates. In many countries foreign investments therefore require government approval before the necessary funds can be taken abroad. Most of the barriers set up have primarily economic reasons, although also cases can be found where the aim is to put pressure on certain governments to change their basic policies. The example of South Africa is here the most striking.

The *immigration barriers,* on the other hand, arise from the receiving country's wish to protect the domestic industry. The argument has then been that distance-related barriers have been reinforced not only by legal procedures but also by duties, standardization rules and other non-tariff barriers (cf. Mattsson, 1972). Many of the immigration barriers are motivated by defence arguments, i.e. that a country needs an industry of its own in times of blockade. Another important argument concerns employment, that a too liberal policy towards foreign entrants may threaten domestic firms and ultimately their labour force. One of the recent examples in this context concerns US and European hesitation about Japanese car import.

It is noteworthy that the emigration barriers of the domestic country and the immigration barriers of a foreign country will reinforce each other. Together they may constitute considerable obstacles to internationalization. It can also be argued that the relative importance of these government related barriers may increase over time, since modern communication technology has tended to reduce the impact of physical distance. Although the distance in itself has not decreased, the increased speed of modern transportation facilities, for individuals as well as for messages, has cut down the costs in terms of time. This in turn has also contributed to reductions of cultural distance. As communication technology develops we may thus expect still further reductions in distance-related barriers. Indeed a retrogression is here unthinkable, whereas a different situation prevails regarding government related barriers. Although they too are now gradually being reduced they may very well be raised once again as a result of political and economic changes. Times of deregulation may be followed by regulation and vice versa.

12.3. General Barriers in Banking

For banks, which are in focus in the present Chapter, the government-related barriers are especially significant. Walter (1985, p. 1) thus characterizes financial services not only as "one of the most structurally complex industries in the world economy" but also as "one of the most heavily regulated". Through their central role both as preservers of trust in the deposit and payment system, and as instruments of monetary policy, the banks constitute some sort of semi-public institutions. It would not therefore be inappropriate to add banks to the earlier list of branches of governments: the legislative, the executive and judicial branches, and the press (cf. e.g. Siebert, Peterson & Schramm, 1956).

The concern for a sound, trustworthy banking system has resulted in the imposition of considerable barriers already at the time of a prospective bank foundation. Contrary to most other industries even domestic banking is subject to establishment control, which is manifested through the charter procedure. Even after such permission has been granted banks are subject to special government treatment in the form of extensive supervision. They are restrained particularly in their risk taking and generally forbidden to undertake other activities than those defined by the charter. Two often mentioned examples of such restrictions are the Glass-Steagall Act and the McFadden Act in the United States, the former preventing commercial banks from operating in investment banking, the latter hindering interstate banking.[3] Certain states, like Illinois, even limit the branching within the state to one unit (cf. e.g. Sinkey, 1986, p. 178-181). Regulations such as these no doubt constitute serious restrictions already on the behavior of domestic banks. Needless to say they have tendencies to become even worse for foreign competitors (cf. below).

In one respect the just mentioned concern for soundness implies a less restrictive government attitude in comparison with other industries. This pertains to the possibility for co-operation between banks. Whereas co-operation between firms in other industries is prohibited (cf. e.g. Singer, 1968) collaboration between banks is permitted in order to smooth liquidity and to spread risks. As a result banking networks not only contain centrally located banks linking depositors and borrowers together, but also include relationships and connections to other banks. Different banks may thus have direct relationships for exchange of financial resources. They may also be connected through customers, who have multiple banking relationships or who obtain long-term financing through placement programs handled by a consortium of banks.[4]

Although banking is under considerable scrutiny even bank regulation has been relaxed in the past decade. This is an international phenomenon,

---

3   It has to be mentioned that considerable efforts are made to repeal these restrictions on banking, and that many observers expect changes to take place in a not too distant future.

4   For a further discussion of relationships and connections in banking networks, cf. Engwall & Johanson (1988).

which is associated with the internationalization of business and the growth of international finance. An important factor is probably also that enough time, more than fifty years, has elapsed since the Great Depression, when many of the regulations were introduced. The present developments can thus be seen as a part of a long-term cyclical pattern of bank regulation, which can be observed in many countries, not least in the United States from 1776 and onwards (Sinkey, 1986, p. 143). Indeed bank regulation seems to be a good example of the fact that organizations tend to abide by procedures which were once implemented to solve urgent problems and that radical shifts in the environment are required for changes (cf. Hedberg, 1981).

For more precision concerning the deregulation process the Swedish case can be used as a representative example. In this context six important steps can be mentioned: removal of deposit interest rate regulation (1978), creation of a money-market (1980), and abolution of liquidity quotas (1983), regulations of interest on loans (1985), credit limits (1985) and currency control (1989) (Lybeck & Hagerud, 1988, p. 16). Together these and other deregulation measures have tended to weaken bank-customer relationships, particularly for the large companies. Some of them have even created banks of their own.

12.4. Barriers in International Banking

The previous discussion stressed the major role of regulation in banking. As a result we would expect government related barriers to be more important than distance related barriers particularly in comparison with other industries. An earlier study regarding the internationalization process of Swedish banks until 1985 (Engwall & Wallenstål, 1988) has also shown that their foreign establishments were not governed by cultural distance[5] to any particular extent. Instead they tended to concentrate their foreign moves to international financial centers. These, in turn, were characterized by their relatively low immigration barriers. A dominant role is played by London, which in 1981 had more than twice as many banks as the second ranked New York. For some places such as Luxembourg and Grand Cayman advantageous banking conditions are particularly worth mentioning.

---

5   They exhibited an internationalization pattern with increasing commitments, however.

These results for the Swedish banks are of special interest, since they indicate that the banks considered it more urgent to be close to the providers of international capital than to their customers. Their foreign establishments thus appear to have been governed by a desire to link up with colleagues in the financial world, whereas the relationships to customers mainly remained in Sweden. The results also point to the existence of a relatively homogeneous international banking culture.

The prominence of distance related barriers even seems to be declining as a result of recent advances in communication technology. In the words of a recent financial journal article (Freeman, 1988):

> The financial markets of the world, isolated by the age-old barriers of time and distance, are now being joined together. Today, the same players can buy and sell the same instruments from country to country, market to market, 24 hours a day, seven days a week. From the satellites high in the sky to the fiber-optic cables deep in the ocean, technology is creating true global markets sooner than anyone would have thought possible.

We may thus conclude that the distance-related barriers tend to be of less importance in banking than in comparison to other industries and that C & C technology is likely to reduce its significance even further.

The main reason for the prominence of the other type of barriers, government related barriers, is the above-mentioned anxiety regarding soundness of banking operations. One particularly vital mechanism in that context has been different kinds of exchange regulations. In terms of *emigration barriers* banks have long been forced to confine foreign operations to those related to export and import trade financing. In many cases these operations have been handled by means of relationships to correspondent banks.   Accordingly one of the largest Swedish banks, Skandinaviska Enskilda Banken, in the early 1980s had relationships to some 2,500 foreign banks (Uggla, 1982, p. 84). With an increasing transnationality of large corporations many banks in developed countries have felt a need to expand their international commitments, but been restricted by emigration barriers. They have undertaken with relative ease the   first   step   on   the   internationalization   route,   i.e.   to   establish representative offices.[6] These have been severely restricted in their work, however, since they have been forbidden to book credits and could only initiate contacts with customers. The next step in bank internationalization has for many banks been participation or wholly-owned subsidiaries, which in most countries require approval of the Inspection Authorities and the Central Bank. A more natural solution from the banks' point of view would have been the creation of branches. But here we again see an example of emigration barriers. Governments prefer subsidiaries, since they are safer than branches inasmuch as they reduce the risk to the share capital. For the banks subsidiaries are a disadvantageous solution to internationalization, however, since they involve higher costs and smaller capacity in international financial markets. The risk reduction argument has thus long prevented banks from opening international branches. The Swedish banks, for instance, were not permitted to open such branches until 1988. They are still under a restriction that their business should be basically related to Sweden.[7] In addition to the emigration barriers banks are also subject to considerable immigration barriers. Among these Walter (1985, pp. 67-80) identifies four types, the chief of which pertains to market delineation, i.e. geographical or client group restrictions on the permitted relationships.[8] Some countries, like Sweden, thus for a long time have not permitted foreign banks to establish subsidiaries. Demands for reciprocity in the treatment of banks, however, have been important to weaken these barriers. In Sweden foreign banks were permitted to open subsidiaries in 1986, but they are still forbidden to have branch offices. Such offices are expected to be allowed in the not too distant future, however. It goes without saying that the planned free market of the European Community in 1992 is important for this development.

---

6 This step in many cases implies the breaking of long lasting correspondent relationships and a move from co-operation to competition. The same is also true, when banks, as some of them have done, move from participation to wholly-owned operations. In these instances one can easily imagine the existence of certain relationship barriers, i.e. inertia in breaking up from long-standing co-operation.

7 The importance of this restriction is difficult to evaluate. For it can be argued that in international competition, one of the most important comparative advantages of a foreign bank is probably its special competence in business related to its own country.

8 These correspond to the Glass-Steagall Act and the McFadden Act in the United States (cf. above).

A second type of discriminatory barrier is composed of limits put on the size of operations of a foreign bank, which leads to a need to set priorities in the bank's network building in a particular country. Thirdly, foreign banks can be disfavoured by funding limits, i.e. by restrictions on the supply side of the financial network. And, finally, there are all sorts of other barriers to the penetration of a national banking network. To this group, which Walter mentions as "nuisance measures", he refers restrictions on the access to infrastructure facilities such as telecommunications, electric power, transportation, etc., but also staffing and managerial restrictions. Thus it frequently happens that banks trying to penetrate a foreign country are curbed by restrictions on the number of qualified foreigners they may employ in the bank. Adding these different barriers together Walter (1985, p. 76) concludes that "foreign-based financial institutions, therefore, operate in one of the most restrictive environments in international trade".[9] Furthermore that "countries that are home bases to highly competitive players in the industry tend to be characterized by relatively liberal policies" (*ibid.*, p. 113). Among those having more restrictive legislation the said development of C & C technology may reduce the impact on the government related barriers by making such control more difficult.

12.5. Implications

An important feature of the development of organization theory in the 1960s was the emphasis on contingencies (cf. e.g. Woodward, 1965 and Lawrence & Lorsch, 1967). Evidence provided from the banking industry in the present Chapter has conveyed a similar picture. It has been pointed out that banks are different, particularly regarding government supervision, which has had effects for their operation in both a national and an international context. In the latter case restrictions on emigration and immigration have been much stricter than in other industries. Distance-related barriers to internationalization, which are usually discussed in the literature, have therefore been found to be less significant. Another circumstance contributing to this conclusion consists in the

---

9   A very special case is constituted by the Islamic countries, which do not have banks of the Western type. The most spectacular difference between the Islamic and the non-Islamic banks is of course the fact that the former does not work with interest rates (cf. further e.g. Mullineux, 1987 and Presley, 1988).

possibilities of the banking firm to employ modern communication technology. This factor goes back to the development of cable and telephone systems, but has certainly become even more important with the advent of modern computer & communication (C & C) technology. It has tended to make distance-related barriers even less significant than before.

Our earlier discussion has not only shown that distance-related barriers are reduced, but also emphasized that the same is true of the government-related barriers restraining emigration and immigration. In terms of our introductory account of actor- and activity-based relationships we could conclude that the earlier world of international banking with a number of government-related barriers no doubt generally promoted actor relationships. Different solutions to emerging problems had to be found on a personal basis. With deregulation and the development of modern communication technology we can expect the actor relationships to decrease in relative importance. This is also in accordance with recent arguments that transaction-based banking has taken the place of relationship banking (cf. e.g. Auletta, 1986 and Mayer, 1984). This does not imply, however, as some argue, that banking networks are gone. Rather it means that they have changed character somewhat. The fact that bank customers are moving around to a greater extent than before has the effect that the industrial networks of banks have widened, the banks and their customers both having more extensive relationships and connections.

In terms of changes in the character of the links we may find two opposite tendencies. On one hand the just mentioned movement towards transaction-based, more free market type, banking will lead to a looser coupling. Bank customers will have a greater tendency to shop around among a number of providers of financial services. But on the other hand the development of C & C networks will involve tendencies in the opposite direction. Banks will both internally and externally exhibit tighter coupling through these physical networks, which may even create traditional economic mobility barriers through their capital requirements. Such barriers even have particular relevance for the internationalization of banks. A special problem occurs in cases when the investments have been made by already established firms, who are then unwilling to admit new entrants at favorable prices. This was the case for instance in Sweden, when foreign banks wanted to gain access to earlier established ATM- and giro-systems.

Finally, it is appropriate to say a few words on the actor-based relationships in industrial networks. The fact that the activity-based relationships are likely to increase does not preclude the existence of actor-based relationships in certain areas. As already shown in Engwall & Johanson (1988) the latter are likely to remain important in areas such as corporate finance and merchant banking. Since these are significant features of international banking, it can even be argued that the actor-based relationships will continue to be stronger in this than in the domestic area. It should also be added that old actor-based relationships may be reactivated if the conditions of international banking become less favourable. The personal network of the international banker will therefore remain an intrinsic asset as it once was in the Middle Ages.

Power Balancing in an International Business Network

Mats Forsgren and Ulf Olsson

13.1. Termination of a Long-lasting Relationship

During the summer of 1988 the Swedish steel and engineering company Sandvik announced that its co-operation with another Swedish engineering company, Atlas Copco would end successively during 1989. This message followed immediately after the latter company's decision to acquire Secoroc, one of Sandvik's main competitors in the rock drilling industry. By so doing, a well known industrial relationship, lasting for more than 40 years, was suddenly terminated. The relationship meant that rock drilling tools produced by Sandvik were marketed through Atlas Copco's foreign market organization, as well as co-operation in developing tools and equipment within the rock drilling area. Both companies regret the discontinuation, which can be illustrated by the following statement of Sandvik's president: "You never change a successful team" (Sandvik Annual Statement 1988).

A change in a relationship between two companies can of course be traced back to factors inherent in the relationship *per se*. Changes in the activities on one or both sides, for example, can reduce the interdependence and the motive for exchange between the actors. But a change in a relationship can also be caused by changes in other relationships of the network which are transmitted to the focal relationship. Atlas Copco's acquisition of Secoroc seems to be the trigger in this case, but what about the underlying factors of the events that followed?

Structural changes in networks, irrespective of the initiating factor, are highly dependent on the type of activity interdependences between actors and and how these interdependences are handled through exchanges. A crucial factor in network analysis is the distribution of power between actors and between clusters of actors i n mixed networks, i.e . networks involving both positive and negative connections (Cook & Emerson, 1984, Yamagashi, Gillmore & Cook, 1988). Changes in relationships of such networks are often caused by the ambition of one actor to increase his power or to restore the balance of power if this has been disturbed for some reason. A reason can be one actor's expanding access to alternative sources of valued resources which can provoke countermoves by other actors trying to engage in new forms of exchange with one another.

This indicates that a survey of the network before the actual change in terms of main actors, activity interdependences, types of exchange relationship and balance of power throughout the system is needed in order to analyse the underlying causes. This will be done in sections 13.2 and 13.3 with respect to the rock drilling industry and the relationship between Sandvik and Atlas Copco. In section 13.4 the changes in this industry will be discussed using power, commitment and uncertainty in relationships as basic concepts.

13.2. The Rock Drilling Network[1]

13.2.1. In General

The rock drilling industry includes producers of rock-drilling tools for mining, tunnelling, civil engineering and oil drilling and producers of diverse machinery for the same purpose, e.g. drilling machines, hammers and rigs. The tools are commodities which are bought constantly and in large amounts by the users while an investment in machinery equipment has an economic life of about ten years. On the user side the main groups are mining and construction companies. Generally the network is characterized by a much lower concentration on the user side than on the producer side.

As a standardized product rock drilling tools are adapted to different types of rock rather than to a special type of mine or rock drilling machinery. In general tools from different producers are substitutable if they are in the same type of product range. A mining or construction company often have two suppliers of tools, one main and one secondary. The technical development of rock drilling tools is chiefly carried out by the producers thereof, although often in co-operation with producers of machinery equipment. Increasing capacity of machinery forces the tool

---

1   Section 13.2 is based on Erland *et al.* 1986.

producer to increase the toughness as well as the wear resistance of the tool, but higher tool quality can provide an incentive to improve the machinery, e.g. by using more hydraulics. The rock drilling tools are usually consumed rather rapidly which means that changes in the quality, e.g. changes in steel alloy or carbide, can immediately be evaluated by the users. The quality, expressed in drilled meters, is decisive for the lifetime of the tools. The less time spent on changes of tools or the less unexpected breaks in the drilling the better. The rock drilling industry is a mature industry with low growth rate and latent over capacity.

13.2.2. The Actors

After the Second World War there was a gradual concentration of the production of rock drilling tools and machinery. At the end of the 1960's the tool production in Sweden was mainly handled by two companies, Sandvik and Secoroc. The development was similar in many other countries. Sandvik and Secoroc effected an early internationalization of their operations by their own establishments or acquisition of companies abroad for production and/or sales. In the mid 1970s the two companies' share of the total world market can be estimated to about 45 per cent (Sandvik 30 and Secoroc 15 per cent). At that time the third largest producer, Boart International in South Africa, only had a few per cent of the world market, mainly in its home market. The remaining production was spread among several small or medium-sized firms.

Since then Sandvik, Secoroc and Boart have increased their shares of the world market for rock drilling tools to around 70 per cent. Sandvik is the largest and Secoroc slightly larger than Boart. During the 1980s Secoroc has been more successful than Sandvik in many countries and increased its share at the latter's expense. Boart has also enlarged its share of the tool market in many countries. Many of the smaller and medium-sized producers have been acquired or have closed and those still producing operate mainly in local markets.

Among the three dominant producers Sandvik is seen as the leading in technology mainly because it is the only company which also produces steel and hard metal. Compared with the other two companies the resources used in metallurgic research are much greater in Sandvik. Secoroc's strength lies mainly in its world-wide selling and service organization including service personnel deployed among important users, while Boart's specific advantage is its dominance in South Africa, a market which has 15 per cent of the total consumption of rock drilling tools in the Western hemisphere.

The production of machinery is also very concentrated. Atlas Copco has been the leading firm internationally for several years but during the 1970s two other companies became large on the international scene, the Finnish firm Tamrock and Boart International. Atlas Copco has a full product line of machinery and equipment for mining and construction. The drilling machines include small machines for hand-use, medium-sized drilling rigs of 15 tons and large rigs of up to 100 tons. These products are sold through the world-wide marketing organization of the Atlas Copco group which means that customers using smaller equipment as well as big mining and construction firms can be reached. Tamrock has a more concentrated production, including large drilling rigs designed primarily for large mining and construction customers. Tamrock's sales organization is more directed to specific customers and has not the same geographic diversity as Atlas Copco's. Boart, finally, has started production of rock drilling equipment during the last ten years, concentrating mainly on smaller machinery. The company is considered technically to be behind Atlas Copco and Tamrock although the gap is decreasing. Boart holds a strong position in South Africa but not in the world market, especially not for large equipment. Atlas Copco and Tamrock together have a market share of about 75 per cent and the rest is spread among 15 or so smaller producers, of which Boart is one.

Technical co-operation between tool producers and machine producers is fairly common, but has not led to any mergers. Up to 1988 Boart was the only company producing both tools and machinery equipment, a situation caused by a development within Boart International. It is important to a tool producer that his products fit into as many different machine brands as possible even if he is engaged in technical co-operation with a certain manufacturer of rock drilling machines. Both Sandvik and Secoroc have for several years had a fairly extensive co-operation with Atlas Copco and Tamrock respectively. In the former case this is a part of the long relationship in selling and marketing. In the latter case it is not so old and extensive and more restricted to technical matters. One important element of the development of the tools is test drilling of new or developed products. These tests are carried out by the tool producer in the customers' or their own mines, often in co-operation with the machine producer. A marketing organization with well-established links to mines and large construction companies is crucial for the sale of rock drilling equipment. Secoroc and Boart have their own marketing organizations while prior to 1988 Sandvik sold the rock drilling tools in their own name but through Atlas Copco's sales subsidiaries.

Atlas Copco's production of rock drilling machinery is carried out in one of the group's divisions, MCT, which is also a wholly-owned subsidiary of Atlas Copco AB. MCT:s turnover, around 3.5 billion SEK, corresponds to 30 per cent of the Atlas Copco group's total turnover. MCT:s executive officer is a member of Atlas Copco's corporate executive committee. Atlas Copco, in turn belongs to the Wallenberg group where it is the only company with connections to the rock drilling network.

Boart International produces tools as well as machines. Thirty per cent of Boart International's turnover pertains to these products. The company is owned by one of the world's biggest mining companies, Anglo American of South Africa.

Sandvik's production of tools is carried out by Rock Tools, one of the group's business areas and a wholly-owned subsidiary of Sandvik AB. The turnover is about 1.5 billion SEK or 10 per cent of the Sandvik group's turnover. The biggest shareholder of Sandvik is Skanska, a construction company. There are no other links through ownership between Sandvik and other actors in the rock drilling network.

Before the take-over of Secoroc by Atlas Copco in 1988 the company was owned by Kinnevik, a business group with the objective to "acquire and manage on a long-range basis large blocks of shares in business firms" (Annual Statement 1988, authors' translation). During the last ten years Kinnevik has invested in companies in the information and insurance industries and today consists of about 20 subsidiaries, controlled directly by its top management, and other "related" companies operating in 13 different industries. By a "related" company Kinnevik means "a company which is controlled by Kinnevik only by membership of the company's board" (ibid.) Secoroc was such a company in the Kinnevik group, with a turnover of about 13 per cent of Kinnevik's total turnover. The biggest shareholder in Kinnevik is Jan Stenbeck and there are no ownership relations to other firms in the rock drilling industry.

Tamrock, finally, belongs to the Finnish Tampella group, operating mainly in the forest industry, making pulp and paper, packaging, machinery equipment and energy equipment for the pulp and paper industry. About 23 per cent of the Tampella group's turnover comes from Tamrock, which is a wholly-owned subsidiary of Tampella. The president of Tamrock belongs to the corporate executive committe of the Tampella group. Tampella has no ownership connections to other actors of the rock drilling network.

The main actors and relationships in the rock drilling network are depicted in Fig 13.1.

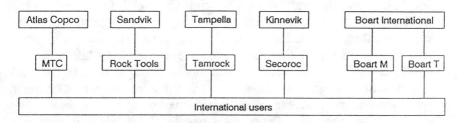

FIGURE 13.1: Main Actors and Main Relationships in the International Rock Drilling Network.

Note: The production of tools and machinery in Boart International is carried out in several companies. For simplicity the production of machinery has been labelled Boart M and the production of tools Boart T.

13.3. The Co-operation between Sandvik and Atlas Copco

The co-operation between Sandvik and Atlas Copco started as early as the beginning of the 1940s. Already then Atlas Copco had a well established market organization directed to the mining industry. The co-operation involved the sale of Sandvik's rock tools through this organization but with its own brand. Successively the co-operation in selling developed into technical co-operation as well. After some years groups were created with members from the two companies working with specific long-range technical and marketing problems. At the time of the cessation of the co-operation there were several such groups. The technical co-operation involved about 10-20 people from each company with frequent contacts within these groups.

The significance of the formal agreement was that Atlas Copco marketed the tools for its own and competitors' machinery to the users while Sandvik handled supply and technical support to customers as well as training of

Atlas Copco's sales staff in the sales subsidiaries. Sandvik sold the tools to Atlas Copco for a certain price and the latter company decided the price-level to the ultimate customers. The difference made up the gross profit of Atlas Copco from this sales. In order to allow scope for contacts between the users and the producer of the tools technicians from Sandvik were gradually placed in many of Atlas Copco's larger sales subsidiaries during the 1970s, although with some resistance because of the contentious issue of price-setting. The sales subsidiaries hesitated to give Sandvik an insight into how the prices to the customers were set. The contacts between Sandvik and the users, however, were usually limited to technical matters, e.g. in handling and maintenance of the tools, while the contacts with buying people on the customer side were arranged by people from Atlas Copco.

The co-operation worked very well during a long period. In the 1980s, however, Sandvik gradually became aware of the importance of letting the tools have a more visible place in the marketing of the rock drilling equipment by the Atlas Copco sales people. Sandvik was increasing its efforts to gain direct contact with the top management level at the Atlas Copco's sales subsidiaries and large mining or construction companies. It became evident to the managers of Rock Tools that the placement of technical service personnel at some of Atlas Copco's sales subsidiaries was insufficient as a system of satisfying the need for information between Rock Tools and the users of rock drilling tools. Within the MCT headquarter there was a unit which handled the selling of Sandvik tools and acted as an intermediary between the sales subsidiaries and Rock Tools. From the latter company's point of view it became more and more clear that contacts with Atlas Copco's sales subsidiaries should be direct and not administered by a unit within MCT headquarter. Sandvik, therefore, wanted to create certain "Sandvik units" within every sales subsidiary. Indeed this was also realized at two of the larger sales subsidiaries. Rock Tools' main competitors had their own sales organizations with their own agents visiting the customers and selling tools only. The Sandvik tool had to compete with the machinery equiment for the customer's time. To a certain extent this was offset by the complementarity of the products but the disadvantage was still there and became more and more important in Sandvik's opinion.

The discussion of Sandvik's contacts with the customers led to a very important change of the whole relationship as late as 1986/87. Agreements were then formulated between Rock Tools and every separate Atlas Copco sales company outside Sweden. These agreements, a total of 53, regulated the price decisions on both sides and the contacts between the people at Rock Tools and the customers. Through these separate agreements price discussions were more easily handled and the relations between users and Rock Tools became better and also more flexible. According to Sandvik this change on the whole solved the problem with relationships to the customers and was favourably regarded by Atlas Copco as well. As late as March 1988 the top manager of MCT in a letter to Sandvik expressed his contentment with the new system. The co-operation between Sandvik and Atlas Copco therefore seemed worthwhile to continue by both parts at that time.

In summer 1988 Atlas Copco announced that the company had bought Secoroc from the Kinnevik group. The bulletin from Atlas Copco stated that Secoroc would continue its operations as before and that the co-operation with Sandvik would not be affected. Shortly thereafter Sandvik announced its cancellation of the Sandvik/Atlas Copco agreement, as from August 1989.

The immediate cause of the cancellation was, according to Sandvik, the acquisition of Secoroc by Atlas Copco. To Sandvik it seemed obvious that in the near future MCT would promote the sales of tools from Secoroc at Sandvik's expense, particularly as it was declared from the outset that Secoroc would be organized as a unit within MCT rather than as a separate company in the Atlas Copco group. From Sandvik's point of view then a breach between Sandvik and Atlas Copco was unavoidable. Rock Tools immediately started to create a sales organization of its own by establishing selling units within Sandvik's market organization in different countries. A technical co-operation with Tamrock was instituted including a formal agreement which was signed in December 1988.

13.4. Relationship Commitments and Network Foci of Power

The rock drilling network consists of few actors, each having a specific role and with well known, long-term relationships between them. A change in such a network tends to provoke countervailing changes which maintain the balance of power throughout the system. Atlas Copco's acquisition of Secoroc brought about changes in other relationships which can be interpreted as such countervailing moves. This will be analysed further in this section.

The rock drilling network is a "mixed" network which means that some of the relationships imply non-exchange with other partners, i.e. they are negatively connected (Cook & Emerson, 1984). For example, exchange between MCT and a specific customer implies non-exchange between Tamrock and that customer at the same time, or exchange between Secoroc and Tamrock means non-exchange between Rock Tools and Tamrock. Negatively connected relationships imply that alternative partners are mutually substitutable. But the industry also contains several positively connected relationships. The technical co-operation between MCT and Rock Tools, e.g., can be expected to have a positive influence on the technical co-operation between Rock Tools and Sandvik and on the same type of relationship between MCT and Atlas Copco.

The relationships depicted in Fig.13.1 have been elaborated to the extent of stating precisely whether the relationship contains financial/ownership exchanges, exchanges within the marketing function, exchanges within technical development function and/or exchanges with users. This is illustrated in Fig. 13.2, which shows the situation before Atlas Copco's acquisition of Secoroc.

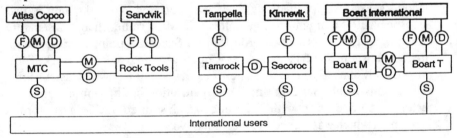

—F— = Financial/ownership exchange
—M— = Exchange in the marketing function
—D— = Exchange in the technical development function
—S — = Exchange with users

Note: See Fig. 13.1

FIGURE 13.2: The International Rock Drilling Network before 1988.

As compared with Fig. 13.1 it is evident that the relationships between the actors are of different kinds and magnitudes in view of the extent to which the exchanges are carried out in terms of the three dimensions above. Purely financial exchanges in which resources in terms of money are exchanged for profits can be said to be equivalent to exchanges of goods for money without any services or specific knowledge connected thereto. In both cases the resources, money or goods, can easily be used in relationships with alternative partners, because the mutual adaptation between the parties, even though it exists, is fairly limited. A network based on financial exchanges is characterized by the autonomy of the actors vis-à-vis each other with high probability of one specific relationship being substituted for another.

Relationships in terms of co-operation in marketing or technical development give rise to exchanges of other resources than money and imply that there are adaptive investments on both sides which makes it difficult to substitute them. The actors in such a network are more dependent on each other and changes in the relationships are less probable, at least in the short run. The dependence can be said to be more specific in this case (Johanson, 1989, p. 72).

This aspect should be attached to Cook & Emerson's concept of commitment in relationships (1984, p.10). Instead of looking upon a series of transactions as independent events the concept of commitment stresses the importance of mutual dependence between actors. Commitment in an exchange relationship means formation of bonds of obligation between exchange partners, bonds which provide the "cement" of these particular structures. The deeper the commitment in an exchange relationship the greater the tendency for the actors to continue the transactions even though the network opportunity structure provides access to alternative exchange relations.

Expressed in terms of commitment exchanges in several functions may be expected to involve deeper commitment than exchanges in few functions because of the greater number of bonds between the partners in the former case. According to the discussion above there is also reason to assume that a relationship based on a pure financial exchange contains less commitment than exchanges within the marketing or development functions because of the higher degree of adaptive investments on both sides in the latter cases.

Figure 13.2 seems to illustrate what Cook & Emerson calls the decentralization principle which means that mixed networks tend to form into systems organized around multiple foci of power (ibid., p. 8). Three different foci of power are apparent; Atlas Copco-MCT-Rock Tools-Sandvik, Tampella-Tamrock-Secoroc-Kinnevik and Boart I-Boart M-Boart T. These subgroups are characterized by each actor in one group being more committed through exchange relationships to actors in the same group than to other actors of the network.

But the figure also shows that the relationships differ in commitment between the subgroups. In the first and the third group there is a rather high degree of commitment between the members. The links between Atlas Copco-MCT and Sandvik-Rock Tools are not only financial but also include exchanges in marketing and/or technical development. This is due to the fact that Atlas Copco and Sandvik, respectively, are fairly integrated companies in which the business areas are functionally and historically linked to each other. As has been described in Section 13.3 the relationship between MCT and Rock Tools was also rather elaborate with intensive co-operation in selling of tools and developing of machinery and tools. In the third group, consisting of Boart International and its companies within the rock drilling business, the commitment between the actors is of the same high degree.

The relationships in the Tampella-Tamrock-Secoroc-Kinnevik group display lower commitment. This is specially so in the Kinnevik-Secoroc relationship. A successive move of the former company during the last ten years towards wholly new business areas, in combination with a more pronounced holding strategy versus its subsidiaries, had led to a pure financial exchange relationship between the two companies, a move which could be traced back to changes in networks not covered in Fig. 13.2. Expressed otherwise, this change had given rise to a much lower probability of Kinnevik continuing its exchange with Secoroc than e.g. Atlas Copco or Sandvik continuing their exchange with MCT and Rock Tools respectively. This holds true for the Tampella-Tamrock relationship as well since this is mainly of a financial nature. Tamrock is rather different from the rest of the Tampella group but compared to the Kinnevik-Secoroc case there is a difference. First of all, Tampella has no intention of being an investment company in relation to its subsidiaries. Tampella is an industrial firm and there are certain connections between Tamrock and other units producing machinery equipment in the group. According to Fig. 13.2 there was also an exchange relationship between Tamrock and Secoroc in the technical field which started about ten years ago. The two companies co-operated in developing and testing machinery and tools in about the same way as MCT and Rock Tools did up to 1988. Unlike the latter relationship, however, the co-operation between Tamrock and Secoroc did not include selling through the same marketing channels. Altogether, the links between the companies in the Tampella-Tamrock-Secoroc-Kinnevik group were weaker than those in the other two groups of the network, particularly in the Secoroc-Kinnevik case.

13.5. Power Balancing

Can we find the causes of the chain of events which started in 1988 by examining the characteristics of the relationships of the network? When trying to find the reason for a change in a specific relationship it is natural to seek the answer in the relationship *per se*. For instance, there were circumstances in the MCT-Rock Tools relationship which could be seen as a threat to the co-operation between the two companies. These circumstances were connected to the growing need for a tool producer to be in continuous touch with large customers, in selling as well as in product development. Rock Tools had become aware of that and the exchange relationship between the two companies had to be developed in that direction in order to function in the future. The problem was that this was more urgent from Rock Tools' point of view than from MCT's so that the organization within MCT which handled the contacts between Rock Tools and the customers had to be renewed.

But as was shown in section 13.3 these problems were solved within the relationship. Rock Tools and MCT agreed to build up separate contracts between every Atlas Copco sales subsidiary abroad and Rock Tools. This system gave Rock Tools direct access to customers without too much interference in the daily sales work of Atlas Copco's sales force. Much work lay behind the construction of these contracts but the system seemed to be mutually satisfactory up to the breach.

Thus, there was no sign of a dissolving factor within the relationship as such. Instead the cause must be traced to changes in connected relationships. The description above indicated the significance of the diminishing commitment of the Secoroc-Kinnevik relationship. Kinnevik has been transformed from an operating to a financial actor in the rock drilling network which in turn gave Secoroc a different position from before. Even if there was a balance of power between the three groups of the network, this change in commitment created a "vacuum" which required measures from other actors insofar as there was a risk of Kinnevik selling out Secoroc. Atlas Copco took action in spite of, and certainly aware of the turbulent situation which would ensue.[2]

Cook & Emerson state that within a network of connected exchange relationships, commitment will evolve in such a way as to promote a power-balance throughout the network (*ibid.*, p 11). Yet in this case the link between uncertainty and commitment is important. Uncertainty relates to the subjective probability of concluding a satisfactory transaction with a partner. By their commitment two actors can reduce such uncertainty. The interesting point in this case is that a reduced commitment in one relationship will increase the uncertainty among actors in connected relationships. More precisely, when Kinnevik was relaxing its ties with Secoroc, the subjective probability of MCT and Rock Tools successfully transacting with each other in the future decreased as the opportunity of incorporating Secoroc in either actor became apparent. If, e.g., Sandvik had acquired Secoroc, there would have been a much smaller chance of MCT continuing its profitable selling of Rock Tools products because an opportunity for the latter company to use Secoroc's sales organization would have emerged. If Tampella had been the buyer, with a consequent development of exchange relationship between Tamrock and Secoroc, this would also have influenced the position of MCT and Rock Tools in the network because of the negative connections between MCT's and Tamrock's customer relationships as well as Rock Tools' and Secoroc's. It is interesting to note that if Secoroc had been bought by a company outside the rock drilling network the relative positions between the groups as well as the actors of the network would have remained intact, at least in the short run. The fact that it was an insider made the chain of countervailing moves that followed logical and unavoidable.

Before that event there was a mutual, balanced dependence in the relationship between Rock Tools and MCT. Rock Tools had access to a world-wide market organization of a complementary product without

---

2   There are certain indications that Sandvik attempted to acquire Secoroc a few years earlier. A reasonable hypothesis is that Tampella also had Secoroc on its list of potential acquisitions.

making large investments and MCT's profit derived largely from the selling of Rock Tools' products. Both actors took advantage of the relationship in product development. The possible alternatives to the relationship on both sides were of about the same magnitude. Rock Tools could build up a sales organization of its own or use Sandvik's, co-operate with Tamrock instead of MCT or establish a relationship with Secoroc. MCT had the opportunity of trying to increase the profitability of its own production to equal its profits from the sales of Rock Tools' products or sell some of the local producers' products. All these alternatives demanded considerable resources but none gave one actor an obvious power over the other or allowed one actor to experience a much higher uncertainty than the other in the relationship.

But Atlas Copco's acquisition of Secoroc drastically changed this situation. A new alternative materialized on the MCT's side of the relationship; a collaboration with Secoroc. So, even if at the time of acquisition Atlas Copco and MCT announced that the event would not influence the relationship with Rock Tools the balance of power between the actors was disturbed and, perhaps more important, the uncertainty on the Rock Tools' side of the relationship increased considerably. Rock Tools interpreted the acquisition as a radical change in the network, meaning that commitment between MCT and Secoroc could be expected in the near future.

In Cook & Emerson's terminology commitment between members of one relation fosters commitment in other relations and the balance of power shifts again towards equality throughout the network (*ibid.*, p.11). The co-operation between Rock Tools and Tamrock which was established immediately afterwards can be seen as such a "fostered commitment", which in this case was combined with a total cessation of the relationship between Rock Tools and MCT. It is important to observe that starting such a countervailing relationship was not important only to Rock Tools but also to Tamrock as a consequence of the new situation.

The network after the acquisition of Secoroc, and the following events are depicted in Fig. 13.3.

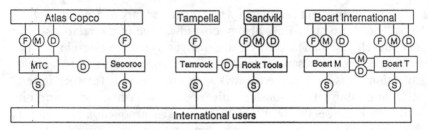

—F— = Financial/ownership exchange
—M— = Exchange in the marketing function
—D— = Exchange in the technical development function
—S— = Exchange with users

Note: See Fig. 13.1

FIGURE 13.3: The International Rock Drilling Network in 1989

As indicated in Fig. 13.3 the rock drilling industry still consists of three groups or foci of power, but two are now composed of different members from before. Through Sandvik's and Tampella's countervailing moves the balance of power between the groups has been restored to the situation immediately before the acquisition of Secoroc. As compared with the original network there is also an increased commitment throughout the system, a natural consequence of one actor, only connected to the network through a financial relationship, being replaced by an insider with a deeper commitment to other actors in the network.

13.6. Concluding Remarks

The tendency to preserve the balance of power between actors can be used to explain changes in industrial networks. There is reason to believe that this is especially so in networks characterized by few actors and deep commitment between actors. Paradoxically, countermoves are more urgent when a change is perceived as a threat to a strong relationship but, by definition, less likely than in a situation with weak relationships. The alternatives which still exist in a deeply committed network, therefore, become important. When Atlas Copco acquired Secoroc the balances of power between MCT and Rock Tools and between Secoroc and Tamrock, were altered to a degree unacceptable to Rock Tools and Tamrock. Rock Tools could not continue its sales through, and technical co-operation with a partner owning the most important competitor. The same argument is applicable to Tamrock's technical co-operation with Secoroc.

But there were alternatives. Through starting a technical co-operation Rock Tools and Tamrock seem to restore the balance of power within the field of technical development and Rock Tool was able to take advantage of Sandvik's extensive market organization.

These alternatives must have been evident to all actors in the network including Atlas Copco, which leads to the question of why Atlas Copco bought Secoroc in the first place. Without giving any complete answer we shall mention one aspect. In a network with few actors and with high degree of commitment between actors there is a tendency in the system to try to reduce the number of low committed actors. The most committed actors are prone to act in such a situation, even if actions from others can be expected to follow. Stability and certainty, a desirable state in a mature industry, is not fully reached until all actors are deeply committed.

14

Entering A Tightly Structured
Network—Strategic Visions or Network Realities
Nils Kinch

14.1. Successful U.S. Market Entry

North America is today the single largest market for Volvo of cars and trucks. It accounts for about 35 per cent of the sale of cars and 32 per cent of the trucks. The first Volvo car was sold in California in 1955 and in less than three years every fourth car produced was delivered there and the company became heavily dependent on this market. Ever since Volvo began to sell abroad in 1928 trucks and buses had completely dominated its export and represented the major part of the turnover. However, the rapidly increasing "American export" turned Volvo into a producer and exporter of cars.

This was a remarkable transformation in a very short time. According to a well-founded opinion it is considered to be a difficult and time-consuming process for a new company to enter a mature market and build up a new system of distribution. The timing of this effort coincided with decreasing sales of cars in the U.S. which caused the domestic manufacturers to cut down their production and lay off workers.

In this context the question arises as to how a small, financially weak, unknown foreign car producer with a ten year old car in such a short time managed to reach this success in "the Promised Land of the Automobiles". How did they proceed and why was it that this introduction in a foreign market differed from the prevailing pattern of a rather less dramatic development of the sales which characterized the remaining Swedish industry entering new markets?

Another issue worth examining is the extent to which increased importance of the American market was planned and expected or just an unforeseen success that emerged through a series of accidental events.

Official accounts of the introduction on the U.S. market convey the impression that this was a deliberate, very carefully planned process. Is this in accordance with what actually happened, or are these "stories" still another example of the justifications and myths of planning commonly cultivated?

To explore the issues raised above the introduction of Volvo in the U.S. market in the years 1955 to 1961 will be examined. In order to enable the reader to understand the context in which this course of events took place a short description of the development of the company up to 1955 and the situation it faced in the mid 1950s will be given. Next the rapid development of the export to the U.S. market and the impact this had on the company as such will be elaborated.

This is followed by a description of the process whereby the venture was organized right from the beginning, based on an interview with the person responsible for the introduction of the Volvo car in the U.S. market. A preliminary draft of the report written in 1955 was also very useful. This account is supplemented by information collected in the minutes from the Joint Board of Volvo. In the concluding section the issues raised will be discussed.

14.2. Volvo Enters the American Market

14.2.1. Volvo's Development until 1955[1]

Right from the beginning the Swedish automobile company Volvo was designed as an export-oriented producer of passenger cars. In 1926 its founder and managing director up to 1956, Assar Gabrielsson, stated that the aim was to produce a car adapted to Swedish conditions. The limited market in Sweden presupposed export of cars as a method rapidly to reach sufficiently large production runs. Cars were mainly sold during spring and summer and in order to even out the variations in sales the export should be directed towards countries below the equator with a season opposite the one prevailing in Sweden. The first-hand interest was concerned with the Argentine and some other countries in Latin America. Of a production target of 1,000 cars in the first year 400 were to be exported. When after

---

1   A more comprehensive account of the development of Volvo is given in Kinch (1987).

three years production had reached 8,000 units 60 per cent were expected to be sold abroad.

The actual development differed from what had been planned. The cars were not accepted by the market and, in order to survive, Volvo soon had to start producing trucks and buses. This business thrived and for many years dominated the enterprise and also accounted for almost all the exports. The sales of these vehicles were more evenly distributed over the year and the need to export to countries below the equator disappeared. Instead, the export was at first directed to the countries close by and later on gradually expanded to more distant markets. However, due to high duties, no vehicles were sold to any large European industrial country with an automobile industry of its own. The vision of a Swedish car industry was not abandoned and Volvo tried out a variety of models over the years. It was not until a small stylish European car was put on the market in 1947 that Volvo had its first real success as a car manufacturer. The main efforts in the post-war period were directed to increase the capacity to cater for the demand for this car on the Swedish market which absorbed almost all of the production.

Around the mid-1950s Volvo entered another phase in its evolution. Until then the post-war period had been dominated by the problem of increasing the production capacity sufficiently to satisfy the rapidly increasing demand. As long as the excess demand persisted the seasonal problems of matching production and sales were easy to solve. However, these problems significantly increased in magnitude when the production capacity was substantially enlarged by a large investment programme in 1954-1956. This coincided with a temporary standstill in the demand for cars in Sweden.

The uncertainty about the development of the market at this time was caused by regulations imposed by the Swedish government to curb the expansion of private automobiles. In 1954 the sales had increased by 50,000, reaching a total of 126,000 cars. At the turn of 1955/1956 Volvo temporarily dismissed workers and cut down the production plans for the coming year. This was due to rumours that the government intended to curtail the sales of new cars from a level of 130,000 in 1955 to about 100,000 in 1956. Out of a total production of 27,900 Volvo cars more than 25,000, or close to 90 per cent, were sold in Sweden in 1955. This implied that Volvo by then was totally dependent on the development of the Swedish market. With a share of the market approaching 20 per cent further growth based on an increased penetration in the domestic market was not very realistic. Thus a continued expansion, which was essential for long-term survival, had to be based on increased efforts in the export market.

Due to the large investment programme Volvo in the mid-1950s was financially weak. The Swedish financial market was regulated and in 1955 Volvo applied to the Central Bank for permission to raise a loan of $ 4 million in the U.S. It was claimed that the company had to give up several export transactions with buses and trucks, as it could not grant conditions of credits to its potential customers, equal to those offered by its competitors. This application mentioned in a short passage that Volvo intended to start export activities in the U.S. Primarily the aim was to sell cars but the company also had diesel trucks in view[2]. With reference to the prevailing credit restrictions this application was rejected by the authorities and the minister for trade even ridiculed the effort to sell Swedish cars in the native country par preference of the automobile industry.

Volvo at this time also lobbied the government for an arrangement with export quotas on a preferential basis with the large automobile producing countries in Europe. The customs duty on cars imported to Sweden amounted to 15 per cent *ad valorem*. At the same time West Germany, the United Kingdom and France had duties in the range of 30-51 per cent. The company stated that it was not competitive on these terms and had refrained from export. However, if Volvo was allowed to import its automobiles into these countries on the same conditions as the foreign industry encountered in Sweden they claimed it would be possible to capture a small amount of the market there as well. The size of the market implied that only a tiny fraction meant a substantial contribution to the sales. Until this was settled Volvo had to look for other markets and in the annual report to the shareholders it was stated: "The company continues to develop its sales organization in the non-automobile producing countries" (AB Volvo, Annual Report to the Shareholders 1954, p.8).

14.2.2. Entering the American Market in 1955

The above passage was written early in 1955. However, somewhat surprisingly in view of this statement, the first Volvo car was delivered to California later in the year. The first official announcement of the

---

2   Volvo, letter to the Swedish Exchange Control Office July 11, 1955.

introduction of Volvo cars was given in a press release dated August 11th. For some months market research had been conducted and the first sample of cars was due to arrive in the middle of August. Imported cars were mainly sold in the coastal districts and Volvo had started in California because it had contact with a distributor who believed in the car. Volvo started on a small scale and did not dare to undertake any commitment regarding the size of expected volumes. It was not possible to judge whether the venture would succeed or not until 6-9 months had elapsed. As soon as the company was convinced that there was a future it would probably try the other coast as well. About five million cars were sold in the U.S. and just one thousandth of this market meant a volume of 5,000 annually, which was adjudged substantial in relation to the conditions prevailing in Sweden[3].

On this occasion it was not mentioned that at the same time a Swedish airman and former test pilot in the Swedish Air Force, Nils Sefeldt had emigrated to the U.S. with the intention of building up a distribution net for Volvo cars in Texas. This business started with a very limited budget which may explain why this organization was not officially recognized by Volvo until 1956.

When the sales increased in 1956 Volvo opened up a sales company in Detroit. Later this organization was transferred to a new head office in Englewood Cliffs, N.J.

In the first year less than 100 cars were sold. The following year the three organizations managed to put slightly more than 5,000 on the market and in the succeeding two years the annual increase in the sales amounted to a full 5,000. In 1959 the sales reached a peak of 18,533 units. By then the export to the U.S. amounted to 105 million SEK which made Volvo the single largest Swedish exporter to this market. The total export to other countries was 207 million SEK and the cars accounted for 60 per cent of the company's export value. The operations in the U.S. were profitable and a dividend of $ 8,000 was distributed to the parent company in 1959.

In the period 1956-1959 Volvo produced 197,000 cars, of which slightly more than 50,000 were delivered to North America. In 1959 this export accounted for 26 per cent, of an annual production of 72,000 cars. The Swedish market still absorbed the major part or 59 per cent of production. Parallel to this development Volvo had organized sales to other countries and this export amounted to 15 per cent of the total production of cars.

---

3   Volvo press release August 11, 1956.

The success in the U.S. was a confirmation of the competitiveness of the Volvo cars. The increased export in 1957 turned Volvo into a producer mainly of cars as had been intended 30 years before. Interestingly enough it was with a layout which closely resembled the original idea. North America was substituted for Latin America but the impetus was the need to increase the production runs and handle the seasonal problems to match production and sales.

14.2.3. The Story as Told by Bertil Bengtsson[4]

The market research in California and the launch of the Volvo organization on the East coast was handled by Bertil Bengtsson. In 1951 he had received a scholarship to spend a year at the Swedish Chamber of Commerce in San Francisco. For some time he worked for a dealer of GM cars and an export/import company which *inter alia* introduced the Nikon camera on the American market. In his opinion this was a good start to doing business in the U.S. After somewhat more than a year and a half Bengtsson was appointed head of the office and stayed until the beginning of 1955. For personal reasons he wanted to return home and had applied for several positions in Sweden and been offered a job as one of four area managers for Volvo there.

In January 1955 a Volvo car had been sent to California and Bengtsson was commissioned to investigate the prospects of selling Volvo cars there. When he returned to Sweden in March 1955 he was "caught" by T.G. Andersson, the Sales Manager of Volvo, and assigned new duties in the Export Department. Andersson had promised Gabrielsson that he would place cars in a country with an automobile industry of its own, and had initiated the market research in California. The car he primarily had in his mind to try for the American market was Volvo Amazon which would be introduced in the following year. The custom duty for cars in the U.S. was only 10% which was an attractive feature as compared with other car producing countries.

In his report on the market for Volvo cars in the Western U.S. Bengtsson gave a detailed description of the relevant conditions. The import of cars amounted to 25,400 in 1954 which corresponded to 0.5 per cent of the sales of domestic cars, some five million units. The sales of imported cars were

---

4   This section is mainly based on an interview with Bertil Bengtsson in London, U.K. on February 6, 1989.

unevenly distributed over the country and the three states in the west accounted for 40 per cent. At the same time only 10 per cent of the domestic cars were delivered there. The import had reached a peak of 29,300 units in 1952. By then the British producers Austin, Hillman, Morris, Jaguar and MG represented 76 per cent of the market. Only two years later this share had dropped to 46 per cent. Of these companies only Jaguar had managed to maintain its level of sales. Against the tide Volkswagen had developed from 600 in 1952 to more than 6,300 units in 1954. That year it had increased by 5,100, the rapid success continued and sales figures exceeding 20,000 units were expected for 1955.

Bengtsson emphasized that Volvo right from the beginning must carefully select dealers with a good reputation, sound financial position and a long-term perspective. The approach adopted by Volkswagen and Mercedes-Benz was favourably described. In contrast it was mentioned that Renault, which had opened a sales company in Los Angeles in 1954 had required dealers lacking in discrimination who were enjoined to place as many cars in the market as possible. The majority of them could be classified as financially weak and it was declared that a large number of cars had been delivered on consignment. Volvo at first could not rely on exclusive dealers and had to accept that they represented other makes. However, in order to attract good dealers and have them promote an unknown make it was suggested they should be given an incentive. This meant that the margin offered to the dealers by Volvo had to be larger than for comparable cars. Renault was priced in the lowest range with $ 1,295 followed by Volkswagen with $ 1,595. The cheapest Chevrolet model amounted to $ 1,995 and the most popular run to $ 2,200. In order to cover the estimated cost Volvo had to set the price at $ 2,045 but the Volvo standard PV 444 did not have a performance matching this price. At this time a tuned up engine which gave 72 instead of 44 hp. had been developed for Swedish police cars. This engine was flown to California and fitted in the test car. With this modification the car ran like a "little bomb" and now justified its price. The car was introduced in competitions and finished first in almost every event in which it participated. This was good publicity and rapidly made Volvo a well known make all over the country.

It was estimated that Volvo after half a year or a somewhat longer period of introduction ought to reach a sale of 400-500 cars annually in the Western U.S. Provided that the new model appealed to the customers and could be priced as the PV 444 it was considered feasible to sell at least twice as many after some years when Volvo had become better known in the market. One of the more prominent distributors interviewed by Bengtsson insisted that by then a level of sales reaching 4,000 should be possible. In order to obtain the expected sales figures for the total market the volumes projected for the western part of the country should be doubled. This rule of thumb applied for most of the other companies. In this way the expected volumes after a period of introduction of some years were in the range of 2,000-8,000 cars annually.

A turnover of 400-500 cars a year required investments in cars and spare parts amounting to about $ 100,000. However, this could be financed with a system of bills of exchange running for 180 days at a favorable interest rate. The transport to the American west coast took 40 days and the importers paid cash on delivery. This meant that if it so desired Volvo could use the borrowed money elsewhere in the business for 140 days.

Bengtsson was given the responsibility to start up the sales of the car in the U.S. and the first distributor attached to Volvo was Auto Import, Inc. in Los Angeles. At first Volvo accepted a trial order of three cars and later gave them the distributorship for the western states. One of the owners—Leo Hirsh—was in the ironware business and imported some articles from Sweden. The other—Gene Klein—was a dealer selling MG sports-cars in three outlets. When Bengtsson had visited Hirsh late in 1954 he had been shown a picture of the Volvo sports-cars with a fiberglass body and asked how contact could be made with the company. Hirsh had repeatedly written letters to Volvo in Sweden but not received any reply. When Bengtsson later studied the correspondence at the export department at Volvo he discovered many letters to the company but few replies. He was told; "There are many writing to us and we can not answer all of the letters—if they persist we pay attention and make contact". According to Bengtsson people at the Export Department were rather indifferent to the possibilities of marketing cars in the U.S. One person had promised to "eat his old straw hat" if Bengtsson managed to sell more than 20 cars over there.

In 1955 Nils Sefeldt also started to sell Volvo cars on a small scale in Texas. He had approached Bengtsson and asked him if he could buy some cars as a way to take money out of the country. He presented Bengtsson his plans to start a business based in Forth Worth, Texas, selling fire-fighting equipment. The latter convinced Sefeldt that it would be more interesting to sell Volvo cars and in this way it started.

Sources based on the accounts given by Sefeldt present a somewhat different picture.[5] Sefeldt had toured the U.S. in 1953 and noticed the growing interest in European cars. This convinced him that it would be possible to sell Volvo there and he decided to emigrate. The authorities denied him transfer of more than $ 600 for each member of the family. Being a family of five he started the venture with only $ 3,000. However, these sources confirm that he was in touch with Bengtsson.

It was more difficult to find a distributor on the East coast and in 1956 when the venture was well under way Volvo set up an organization of its own. This was located at the purchasing office which Volvo for many years had had in Detroit. At the age of 31 Bengtsson was appointed as manager of this unit and he was also responsible for the export to the U.S. from Sweden.

By now Volvo had three organizations operating on the North American continent. In its own company Volvo had engaged Americans with experience from the automobile industry, and by June it had obtained 11 dealers in the eastern states. In the Western part the number of dealers amounted to 40-50. A small unit had been established in Texas but Volvo still lacked an organization in the Midwest.

The cars had to be modified to a certain extent to meet the American standards. Indicators, headlights and windscreens had been changed. In order to protect the cars from serious damage caused by minor collisions with the higher American vehicles the bumpers also had to be modified. This adjustment work was mainly carried out in the U.S. at first. The standard fittings as well as the colours suited to Swedish conditions did not appeal to the American consumers. They wanted bright plastic upholstery and the most popular colours were white and red. These adaptations were gradually introduced.

In September 1956 Gunnar Engellau succeeded Assar Gabrielsson as Managing Director of Volvo.[6] Since April he had devoted much time to the "American export" and twice travelled there to help organize the business. According to the statements he made to the Joint Board of the company

5   Fact Sheet: Nils Olof Sefeldt, November 18, 1985, prepared for a press release.

6   In this passage Bengtsson's story has been supplemented by information collected in the minutes from the Joint Board of AB Volvo.

Engellau firmly believed in a growing market for European quality cars in the U.S. and stressed the importance of being sensitive to the demands of the customers. The entire import still only represented "a drop in the ocean" compared with the total production of the American manufacturers. There was a possible danger that the domestic companies would develop a small car, but as long as Volkswagen or Volvo did not sell more than 100,000 cars annually this step would probably not be taken. Gabrielsson had maintained that the importers should be independent of Volvo but this policy was changed and Volvo came closer to the market and in later years set up a number of sales companies.

In Bengtsson's opinion the former managing director had allowed the technicians in Gothenburg too much influence and they were unwilling to adapt the cars to the desires of the American customers. The export of cars had been very marginal and not handled on business lines. Cars were sold as unsophisticated products, "like potatoes". The responsibility of the company did not extend beyond the front door of the factory and the distributors were free to develop the business according to their own ideas. Engellau backed the introduction, "disciplined" the technicians, and released Bengtsson from the task of organizing the adjustment of headlights etc. in the U.S.

When he developed the network of dealers Bengtsson had the VW organization in mind. This company had been the most successful of the imported makes and had strict rules for the equipment of the dealers. Volvo chose to design standard signboards in blue and white and worked out a layout of the garages etc. in order to create a distinctive Volvo profile. The company was very strict with the requirements which a prospective dealer had to fulfil in order to be eligible to sell Volvo cars. It was essential that he be able to provide sufficient service. A dealer had to buy at least three cars and a kit of spare parts all of which had to be paid for in cash on delivery. Volvo did not make an effort to attract dealers and as it was considered to be difficult to be accepted Bengtsson claimed that many wanted to sign up for the company. Volvo also arranged a business management system for the dealers and helped them to organize their business.

These measures were not accepted by all at the Volvo headquarters in Gothenburg. According to Bengtsson the standard procedure on the export sales had been not to take any responsibility for the product beyond the factory doors. He insisted that it was important to follow the product to the ultimate customers in order to know their preferences. The margins on a standard model were rather low but if the customers could be persuaded to accept some of the extra equipment offered this would substantially increase the profitability. Thus by knowing the customer it was possible to achieve a better price level, and it also helped to organize the service and spare part business in a profitable way. If the customers were satisfied the rate of re-purchase would increase and the dealer prosper. After approximately two years about 450 dealers had been tied to the organization and as they carried the financial burden they were eager to get the cars rapidly on the market. The sales company of Volvo had a comparatively large stock of spare parts and organized training in the service of cars.

At the beginning the finance of the dealers' stock of cars was a major problem. It was considered risky to finance a dealer promoting a new make where no price level for used cars had yet been established. This almost blocked the whole venture. However, Bengtsson managed to gain access to the Chief Executive Officer of Universal CIT, who specialized in credits to the automobile industry and they worked out a "floorplan" for the Volvo dealers.

In order to keep up the production in the factories in Sweden Volvo at times "forced" cars on the American organization. When the Suez crisis broke out in November 1956 rationing of gas and restrictions on driving at weekends, were enforced in Sweden. The sale of cars slumped and Volvo had to cut down production. At that time there was an excessive demand for labour in the remaining industry and the Volvo management feared that the workers would be absorbed by other companies if the assembly lines temporarily closed down. Volvo wanted to keep the organization intact and the export to the U.S. helped to overcome the crisis in which it was innocently involved. The delivery to the U.S. was a problem and in 1956 Volvo chartered a ship which could load fully 600 cars. According to Bengtsson sometimes, during this period, he was instructed by cable to organize the unloading of cars in places where Volvo did not have any organization. The vessels were not adapted for transport of automobiles and the cars arrived in bad condition. However, these forced deliveries were made out of necessity to avoid the dismissal of workers.

In 1958 a new manager was appointed as head of the American Volvo organization and Bengtsson was engaged elsewhere in the company but still had the overall responsibility for the venture. When the American automobile manufacturers introduced the "compact cars" in 1960 the sale of imported cars slumped. Renault and Peugeot which had built up large sales were badly hurt and compelled to re-ship large quantities of unsold cars to Europe. The sales of Volvo cars dropped as well and Bengtsson was again attached directly to the U.S. organization. It was important to convince the dealers that Volvo had a long-term perspective and intended to stay on the market and weather the crisis. The company managed to keep most of the organization intact. This was facilitated by the investments which the dealers had been obliged to make in spare parts and other facilities which made it uneconomical for them to withdraw.

However, the distributor in California was severely hit by the crisis. In 1958 Hirsh and Klein had sold the business with a good profit to the Swedish businessman Axel Wennergren unbeknown to Volvo. Wennergren had large plans to develop British Columbia and had started the Canadian distributor net in 1957. The company was left with about 1,500 unsold cars and asked Volvo to buy them out. A new company, Volvo Western Distributing, Inc., was established in 1961 and with a reduced organization the operation soon became profitable again. Moreover the Canadian distributor faced problems in 1961 with a stock of more than 1,200 unsold cars. The cars were bought back by Volvo at a discount of 25-30 per cent as they were in sore need of re-conditioning. In order to obtain working capital Bengtsson tried to induce the old bank to offer financing of the cars to their full value. They did not accept this idea but Bengtsson managed to convince another bank to consent to this arrangement. The business was moved from Vancouver to Toronto and the turnover increased substantially when it was operated by Volvo.

The attempt to introduce trucks in 1958 did not develop as planned. Volvo began to market trucks for long distance traffic. A car was sold on the West coast and used on the route between Los Angeles and Alaska. The vehicle was not adapted for this kind of service and Volvo could not offer the required maintenance. The engine lacked the required power and could not run at high speed for so long a time. The truck stopped every now and then in the woods and the service team had to drive for days to fix the vehicle. Volvo left the market in 1961 and the unsold trucks were re-shipped.

14.3. Entering and Remaining in a Tightly Structured Network

How can it be explained that Volvo in a relatively short period could reach and maintain a foothold in a tightly structured network such as that of cars in the U.S. This is elaborated in the first section below. Next the question is raised of the extent to which the introduction and rapid success can be characterized as intended by the management of Volvo or as the unexpected consequence of a number of more or less accidental events.

The American market for cars in the mid 1950s can be characterized as a rather tight network (Hammarkvist *et al.*, 1982 p. 27). The companies dealing with American cars had fixed, well defined roles in relation to each other. The way the business was handled followed well established rules. The big three — GM, Ford and Chrysler — dominated, and accounted for more than 90 per cent of the sales. The basic properties of the cars offered and the organization of the manufacture and distribution were more or less identical regardless of make. Large gas-consuming cars with annual changes in the styling were put on the market in large numbers. The marginal manufacturers followed more or less the same strategy as the big three but suffered from cost disadvantages due to inadequate production runs. The alternatives open to the customers looking for something different were rather limited.

Over the years very stable, close relationships had developed between manufacturers, dealers, service facilities and customers. Through interaction they had adapted to each other which resulted in investments of various kinds specific to this exchange and promoted trust and loyalty in the relationship. This involved a high probability that those involved in the car-business would continue to co-operate closely also in the future. As long as the prevailing rules of the game were beneficial to the main actors involved, the network would be stable and very difficult for an outsider to enter.

However, it can be claimed that besides a situation characterized by loose ties between the actors, it may be easier to enter a tightly structured network compared with a situation in between. If the new entrant can somehow complete the existing structure it may be integrated in the net. However, another reason more relevant in this case is that a highly structured situation often creates discontent by actors disfavoured by the way the network is handled. There is no alternative offered by the established actors for groups wanting a different solution. This may make them leave the traditional outlets once they are given an alternative. A moderately tight network on the other hand opens up alternatives for those involved and an outsider cannot, to the same extent, rely on dissatisfied actors. Adaptations, trust and bonds of loyalty tie them together and time-consuming efforts and large investments are needed in order to establish a position. Thus, somewhat paradoxically, it may be argued that a very tightly structured network opens the possibility for new entrants playing a different game.

This is exactly what happened. The sale of imported cars was up to 1955 very marginal and fragmented over a wide range of makes. The vehicles put on the market ranged from sports models to very expensive cars, most of which did not represent an alternative for the public at large. The importers and dealers involved in the business were mostly poorly organized and had weak financial standing. They also lacked a widespread net of service facilities and their stock of spare parts was inadequate. The British producers of family cars which first entered the market and received some attention did not meet the quality standards required by the customers. The situation changed drastically when Volkswagen entered the market with a car of excellent quality and a well organized launch. The car received much attention in the press which partly explains its rapid success. In 1955 the import of cars amounted to 57,000 and out of this Volkswagen sold 30,000 cars and their sales volume almost doubled in the following year. Volkswagen was followed by other European manufacturers and the sales of imported cars multiplied and reached a peak of 668,000 in 1959.

The new vogue for imported cars also attracted new dealers. The margins on the American cars were very low due to the keen competition and the most profitable part of the business was the financing of the hire-purchase contracts. Dealers with a good financial position set up new retail units promoting imported cars side by side with their old units. Companies dealing with used cars or running service units which had not been allowed access on equal terms to the network of American manufacturers now saw a possibility to extend the business into the sale of imported cars.

In a very short period the structure of the network for imported cars changed so that its relative importance increased and developed into a threat to the American manufacturers.

When the American manufacturers in 1960 introduced "the compact car" the import slumped. The volume dropped to 444,000 and when the stocks were decreased in 1961 slumped to 279,000 units or substantially less than 50% of the volumes reached in 1959.[7] Many of the European companies which had surfed on the vogue for imported cars were severely hit when the American competitors retaliated. In the short period that had elapsed trust and loyalty had not yet developed sufficiently and many of the dealers were not commited enough to stay in business when problems arose. Some of the companies had overexploited the situation, expanded too rapidly and not given adequate attention to organize the network of dealers and service facilities. This short-sighted behaviour implied large costs later on. Easy come – easy go! What had been easily obtained at first was lost in an even shorter period. Facing losses the dealers quit the business and for some manufacturers the only solution was to ship large quantities of unsold cars back to Europe. This also created bad will with the customers and hampered a come back when the market, after some years, recovered.

In relation to its size the export to the U.S. was very important for the Volvo company. However, compared with the total import to the U.S. its sales only represented a minor fraction. The Volvo models were initially segmented as a kind of sports car and thus not directly competing with the new compact models. Sales at once dropped with about 5,000 units in 1960 and some of the actors involved were badly hit. The distributors in California and Canada faced serious problems during the slump and had to be taken over by Volvo in 1961. Compared to the total setback and the problems other makers experienced this loss of sales was marginal to Volvo and could be compensated in other recently opened export markets. With a foothold in its own American organization Volvo had deliberately made a great effort to develop the network of dealers and service facilities. They also claimed to have set high standards for the ones chosen right from the beginning. Furthermore Volvo had made the dealers invest in the relationship and tried to create a distinctive Volvo identity. These investments had a limited value once the dealers left the venture and thus tied them to the Volvo company.

---

7   The figures are collected from World Motor Vehicle Data 1988.

14.4. Strategic Planning or Swift Footwork

In retrospect it may seem logical that Volvo should try to export cars to America as all other large markets were protected by high import duties. Volkswagen had shown in 1954 that a well organized launch of a quality car could pay off in rapidly increasing sales figures even in a declining market. In 1955 the import of cars more than doubled and the success of Volkswagen continued. However, the impression obtained in this case is that Volvo took this step rather reluctantly and that the positive result was unexpected. The success exceeded the most daring expectations laid down at the beginning.

The first figures mentioned in 1955 indicated an expected volume of 5,000 cars. In the market research Bengtsson had projected a level of the sales in the range of 2,000-8,000 cars after a couple of years but this volume was surpassed in less than two and a half years. The uncertainty concerning the project is clearly revealed when the minutes of the Joint Board of AB Volvo are scrutinized. In September 1955 the project was presented as an experiment and the outcome could not be judged until 6-9 months had elapsed. With a positive response the business might be extended to include the Eastern states as well. In March 1956 it was somewhat reluctantly stated that a volume of 2,000 was in reach for 1956. The possibility that the company could delay the seasonal cut-back of production in the fall was promised in June conditional on a continued positive development of the export to America. In October the estimates for 1956 had been augmented to 4,000 cars. At the end of the year the new managing director Gunnar Engellau admitted that the export to America had helped and would help the company to settle the problems it faced due to the Suez crisis. Engellau expected Volvo to sell fully 5,000 cars or 2 1/2 times more, than he had promised the Board of Directors at the beginning of the year. Thus the expectations gradually rose in response to increasing sales figures. The result obtained at the close of the year came as a surprise and surpassed by good margin the most daring forecasts made at the outset.

In less than three years the North American market achieved a "strategic" status for Volvo and has been of significant importance to the company's development ever since. To what extent was this a result of carefully hatched plans or an ability to take advantage of the opportunities as they arose?

First it must be recognized that export to an automobile producing country was in conflict with Volvo's officially stated policy. This argument should not be stretched too far as there is good reason to believe that the "policy" was a way to rationalize the actual pattern that had emerged (Mintzberg 1978) and turn necessity into a virtue (Kinch 1987). However, this kind of statement might have limited the focus of attention of the export department of Volvo and partly explain why outsiders played such an important role in the creation of the new market. The Sales Manager of Volvo is said to have promised to open up a market in an automobile producing country. When Bengtsson was employed by Volvo a person with detailed knowledge of the U.S. emerged and the Sales Manager had him carry out market research in California.

At this time Volvo was also approached by Nils Sefeldt who applied for a dealership in Texas and adjoining states. Thus, two establishments started in parallel and outsiders played an important part in launching the business. Bengtsson carried out the market research and organized the introduction. As newly attached to Volvo and with a long experience of the institutions and business practice in California he could serve as a weak tie between Volvo and the actors in the network for cars in the U.S. (Granovetter 1973). He was new to the company, young and enthusiastic about the idea, not caught in old traditions, and swiftly took the opportunities as they arose. The product, sold as a family car in Sweden, was positioned as a sports car in the U.S. and adapted to cater to the desires of the customers. Once the venture was off and running a sales unit was established and investments made in building up relationships to dealers. This was also contrary to Volvo's established policy of selling through independent distributors on the export markets. The Volvo car also for the first time since the 1920s took part in various competitions.

The timing of this venture was just right as the demand for imported cars rapidly increased, largely as a consequence of the success of Volkswagen. At this time the Swedish government considered imposing different measures to curb the expansion of automobiles which gave Volvo a major incentive to increase the exports. Alongside with the efforts in the U.S. other attempts were made elsewhere as well. With the rapid development of the sales in America these measures temporarily had to be cut back. The venture was certainly accelerated in 1956 by the temporary slump in the sales of cars in Sweden. When the market recovered at the beginning of

1957 the problems were reversed. Volvo could not cater for the demands made simultaneously by the Swedish and American markets. Engellau stressed the importance of keeping the American export alive and claimed that the Swedish market could never absorb the full production in the second half of the year.

Of importance for the rapid development of the introduction was probably also that the venture coincided with a change of management in Volvo. When Gabrielsson in September 1955 presented the American experiment he emphasized that Volvo "must not expose itself to large risks, but develop the market stepwise".[8] At this time the venture was presented as just one in a number of forward thrusts to try out the possibilites of extending the market. In September 1956 Engellau succeeded him and gradually new persons were brought into the company. Engellau had a personal stake in the American venture as for a couple of months he had been actively organizing the introduction. As newly assigned Managing Director he further desired to "win his spurs" and gave priority to the export to America. At times he forced cars onto the market and early in 1958 built up a stock of cars in the U.S. to match an expected increase in sales later in the spring season. He was younger, more aggressive and more prone to take risks, than Gabrielsson. According to one source he may also have had increased ambitions for the company and realized the need to gear up the expansion as a means to long-term survival.[9] Gabrielsson's policy not to engage in the distribution of the vehicles, if this could be avoided, was abandoned. Sales companies were established in a number of countries and new markets for cars opened up. To conclude this paragraph it may be argued that the mode which best describes what happened is that of "swift footwork" rather than strategic planning. The scope and the importance of the venture were not conceived at the outset. The impression obtained is that right from the beginning there was a number of lucky circumstances that set the project off and running. Once the opportunities arose they were cleverly and consistently exploited. Sometimes bold measures were taken and earlier policies and routines abandoned. The result was as far reaching as it was unexpected.

---

8 Minutes from the Joint Board of AB Volvo, September 26, 1955, p. 6.

9 Ulf af Trolle, SvD 88-01-08, in memory of Gunnar Engellau.

14.5. Managing in a Network — Strategic Vision Beaten by Network Realities

The majority of the management oriented literature on strategy and corporate development emphasizes the importance of top down planning, goal directed behavior, and is often based on a rather unsophisticated view of organizations and environments. The unsupported assumption made in these accounts is that strategies and consequences are tightly linked as if managerial intentions can be smoothly translated into organizational outcomes (Aldrich,1986).

A quotation from the customer magazine of Volvo describing the introduction of cars in America written in 1959 illustrates this way of thinking.

> "Before the important step across the Atlantic was taken by Volvo the market in America had been carefully investigated. In advance it had practically assured itself a net of distributors and had devoted considerable time to solve the problems related to service and the like. So when the first load of cars arrived in America, Volvo could press the button and the machinery worked" (*Ratten* 1959:1,p.8).

In this account the uncertainty expressed when the venture was first suggested is forgotten and the problems arising from the introduction of the trucks not mentioned. The picture presented is touched up to fit the image of a carefully planned and implemented strategy. This rational approach to strategy is constantly challenged by empirical research maintaining the importance of emerging strategies and claiming that policies and strategies are often formulated in retrospect to justify the pattern which has eventually developed (Mintzberg, 1978; Mintzberg & McHugh, 1985; Salancik & Meindl,1984).

In the development of a company purposeful actions are certainly of significance. But factors outside the control of management, the impact of unforeseen events, and chance may also be of critical importance. As the company is tied to a network the behavior to some extent is conditioned on actions taken by other actors and strategy cannot be pursued unilaterally. The pattern which emerges may differ substantially from what had been planned (Kinch 1987). Sometimes accidental occurrences and behaviour in opposition to the official policy may dramatically change the scope and direction of a venture. It has already been mentioned that Volvo was forced to acquire the distributors in California and Canada as they failed when the market slumped.

Beginning in 1962 the total import as well as the Volvo export gradually recovered and by 1965 approached the volumes attained in 1959. Then the sales steadily increased until 1973 when slightly more than 61,000 Volvo cars were sold. The forecast indicated that a volume of 100,000 units was within reach and this initiated a decision to start up the first assembly unit operated by a foreign manufacturer of cars. This would be the single largest investment made by the company. However, due to decreasing sales in the years which followed, this plant was never opened. This time the drop in sales was not related to a setback in the total market but caused by problems with the product as such. Major efforts to improve the quality of the existing models were made as well as the introduction of a new up-market car especially designed for the American customers. In the 1980s the position of Volvo radically improved. The sales to North America surpassed the sales in Sweden and a peak of 111,000 units was obtained in 1986.

The network for trucks was not as firmly structured as that for cars. The customers were offered a range of solutions to their transport needs. Trucks were bought more for economic reasons and not so much influenced by the "whims of fashion". The quality of the trucks offered by Volvo did not match the local needs and in the 1950s Volvo could not establish the necessary service facilities to attract enough customers. This was repeated when the company in 1975 made a new attempt to enter the market. It now intended to start with trucks for short distance distribution operating within a radius of 200 kilometers. By gradually opening up new units this would enable the company to establish a service organization covering most of the country. This process was very slow and in order to speed it up Volvo allied itself with Freightliner, a producer of long-range trucks, which was looking for a partner which manufactured trucks for short range services. This co-operation ceased shortly afterwards when the company was acquired by Mercedes-Benz. In this situation, White Motors, a former partner to Freightliner, which had gone into the hands of the receivers was acquired by Volvo. The company was restructured and Volvo became engaged in the production of trucks in the U.S. Shortly afterwards a co-operation with GM concerning heavy trucks was established. Thus, the further development was also characterized by unexpected events. What had been intended, e.g.

the manufacture of cars in the U.S., did not materialize, but due to external circumstances Volvo instead later started the production of trucks.

Thus when the story of Volvo in the U.S. is continued we are presented with another series of illustrations where strategic visions yield to network realities. The development of the company seems to be more dependent on the ability to handle the long-term relations and respond to unplanned events as they arise rather than on strategic visions and carefully planned strategic moves. This rather erratic development is not unique to Volvo. A classical case in this vein is the description by Pascale (1984) of Honda's introduction of motorcycles on the American market in 1959. The Volvo case may be added to the empirical evidence illustrating this phenomenon.

15

Taking a Position in a Structured Business Network

Nazeem Seyed-Mohamed and Maria Bolte

15.1. Positioning in Business Networks

Each firm in the business network occupies a position in it. The positions are interconnected and form the structure of the network within which business takes place. The structure of the network, the resource exchange activities between the positions, and the individual relationships between the actors determine the opportunities and constraints for actions in the network. Thus, a firm which controls a unique resource required by other actors in the network will be able thereby to strengthen its existing relationships and also to initiate new relationships with firms who need that resource. However, the action to use this resource to strengthen its position seems to depend much on how the individual actor interprets the value of that resource in terms of the other actors' need.

This chapter is about how an industrial firm establishes, maintains and develops its position in a foreign business network. The paper begins with a theoretical section about positions in networks. This section is intended to give a brief introduction of the concept related to the subsequent case study. The case study which follows deals with a Swedish compressor manufacturer's endeavour to enter the American industrial compressor market.

A firm in an business network has a number of exchange relationships with other firms. Thus each firm has a position directly dependent upon its relationships with counterparts, and indirectly dependent upon the counterparts' relationships with others in the network. As it is possible to define all the actors' positions in this manner, the concept can be used to characterize network structure and network distance between the actors (Johanson & Mattsson, 1990). Time and commitments are necessary to build up exchange relationships and to shape the positions of the firms. The position of the actor in the network and its operative environment is important for future action. This could involve initiating new relationships and improving old ones.

Each firm has a position with direct exchange relationships with some actors and connected exchange relationships with other actors. The connectedness implies that exchange in one is conditioned—facilitated or hindered—by exchange in the other relationship. Therefore a connected relationship can be positively or negatively connected depending on whether the connected exchange relationship is a complementary supplier or a supplier producing substitutable products. These types of interrelations between firms connect their resources in industrial activities. If the resource interdependences are strong, or if the positions are 'close' to each other in the exchange activity chain, or if they are more specialized in relation to each other, or if the production system is more concentrated the stronger will be the interrelations and the more structured the network will tend to be.

In addition to the activity dependent relationships there could also exist strong personal interrelationships (or firm specific dependencies) which are more or less important. Firms develop these interrelations as a result of doing business with each other for long periods. During these periods the actors gain knowledge about each other and build up trust about what one will perform to satisfy the needs of the other. The emergent trust will make the actors more willing to commit resources which are investments to strengthen the business relationships. This could further promote the dependences between the actors in the network.

When the business interdependences are heavy and tightly knit and when social relationships are strong the positions of the actors become closely linked by various bonds of dependences which consequently could function as high barriers to entry to newcomers. An outsider will find it difficult to initiate exchange relationships with the firms which are already in the network. These firms in exchange relationship within the network will either find it difficult to switch partners because of strong activity interdependences and strong resource commitments or else they might find no good reason to turn to a newcomer of whom they know little or nothing. In such instances the company which wants to enter into exchange relationships with firms engaged in the network will either have to 'buy' into already established positions or else make long-term investments to win acceptance. A foreign firm, for example, cannot choose an entry mode without seriously taking into account the existing structure of the network.

The structure of the network however is more or less invisible for an outsider. This is simply because of the business logic in industrial activities. The actors who occupy positions in the network have specific knowledge of their own and sometimes also their counterparts' exchange activities. This knowledge has been acquired gradually and incrementally by the logic of learning by doing, which subsequently enhances the process of doing by learning. More or less as a result of this specificity in the exchange relationships the structure of every business network is unique and cannot be easily discerned by an outsider. As a result an actor can normally accumulate information about the structure and the functioning of the network only by active participation in the network dynamics.

Firms in networks are continuously in action in order to maintain or strengthen their position. The reason is that firms in a network have gained their position because of their interdependences with other positions in the network and also as a result of their previous actions. The action of the firm will depend more or less on how it evaluates information to which it has access about the need uncertainties of its counterparts or potential exchange partners, the qualitative and quantitative resource of firms holding equivalent positions, and its evaluation of its own resources. In other words, the firm's action will depend on how it evaluates its position and its link to the environment in which it operates. Depending on how it evaluates the situation it can make functional moves which only firms within the network can effect because of its knowledge about the network and its operations. In this manner a firm can gradually build up a position in the network. Every process is cumulative and can improve the firm's position.

15.2. Atlas Copco and the U.S. Compressor Network

15.2.1. The Background

Atlas Copco AB is a Swedish firm, one of the largest in the world in the group's traditional lines of business: compressors, mining & construction equipment, industrial automation and production equipment. The company sells approximately 3,000 products and services to over 250,000 registered customers in more than 50 countries (Annual Report, 1987). International sales account for over 92 per cent of the group's turnover.

Atlas Copco AB first entered the American market in the 1940s. The products which were introduced at that time were machinery and equipment for the mining and construction industry. The operation was very restricted and the sales directed towards end-users such as mining and construction companies. Notwithstanding that these businesses were dominated by giant American firms Atlas Copco was able to increase sales in competition with the local products. In this instance Atlas Copco adopted a marketing technique which had helped them in Europe and in Canada. This involved demonstrating to prospective customers the advantages of the Atlas Copco products vs competing brands (a detailed presentation of this interesting marketing concept is to be found in Ramström, 1974). The Swedish firm had the advantage of a new technology which was a result of a combination of carbide drill steel and the Atlas Copco drilling machine.

The American compressor network, like most of the other industrial networks, have traditionally been dominated by very large domestic firms. A few of them have been in the business for over 100 years. These firms together form a compressor network with distribution and service channels spread across the states.

In the 1960s five major producers controlled 80 per cent of the industrial compressor market. The market shares of these firms are listed in Table 15.1.

TABLE 15.1: Five Major Producers in the American Compressor
Market in the 1960s.

Firm	Market share (in %)
Ingersoll-Rand	25
Joy	20
Dresser	15
Gardner & Denver	10
Worthington	10

Source: Interview (the proportions are approximates).

The manufacturers sold over 90 per cent of their output through independent distributors. The distributors who sold products originating from these five firms were authorized firms and reputed to provide excellent service to customers. The manufacturers normally had one distributor in each town. Each distributor usually carried products from only one manufacturer. However, if product items which were not produced by the particular manufacturer entered the market then they also supported them as complementary products. It was very unusual for any reputable distributor to support two competing brands from two different suppliers. The manufacturers, in turn, avoided selling to two distributors if there was evidence that they would compete for the same customers.

The compressor market and the relationship between the actors can be portrayed as in Figure 15.1.

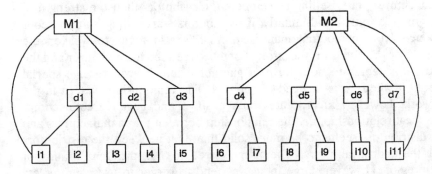

FIGURE 15.1: The American Compressor Network

There are three sets of actors: the manufacturers (M), the distributors (d) and the industries (i) which ultimately use the compressors. The manufacturers are dependent on the distributors for (1) distribution (2) service to users (3) storage and (4) information access regarding customer needs. The distributors, in turn, receive some exclusive right to sell a particular manufacturer's compressors and spare parts. Furthermore, they can also depend on the manufacturer to provide their personnel with free training in technical and management issues. Additionally, when sales are directed to important customers the manufacturer will provide technical support. The end-users, in turn, are dependent on the distributors to obtain service and spare parts if there are any breakdowns. Major industries, which purchase compressors directly from manufacturers, can also depend upon the local distributors for services and spare parts.

The manufacturers, the distributors and the industries respectively are also connected to each other although they do not have any direct business transactions. Most of the firms are members of various organizations and have the possibility of meeting and exchanging ideas and information.

This relationship pattern between manufacturers, distributors and end users has emerged as a result of their doing business with each other. The actors have some form of prescribed roles—network identity—which stipulate what each can, will and probably must do for the others. The whole network is structurally consistent with clique-like formations where each clique is clustered around a single manufacturer. The strength of the clique seems to be based on mutual support. If, for example, the manufacturer starts selling to competing distributors then the strength of the group is impaired. Similarly, if distributors start selling homogeneous products from competing manufacturers this also tends to weaken the group. For the end user, the strong bond between the manufacturer and the distributor seems to be a form of guarantee that he will receive special attention when he is in need of services. The relationship pattern in the network, however, incorporates both positive and negative connections. The focal relationship, i.e. the relationship between the manufacturers and the distributors seems to be more solid than that between the distributors and the industrial users. The user is free to use different brands of compressor. However, large industries tend to prefer to use compressors from one distributor with whom they have long term relationships.

In the 1960s two major events, both with technical foundation, created some turbulence and generated some changes in the network relationships. One was the innovation of the oil fluid compressor. This was judged technically superior to the piston compressor which until the 60s was the principal technology used in the industrial compressors. The technical base for the new compressor originates from the so-called rotary screw technology which was invented by a Swedish firm and subsequently sold on licence all over the world. The oil fluid compressor had comparable advantages; relatively easy to replace, much lighter and very smooth running which is important from the point of view of the work environment.

The commercial importance of this technical development is interesting. The oil fluid compressor was invented by a few engineers who were then working for Joy, a compressor manufacturer. They resigned and started a new firm, Sollair. Within a very short period Sollair, with licenced technology, was able to capture a large segment of the market and became the market leader for compressors. The old giants like Ingersoll-Rand were initially caught off balance but able to mend the damage by following suit and producing oil free compressors themselves.

The other major event was the introduction of oil free compressors by Atlas Copco. The technological base for this product is the so-called dry screw technology and was also developed in Sweden. The major attribute of the product is that it eliminates the need to use lubricant. The significance of this differentiated product for Atlas Copco's position in the U.S. market will be examined in more detail later on in this Chapter.

Today, the market structure has not changed significantly since the 60s. Eighty per cent of the market is still shared by five large firms. Two of the original firms have merged and one new firm, Sollair, was able to create and build up a position of strength in the compressor network. They were able to offer a unique resource and thereby succeeded in attracting other firms to start doing business with them.

15.2.2. The Initial Steps

In 1956 Atlas Copco acquired a compressor manufacturing plant in Belgium. Almost all the production output was sold to the U.S.S.R., which was a tremendous market. Suddenly, in the 60s, the Soviets stopped buying and that was that. They did not buy any more compressors from the Belgium plant. Thus, Atlas Copco had the production resources but they had to find new markets. The U.S. market seemed to be attractive since Atlas Copco felt they had already a good establishment in the U.S., albeit for other products, and also the production capacity in the Belgium plant to back up sales.

In the 1960s Atlas Copco made its first serious effort to enter the industrial compressor market in the U.S. For the next 10 years the firm tried to build up its own sales organization and a distribution net but with very little success. The reason was simple. Mr Jonsson, a director of Atlas Copco who had worked within the project recalls

> ..everytime we try to break into a distributor and ask him to sell Atlas Copco compressors, the first thing he said to us was "Atlas Copco ? Who is that ?" and then he proceeded "O.K. if we sell the A.C. compressors, I will lose my old

brand that I am selling now. And I have over 500 compressor customers who use the brand I sell. They come for service and buy spare parts from me. That is my bread and butter".....

This explains the complicated interconnections between the products and the actors. The distributors do not make much profits from the sale of a new product. But when they manage to sell one to an industry then they have a guaranteed sale of spare parts and complementary service. It is from the spare part and service business they make their profits. If a distributor sells competing brands he is liable to lose the dealership for one of the brands. Atlas Copco, being a foreign and unknown firm without any local reference was not an attractive alternative and the dealers found a change of supplier unwarranted.

In 1971 Atlas Copco undertook a pilot project to promote sales on the east coast. They concentrated on Metropolitan New York, Baltimore and one other city. Special American sales personnel were hired to visit industries and distributors. The promotion project revealed some important facts. The distributors were not unwilling to buy from Atlas Copco. However, they never substituted the assortment they were already supporting. If they found some products which were interesting they were more responsive. As an interviewee said

'they only plucked the cream of our product assortment and that was it!'.

At any time when they were able to sell their full assortment they found these distributors not to be reputable in the market. Mr Nilsson, a Atlas Copco manager, recalled

'....it was not to the first or second rate distributors — It was only the fourth rate distributors who wanted to sell our products'.

The result of the initial endeavor and the lessons from it were clear. The intentions of Atlas Copco when they entered the market were to establish serious relationships with dealers and users which could give them a foothold in the market. However, the structural nature of the market did not permit the entry of a newcomer with almost homogeneous products. The distributors were not interested in switching to a new supplier. Whatever products they bought from Atlas Copco pertain to a marginal, short term level. Thus, there was a mismatch in the intentions of both parties. At this stage Atlas Copco realized that it was a very tough assignment to raise a functional and serious distribution network from scratch.

15.2.3. A Breakthrough

The sales promotion efforts and prior experience strongly indicated a 'face', as Atlas Copco puts it, was necessary in the market. Atlas Copco did not have this 'face' or 'position' in the market since hardly any industrial firms used their compressor machines. In other words, Atlas Copco did not have the same type of relationship with distributors or end-users as did local manufacturing firms. The dilemma was how to build up such relationships in a short time. An opportunity more or less materialized when Worthington, one of the four large compressor manufacturing firms was put up for sale.

Worthington was a good old American firm which had been manufacturing and supplying compressors through distributors who were generally thought to be in good standing in the areas they served. Furthermore most of the distributors had been selling Worthington compressors for a long time. The manufacturing plant was situated in Massachusetts, a town in the middle of the 'rust belt'. In the 70s this whole area was afflicted by structural problems, partly as a result of the strong dollar. Worthington's was suffering a dual predicament because it had not kept up with the technical changes necessitated by the introduction of oil fluid compressors. The Worthington ownership was a conglomerate firm and unwilling to invest further in the industry. As a result of all these circumstances it became certain that Worthington would either change ownership or be closed down.

Atlas Copco bought Worthington in 1971. For the former, it was not the physical assets which were important. They could have built a modern plant at a reasonable cost. The value of the acquisition was that a distribution network with hundreds of distributors could be secured overnight.

Following the acquisition some quick changes were made in the organization. The number of employees was reduced from 800 to 300. The management staff too was gradually changed. Worthington, being a traditional American firm, had only Americans on its staff. Atlas Copco introduced Swedes, Italians, Belgians etc. so that the firm could be integrated with European management and technology.

The acquisition of the Worthington operation gave Atlas Copco the necessary recognition as well as a position in the compressor network in the U.S. Worthington's geographical coverage, i ts production unit, the staff of technical and managerial personnel could be put into operation within a relative short time. However, Worthington's specific relationships with independent distributors was perhaps the most important asset Atlas Copco inherited. Through the acquisition the latter was able to take over a position which has been formed as a result of several years of exchange relations with distributors and industrial users.

15.3. Relationships with Distributors

The distributors had for some time perceived some degree of uncertainty over their relationship with Worthington, due naturally to causes mentioned earlier in this Chapter. Therefore, for the dealers it was apparently a positive solution when Atlas Copco took over the Worthington operation.

From the start, directly following the acquisition, Atlas sought to maintain and develop the Worthington relationship with the distributors. They continued to supply Worthington compressors and original spare parts. In addition, the distributors were given the option to stretch their assortment with a wider product range consisting of Atlas Copco compressors and spare parts. This included oil free compressors as well. This proved to be popular because the distributors, as well as Worthington products, could also carry an additional brand in their assortment without any conflict of interest. However, it should be pointed out that some of the Worthington distributors carried the oil free compressors from Atlas Copco in their inventory before Worthington changed ownership.

Atlas made additional investments to demonstrate to the distributors that they were, at least, as serious as the other American suppliers. Importance was attached to providing the distributor with superior value from the re-sale and through support programmes. They included training for personnel, seminars, distribution councils, distributor communication programmes and newsletters. To carry out these activities American advertising agencies and an American communication manager was hired. An editorial network with the trade press was created. All these activities aimed at promoting knowledge about Atlas Copco and their activities.

Successful distributors and important industrial users were taken to Antwerp in Belgium where they were shown around the very modern and sophisticated factory. This factory was in stark contrast to the Worthington plant which was obsolete. By showing the Antwerp factory Atlas wanted to reduce their perceived uncertainty in using Atlas as a supplier. In retrospect, Atlas Copco management felt that this was a vital step as a very strong 'buy American' attitude was prevalent at that time.

Atlas provided a free training program to their distributors and their servicemen. In the training programmes the distributors' technicians were introduced to Atlas Copco products. The education had some elements of specificity because Atlas Copco was the only supplier of oil free compressors at that time. The oil free compressor had a strong impact on Atlas Copco's future advancement. We shall return to this important issue in a separate section.

A parallel service contract was made available to the end-users through the distributors. This raised the service standards of the distributors since they can now afford to provide customers with extended options.

The spare part supply was considerably improved so that the customers could rely on obtaining necessary items without delay. Storage warehouses were built such that the efficiency of the distribution network was enhanced. For instance, if a distributor lacked any special spare part he could procure it overnight irrespective of his location in the country.

All these measures together were intended to increase the partnership advantage and demonstrate to the distributors that they are here to do serious business. Atlas Copco wanted to convey that they can match the standards of any other strong American supplier. In this way they sought to maintain the position Worthington had created by meeting their commitments to the distributor firms.

15.4. Relationships with End-Users

The problem was how to build up a new trade name and a brand loyalty among the end-users. One important aspect was to study the buying process of the industrial user. The buying process somehow reflects the needs of the end-user, the circumstances surrounding the need and the span of time between his need and his purchase. As result of a research study it became apparent to Atlas Copco that it was only when the compressor broke down or did not function properly that the customer was motivated even to think about it. The period between the user's perception of a need to buy a compressor to the execution of the purchase was very short. Based upon this information the firm decided that the best possible way for them to deliver the message, and to influence the potential customer about which brand to choose, was to keep in constant touch with him. Hence, they changed the advertising message from explaining what the compressor could do to emphasizing the importance of keeping the compressor in operation and thereby guarantee a continuous production flow. Atlas Copco passing these messages also offered inspections, guidelines, checklists etc to help the user to keep his compressor system in order. The idea was that once you are inside the firm you may be sure that repeat orders will be yours.

When Atlas Copco took over Worthington, they knew that loyalty among end-users was inconceivable if it was to be conveyed only through distributors. If the latter decided to change brand name or something similar happened there was risk of losing customers. As a result one of the strategic questions taken up for discussion was how to handle the advertisement. Should they advertise directly in magazines directed to end-user categories, or should they provide the distributor with advertising material where he could put his own name in the corner before mailing it to customers? On the whole the second option was adopted and Atlas Copco paid 50 per cent of the advertising cost undertaken by the distributor. The advantage of going through the distributor is that it creates a feeling of trust as well as revealing to the end-user that the manufacturer and the distributor are working as a team. This in turn might decrease his perception of brand uncertainty. Working in close co-operation with the distributor and also having a foot inside the end-user's workshop gives the spin off of deep involvement in the market and thereby also access to inside information.

Another detail in the interaction with the users was to inform them of the technical features of the product. The product used in Europe is quite different from American standards. As an example, the pressure vessels had to be remodified to pass American specifications. Similarly all the technical specifications had to be changed to suit the electrical standards; for e.g. 220 to 120 volts.

This section illustrated the process which Atlas Copco followed to establish and enforce relationship with end-users. The policy adopted to reach the end- user was to work closely with the distributors. The idea of continuously exchanging information with the end-user also gives a closeness which would be difficult to achieve otherwise, e.g. through a public advertisement campaign.

15.5. Atlas Copco Strengthens its Position

In the 70s the market could be said to be dominated principally by two types of compressor. One was based on the rotary-screw technology with oil fluid operation and the other on dry-screw technology which did not use any lubricant in operation. The former contained oil which was considered desirable in industries such as engineering workshops. However, these compressors were totally unfit for use in certain industries such as the pharmaceutical, textile, food industries etc. If the oil infiltrates into food, beer, or aspirin etc. this will have serious consequences. Thus, for these groups oil free compressors were most preferable.

When Atlas Copco took over Worthington the American firms were producing and delivering an oil free compressor which was limited to the upper size levels. Further, the oil-filtering technology was not 100 per cent reliable. A filter can leak which meant that batches of a product could be destroyed. After entering the market and meeting with customers, Atlas Copco realized that the largest group of purchasers of oil free compressors were in fact in need of intermediate size and not the large sized compressors.

Atlas solved this problem by introducing a completely oil free compressor of medium size which, in fact, they were already selling in Europe. When they introduced this particular product the American manufacturers did not take them seriously. A former employee of one of the American firms who now works for Atlas Copco recalled

> "when they came out with the oil free compressor we were laughing. We had made some studies and concluded the product not attractive from an economical point of view. And then we also concluded that the market was not big enough.."

However, the result was somewhat similar to that of the oil fluid compressors, albeit not that revolutionary. Atlas Copco managed to create a unique niche for this product in the industries which needed such machinery. The price was set at a premium of 25 to 30 per cent relative to oil fluid compressors. Nevertheless, the product caught up with the users and Atlas Copco has a very large market share in this sector. In fact they are the market leaders in the oil free section of the compressor market.

The introduction of the oil free compressors also helped Atlas Copco to forge new relationships with firms, especially in Silicon valley. When computer printed circle cards were manufactured an expensive nitrogen cleaning process was used. Compressed air could have been an alternative but oil infiltration had constrained its use. When Atlas Copco introduced the oil free compressor, which was also cheaper than the nitrogen gas compressor, the product was unbeatable. This association was an important breakthrough for the firm and helped to spread their name into other industries as well. It follows the saying 'It is easier to filter downwards than climb upwards.'

15.6. Market Entry and Network Structure

The literature dealing with foreign market entry strategy reports various techniques whereby individual firms "engineer" their way into foreign countries and how they single-handedly use different marketing tactics to penetrate the market. The case study presented here however indicates that the strategic choice available for the firm is to adapt to the prevalent industrial network structure. The positions of the individual firms are embedded within this structure and connected to each other in different dependence relationships. Because of these interrelationships, which are based more or less on business logic and interpersonal relations, the actors find no incentive to break old relationships. Unlike markets the networks have a history. Positions emerge as a result of this historical process. The actors who hold these positions have access to other actors holding other positions which opens up possibilities for action which effectively excludes outsiders. Within the network each firm has the possibility to approach actors and obtain information which they can utilize to improve their own position.

Atlas Copco was already a well established firm in the U.S. before they decided to sell industrial compressors. Nevertheless they were unable to utilize their marketing organization in the country to activate the necessary relationship with distributors and end-users. The customer groups belonged to a network which was only weakly connected to the other networks in which Atlas Copco was operating. Further, the sales force, the technicians etc cannot easily be converted from selling tools to selling compressors. As a manager puts it "if we sent sales people from the same organization they would have come into conflict. You have to sell 300 industrial tools to match the sale of one compressor". A co-ordination would have generated conflicts among those who were involved in the sales because of the imbalance in satisfaction which would have ensued from differences in performance levels.

The interdependence between the firms in the American compressor network has developed as a result of their doing business with each other for a considerable length of time. In consequence of this process the actors have also come to know and value the other actors. Furthermore, the actors are closer to each other because they are connected to each other more or less directly and not widely dispersed. Moreover, each actor is more or less specialized in the sense that the activity of the actor strengthens rather than weakens the position of the other firm. All these signify that the firms have defined roles and the relationships between the positions have formed a strong network structure.

Given this structure the best way for Atlas Copco to build up relationships in a short time was to take over another firm's position. This action had little effect on the network structure. Only the actors changed while the position itself remained intact. The significance of this action for Atlas Copco was that it was able to acquire a position which had developed as a result of many years of doing business with the other actors in the network.

Most of the subsequent exchanges Atlas Copco had with distributors and end-users can be characterized as normal and proper business conduct in industrial networks. All the other major actors in the compressor network were giving similar value to distributors and end-users in return for selling their products. However, Atlas Copco made an extra effort to reduce the uncertainty among the actors because they were a foreign firm as well as being a relatively new and unknown actor in the market. It is analogous to soliciting a new friendship. You have to demonstrate who you are, what you are and what you can do in order to win the initial acceptance. Once accepted you are already inside and can enjoy the benefits and shoulder the paucity that characterize the exchange relations in the network.

The introduction and marketing of the oil free compressor furnish evidence of how Atlas Copco could profit from being an active player in the network. Through information exchange and close co-operation with others they were able to identify specific need uncertainty within important market segments. By properly understanding the need they were able to design a product specifically suited to meet it. This gave them entry to new and valuable relationships with important customers.

Briefly this case exemplifies some significant facts about network structures in general and positions in particular. Strongly structured networks can present barriers to new entrants. A contemporary firm can have a better chance to overcome this barrier if it understands the nature of the network structure. For Atlas Copco it took some time to realize that it was almost impossible to start from scratch although it is a relatively large international firm with considerable resources.

However, it should be admitted that if the resources needed are not congruent between actors embedded within the network then the stability of the linkages between the positions will be frail. Further, the links which join two positions will be stronger if they are multiple. This is valid only if actors within the same firm are also closely connected. Otherwise, conflicts can break up old relations and pave the way for new ones (e.g. Sollair – here the technicians who broke away to start the new firm would have had access to network information and contacts with counterparts before hand). Moreover, a firm's position is not just provided. It has to be associated with the other positions. This could only be achieved by managing the needs of the other position. By doing so a firm will be indirectly preparing its own position.

Furthermore, the information about network exchanges and access to actors which is available for a member of the network is rarely at the disposal of an outsider. While performing activities you are also noticed and diverse bonds may be generated. These bonds can be the source of information yielding further knowledge and possibilities which could be strategically utilized to strengthen a firm's position (e.g. introduction of oil free compressors).

This case study indicates that firms entering a foreign industrial network must go through a gradual process of learning to manage exchange activities and subsequently build up relationships. They are thereby able to improve their position in stages. These findings raise some interesting questions.

One of them is whether it is possible for firms to make long-term strategic plans and engineer their operations according to a masterplan. In our case the answer was no. Atlas Copco was a relatively large firm when they entered the American compressor market. However, the firm had to go through a gradual process and gain insight about the functional structure of the compressor network. It is only through this process that they realized the importance of acquiring a local manufacturing firm. The other question is, whether it is necessary, albeit not uncommon, for a firm to go through various stages of internationalization, starting from direct export, then enlisting an agent, a joint venture etc, to establish a market position. The case study presented here indicates that it is not necessary and may be inapposite. The correct mode of entry is determined by the structural characteristics of the network itself and not by an individual firm. Atlas Copco did not go through the various stages but made a hop, skip and a jump to gain a foothold by buying an already established position. In this case it seems to be the appropriate move considering the alternative painful process of trying to build up its own position from scratch.

REFERENCES

Aldrich, H.E. (1979). *Organizations and Environments*, Englewood Cliffs, N.J.: Prentice-Hall.

Aldrich, H. E. (1986). *Population Perspectives on Organizations*. Universitatis Upsaliensis, Studiae Oeconomiae Negotiorum, **25**: Uppsala.

Aldrich, H. and D. A. Wetten (1981). Organizations-sets, Action-sets, and Networks: Making the Most of Simplicity. In Nyström, P. and W. Starbuck, (eds.), *Handbook of Organization Design*, **1**: New York: Oxford University Press.

American Express (1987). *Resa i affärer* (Business Travelling). Stockholm.

Auletta, K. (1986). *Greed and Glory on Wall Street. The Fall of the House of Lehman,* New York: Random House.

Bain, J. S. (1968). *Industrial Organization* (2nd ed., 1st ed., 1959), New York: Wiley.

Beckerman, W. (1956). Distance and the Pattern of Intra-European Trade, *Review of Economics and Statistics,* **38**: 31-40.

Behrman, J.N. and H. Wallender, III. (1976). *Transfer of Manufacturing Technology within Multinational Enterprises.* Cambridge: Ballinger.

Belshaw, C. S. (1965). *Traditional Exchange and Modern Markets.* Englewood Cliffs, N.J.: Prentice Hall.

Boddewyn, J. J. (1988). Political Aspects of MNE Theory. *Journal of International Business Studies,* Fall, 341-363.

Borg, M. (1988). *International Transfers of Managers in Multinational Corporations.* Acta Universitatis Upsaliensis, Studia Oeconomiae Negotiorum **27**, Almqvist & Wiksell International, Stockholm.

Carlson, S. (1951). *Executive Behavior : A Study of the Workload and the Working Methods of Managing Directors.* Stockholm: Strömbergs.

Carlson, S., 1966, *International Business Research,* Acta Universitatis Upsaliensis, Studia Oeconomiae Negotiorum **1**: Stockholm: Almqvist & Wiksell.

Carstairs, R. and L. Welch (1979). Foreign Licensing: A Stepping-stone Strategy. Working Paper **1979/2**, Centre for International Business Studies, University of Uppsala.

Carstairs, R. and L. Welch (1981). Licensing and the Internationalization of Smaller Companies. *Working Paper Series* **81/4**, Oslo: Bedriftsøkonomiskt institutt.

Casson, M. (1979). *Alternatives to the Multinational Enterprise*. London: The Macmillan Press.

Cateora, P. (1966). *International Marketing*. Homewood, Ill: Richard D. Irwin, Inc.

Caves, R.E. (1982). *Multinational Enterprise and Economic Analysis*. Cambridge: Cambridge University Press.

Cleveland, H., B. Van and T. F. Huertas (1985). *Citibank 1812-1970*, Cambridge, Mass.: Harvard University Press (Harvard Studies in Business History **37**).

Contractor, F. J. (1981). The Role of Licensing in International Strategy, *Columbia Journal of World Business,* **16**: 73-83.

Cook, K.M. and R. M. Emerson (1984). Exchange Networks and the Analysis of Complex Organizations. *Research in the Sociology of Organizations*. **3**: JAI Press.

Coser, R. (1975). The Complexity of Roles as Seedbed of Individual Autonomy. In L. Coser (ed.), *The Idea of Social Structure: Essays in Honor of Robert Merton.*, New York: Harcourt Brace Jovanovich, 237-263.

Cunningham, M. T. and E. Homse (1982). An Interaction Approach to Marketing Strategy. In H. Håkansson (ed.), *International Marketing and Purchasing of Industrial Goods: An Interaction Approach*. Chichester: J. Wiley.

Dilworth, J. D. (1985). Centralized Project Management, *Journal of System Management* **36**: 30-35.

Doz, Y. (1986). *Strategic Management in Multinational Companies*. New York: Pergamon Press.

Engwall, L. and J. Johanson (eds.), (1980). *Some Aspects of Control in International Business*. Acta Universitatis Upsaliensis Studia Negotiorum **12**, Uppsala: Almquist & Wiksell.

Engwall, L. and J. Johanson (1984). Mobility Barriers in Organizations. In I. Hägg and F. Wiedersheim-Paul (eds.), *Between Market and Hierarchy,* Department of Business Studies, Uppsala University, 29-38.

Engwall, L. and J. Johanson (1988). Banks in Industrial Networks. Paper Presented at the Conference "The Firm as a Nexus of Treaties" at the Swedish Collegium for Advanced Study in Social Sciences in Uppsala, June 1988.

Engwall, L. and M. Wallenstål (1988). Tit for Tat in Small Steps. The Internationalization of Swedish Banks, *Scandinavian Journal of Management,* 4: 147-155.

Erland, O., M. Forsgren and U. Olsson (1986). *Nordisk handelsbojkott mot Sydafrika.* Ds UD 1986:9, Stockholm: Liber.

Foord, R. C. (1988). *Organization Theory,* Harper & Row, N.J.

Ford, D. (1979). Developing Buyer-Seller Relationships in Export Marketing. *Organisation, Marknad och Samhälle,* 16, 5: 291-307.

Ford, D. (1982). The Development of Buyer-Seller Relationships in Industrial Markets. In H. Håkansson, (ed.), *International Marketing and Purchasing of Industrial Goods,* Chichester: John Wiley & Sons.

Forsgren, M. (1989). *Managing the Internationalization Process. The Swedish Case.* London: Routledge.

Forsgren, M. and J. Johanson (1975). *Internationell företagsekonomi.* (International Business Economics). Stockholm: Norstedts.

Forsgren, M. and N. Kinch (1970). *Företagets anpassning till förändringar i omgivande system.* (The Adaptation of the Firm to Changes in Surrounding Systems). Acta Universitatis Upsaliensis. Studia Negotiorum 2, Uppsala: Almqvist & Wiksell.

Forsgren, M., U. Holm and J. Johanson. (1990). Internationalization of the Second Degree. Paper presented at the AIB Regional Conference, University of Strathclyde, Glasgow.

Freeman, H. L. (1988). Barriers to Global Markets. *Institutional Investor,* 22: 32-33.

Gårdeborn, I. and E. Rhenman (1974). *Internationaliseringsstrategier i konsultbranchen – en programutredning,* SIAR; Stockholm.

Giddens, A. (1984). *The Constitution of Society,* Cambridge: Polity Press.

Goodman, R.A. (1981). *Temporary Systems Professional Development Manpower Utilization*, Praeger, N.J.

Granovetter, M. S. (1973). The Strength of Weak Ties. *American Journal of Sociology*, **6:** 1360-1380.

Granovetter, M. S. (1982). The Strength of Weak Ties: A Network Theory Revisited. In P. V. Marsden and N. Lin, *Social Structure and Network Analysis*. Sage Publications, Beverly Hills, 105-130.

Grossman, P. Z. (1987). *American Express — The Unofficial Story of the People Who Built the Great Financial Empire*. Crown Publishers.

Grubel, H. G. (1968). Internationally Diversified Portfolios: Welfare Gains and Capital Flows. *American Economic Review*, 1299-1314.

Gudykunst, W.B. and Y. Y. Kim (1984). *Communications with Strangers — An Approach to International Communication*, New York: Random House.

Hadjikhani, A. (1985). *Organization of Manpower Training in International Package Deals*, Acta Universitatis Upsaliensis, Studia Oeconomiae Negotiorum, **21,** Almqvist & Wiksell, Stockholm.

Hägg, I. and J. Johanson (eds.), (1982). *Företag i nätverk — ny syn på konkurrenskraft* (Firms in Network. A New Approach to Competitive Strength), Stockholm: SNS.

Håkansson, L. (1980), Multinationella företag: FoU-verksamhet, tekniköverföring och företagstillväxt — en studie av svenska storföretag och utlandsägda företag i Sverige. SIND 1980:4. Stockholm: Liber.

Håkansson, H. (ed.), (1982). *International Marketing and Purchasing of Industrial Goods. An Interaction Approach*. Chichester: J. Wiley.

Håkansson, H. (1985). The Swedish Approach to Europe. In P.W. Turnbull and J-P. Valla (eds.), *Strategies for International Industrial Marketing*, London: Croom Helm.

Håkansson, H. (ed.), (1986). *Industrial Technological Development, A Network Approach*, London: Croom Helm.

Håkansson, H. (1989). *Corporate Technological Behavior: Cooperation and Networks*. London: Routledge.

Håkansson, H. and J. Johanson (1988). Formal and Informal Cooperation Strategies in International Industrial Networks. In F. J. Contractor and P. Lorange (eds.), *Cooperative Strategies in International Business*, Mass.: Lexington Books.

Håkansson, H. and I. Snehota (1989). No Business is an Island: The Network Concept of Business Strategy. *Scandinavian Journal of Management,* **5,** 3: 187-200.

Håkansson, H. and C. Östberg (1975). Industrial Marketing – An Organizational Problem?" *Industrial Marketing Management,* **4:** 113-123.

Hallén, L. and F. Wiedersheim-Paul (1979). Psychic Distance and Buyer-Seller Interaction. *Organisasjon, Marked og Samfunn,* **16:** No 5.

Hallén, L. (1982). *International Industrial Purchasing. Channels, Interaction, and Governance Structures.* Acta Universitatis Upsaliensis, Studia Oeconomiae Negotiorum **13.** Stockholm: Almqvist & Wiksell International.

Hallén, L. (1986). A Comparison of Strategic Marketing Approaches. In P.W. Turnbull and J-P. Valla (eds.), *Strategies for International Industrial Marketing,* London: Croom Helm.

Hallén, L. and J. Johanson (1989). Introduction: International Business Relationships and Industrial Networks. In L. Hallén and J. Johanson (eds.), *Advances in International Marketing,* **3.** Greenwich, Conn.: JAI Press Inc.

Hallén, L. and M. Sandström (1988). Relationship Atmosphere in International Business. Paper presented at the IMP Conference, Manchester.

Hallén, L., J. Johanson and N. S. Mohamed (1987). Relationship Strength and Stability in International and Domestic Industrial Marketing. *Industrial Marketing and Purchasing,* **2, 2:**22-37.

Hallén, L. and F. Wiedersheim-Paul (1982). Psychic Distance in International Marketing. *Working Paper* 1982/3, Department of Business Administration, Uppsala University.

Hammarkvist, K-O., H. Håkansson and L-G. Mattsson (1982). *Marknadsföring för konkurrenskraft* (Marketing for Competitive Power). Malmö: Liber.

Hamilton, C. B. (ed), (1989). *Europa och Sverige* (Europe and Sweden), Stockholm: SNS Förlag,

Hayden, E.W. (1976). *Technology Transfer to East Europe. New York: Praeger.*

Hedberg, B. (1981). How Organizations Learn And Unlearn. In P. C. Nyström and W. H. Starbuck. (eds.), *Handbook of Organizational Design.* **1:** *3-27. Adapting Organizations to their Environments,* Oxford: Oxford University Press.

238 REFERENCES

Hedlund, G. (1986). The Hypermodern MNC — A Heterarchy? *Human Resource Management,* Spring, **25**: 9-35.

Hedlund, G. and P. Åman (1983). *Managing Relationships with Foreign Subsidiaries — Organization and Control in Swedish MNCs.* Stockholm: Sveriges Mekanförbund.

Hildebrand, K.-G. (1971). I omvandlingens tjänst (In the Service of Change), Stockholm: Seelig.

Hirschman, A. O. (1970). *Exit, Voice and Loyalty,* Cambridge, MA: Harvard University Press.

Hofstede, G. (1980). *Culture's Consequences: International Differences in Work-Related Values,* Beverly Hills, London: Sage Publications.

Hörnell, E. and J-E. Vahlne (1973). Svenska dotterbolag i utlandet (Swedish Subsidiaries Abroad). In E. Hörnell., J-E. Vahlne and F. Wiedersheim-Paul, *Export och utlandsetableringar* (Export and Foreign Establishments), Uppsala: Almquist & Wiksell.

Hörnell, E. and H. Didner (1988). *Svenska aktier i utlandet. Fallet Pharmacia* (Swedish Shares Abroad. The Pharmacia Case). Uppsala: SNS.

ILO, (1984). *Technology Choice and Employment Generation by Multinational Enterprises in Developing Countries,* Geneva.

IVA (1989). Forskning och Utveckling i Utlandet — En studie av svenska multinationella företag; IVA-PM, 1989:1, Stockholm: Ingenjörsvetenskaps-akademien.

Jansson, H. (1985). Marketing to Projects in South East Asia, IMP Research Seminar. In L. Hallén and J. Johanson (eds.), *Networks of Relationships in International Industrial Marketing.* Advances in International Marketing, 3, Greenwich, Conn: JAI Press.

Jansson, H. (1988). *Strategier och organisation på avlägsna marknader: Svenska industriföretag i Sydöstasien* (Strategies and Organization in Distant Markets), Lund: Studentlitteratur,

Joachimsson, R. (1984). Utlandsägda dotterbolag i Sverige. En analys av koncerninterna transaktionsmönster och finansiella samband. *Nordiska skattevetenskapliga forskningsrådets skriftserie,* (Foreign-owned Subsidiaries in Sweden) NSFS 14. Stockholm: Liber.

Johanson, J. (1966). *Svenskt kvalitetsstål på utländska marknader* (Swedish Special Steel in Foreign Markets), Uppsala: Department of Business Studies.

Johanson, J. (1989). Business Relationships and Industrial Networks. In O. Williamson, S.-E. Sjöstrand and J. Johanson, *Perspectives on the Economics of Organization*. Lund: Institute of Economic Research, Lund University.

Johanson, J. and L-G. Mattsson (1984). International Marketing and Internationalization Processes — Some Perspectives on Current and Future Research. In P. Turnbull and S. Paliwoda (eds.), *Research in International Marketing*. London: Croom Helm.

Johanson, J. and L-G. Mattsson (1985). Marketing Investments and Market Investments in Industrial Networks. *International Journal of Research in Marketing*, **2**: 185-195.

Johanson, J. and L-G. Mattsson (1988). Internationalization in Industrial Systems — A Network Approach. In N. Hood and J-E. Vahlne (eds.), *Strategies in Global Competition*, New York: Croom Helm.

Johanson, J. and L-G. Mattsson (1990). Strategic Actions in Industrial Networks. A Framework. In B. Axelsson and G. Easton (eds.), *Industrial Networks — The New Reality*. London: Routledge.

Johanson, J. and F. Wiedersheim-Paul (1975). The Internationalization of the Firm — Four Swedish Cases, *Journal of Management Studies*, **12**: 305-322.

Johanson, J. and J-E. Vahlne (1977). The Internationalization Process of the Firm — A Model of Knowledge Development and Increasing Foreign Market Commitments, *Journal of International Business Studies*, **8**: 23-32.

Jungerhem, S. (1988). Kontorsnätens drivkraft (The Driving Force of the Office Networks), *Manuscript*, Department of Business Studies, Uppsala University.

Keegan, W. (1974). *Multinational Marketing Management*. Englewood Cliffs NJ: Prentice Hall.

Keegan, W. (1989). Global Marketing Management. Englewood Cliffs, NJ: Prentice Hall.

Kinch, N. (1974). Utlandsetableringar inom massa och pappersindustrin. En studie av olika metoder att hantera en osäker marknad" (Foreign Subsidiaries within the Pulp and Paper Industry). In J-E. Vahlne. (ed.), *Företagsekonomisk forskning om internationellt företagande* (Business

Administration Research on International Business), Stockholm: Norstedts, 61-65.

Kinch, N. (1987). Emerging Strategies in a Network Context: The Volvo Case. *Scandinavian Journal of Management Studies,* May, 167-184.

Kinch, N. (1990). Strategic Illusion As A Management Strategy. Forthcoming in *Journal of Management Studies.*

Laage-Hellman, J. (1989). *Technological Development in Industrial Networks,* Acta Universitatis Upsaliensis. Comprehensive Summaries of Uppsala Dissertations from the Faculty of Social Sciences, **16**, Stockholm: Almqvist & Wiksell.

Langlois, S. (1977). Les réseaux personnels et la diffusion des informations sur les emplois". *Recherches Sociographiques* 2:. 213-345.

Larsson, A. (1985). *Structure and Change. Power in the Transnational Enterprise,* Acta Universitatis Upsaliensis Studia Oeconomiae Negotiorum, **23**, Stockholm: Almqvist & Wiksell.

Lawrence, P. R. and J. W. Lorsch (1967). *Organizations and Environments,* Cambridge, Mass.: Harvard University Press.

Lindblom, C. (1959). The Science of Muddling Through", *Public Administrative Review,* **19**:. 79-89.

Lovell, E. B. (1969). Appraising Foreign Licensing Performance. *Business Policy Study* **128**. New York: National Industrial Conference Board.

Lowe, J. and N. K. Crawford (1984). *Innovation and Technology Transfer for the Growing Firm — Text and Cases.* Oxford: Pergamon.

Lybeck, J. A. and G. Hagerud (1988). Penningmarknadens instrument (The Instruments of the Money Market), Stockholm: Rabén & Sjögren

Markowsky, B., T. Patton and D. Willer (1988). Power Relations in Exchange Networks. *American Sociological Review,* . **53**: 220-236).

Mattsson, A. (1972). *The Effects of Trade Barriers on the Export Firm,* Acta Universitatis Upsaliensis. Studia Oeconomiae Negotiorum **5**, Uppsala: Almqvist & Wiksell.

Mattsson, L.G. (1979). Cooperation between Firms in International System Selling. In L-G. Mattsson and F. Wiedersheim-Paul (eds.), *Recent Research on the Internationalization of Business,* Acta Universitatis Upsaliensis, Annum Quingentesimum Celebrantis **13**, Stockholm: Almqvist & Wiksell.

Mattsson, L-G. (1989). Development of Firms in Networks: Positions and Investments. In L. Hallén and J. Johanson (eds.), *Networks of Relationships in International Industrial Marketing,* Greenwich, Conn: JAI Press.

Mayer, M. (1984). *The Money Bazars. Understanding the Banking Revolution Around Us.* New York: Dutton.

Maynard, C. (1983). *Indonesia's Countertrade Experience.* New York: The American Indonesian Chamber of Commerce.

McCall, J. B. and M. B. Warrington (1984). *Marketing by Agreement. A Cross-cultural Approach to Business Negotiations.* Chichester: Wiley & Sons.

Merton, R. K. (1957). *Social Theory and Social Structure.* Free Press, New York.

Mintzberg, H. (1978). Patterns in Strategy Formation. *Management Science,* 24:934-948.

Mintzberg, H. and A. McHugh (1985). Strategy Formation in an Adhocracy". *Administrative Science Quarterly,* 30:160-197.

Mullineux, A. (1987). *International Banking and Financial Systems: A Comparison. London: Graham & Trotman.*

Newcomb, T. M., R. H. Turner and P. E. Converse (1965). *Social Psychology,* New York: Holt, Rinehart and Winston, Inc.

Nordström, M. and M. N. Seyed (1987) *Positionsförändring i nätverk vid samgående,* Internal Paper, Department of Business Studies, Uppsala University.

Pascale, R.T. (1984). Perspectives on Strategy. The Real Story Behind Honda's Success". *California Management Review,* 26(3):47-72.

Penrose, E. T. (1966). *The Theory of the Growth of the Firm.* Oxford: Basil Blackwell,

Perichitch, M. (1976). *Transnational Operation of U.S Engineering Consulting Firms,* OECD Development Centre, Paris.

Pfeffer, J. (1981a). *Power in Organizations.* Boston: Pitman.

Pfeffer, J. (1981b). Management as Symbolic Action: The Creation and Maintenance of Organizational Paradigms. *Research in Organizational Behaviour,* 3:1-52. Greenwich, Conn.: JAI Press Inc.

242 REFERENCES

Pfeffer, J. and G. Salancik (1978). *The External Control of Organizations.* New York: Harper & Row.

Porter, M. E. (1980). *Competitive Strategy,* New York: Free Press.

Porter, M. E. (1983). (The Technological Dimensions of Competitive Strategy. Research on Technological Innovations. *Management and Policy.* 1. *Greenwich, Conn: JAI Press.*

Porter, M. (1986). Competition in Global Industries: A Conceptual Framework, in M. Porter, (ed.), *Competition in Global Industries.* Boston: Harvard Business School Press.

Ramström, D. Atlas in the World Market Place. In T. Gårdlund, L. Janelid, D. Ramström and H. Lindblad, H., *Atlas Copco 1873-1973,* Örebro: Ljungbyföretagen.

Robinson, R.D. (1980). Background Concepts and Philosophy of International Business from World War II to the Present. *Journal of International Business Studies,* Spring/Summer 1: 13-21.

Robock, S. H. and K. Simmonds (1989). *International Business and Multinational Enterprises.* Homewood: Irwin.

Root, F. R. (1982). *Foreign Market Entry Strategies,* New York: AMACOM.

Rugman, A.M., D. J. Lecraw and L. D. Booth (1985). *International Business. Firm and Environment.* New York: McGraw-Hill.

Ratten 59:1, The Customer Magazine of AB Volvo.

Sahal, D. (1980). Technological Progress and Policy. In D. Sahal, (ed.), *Research Development and Technological Innovation,* Lexington: Lexington Books.

Salancik, G. R. and J. R. Meindl (1984). Corporate Attributions as Strategic Illusions of Management Control. *Administrative Science Quarterly,* 29:238-254.

Scherer, F. M. (1970). *Industrial Market Structure and Economic Performance,* Chicago, Ill.: Rand McNally.

Sharma D. D. (1985). Technical Consultancy as a Network of Relationships: A Case Study. In: J. Johanson and L. Hallén, (eds), Networks of Relationships in International Industrial Marketing 3: Greenwich, Conn: JAI Press Inc *Advances In Marketing,* JAI press (forthcoming).

Sharma, D. D. and J. Johanson (1983). The Foreign Operations of the Swedish Technical Consultancy Firms: An Empirical Study. *Working Paper* No. 5, Department of Business Administration, Uppsala University.

Sharma, D. D. and J. Johanson (1984). Swedish Technical Consultants: Task, Resources and Relationships – A Network Approach. Paper presented at the International Seminar on Industrial Marketing, Stockholm, August 29-31.

Siebert, F., Peterson, T. and W. Schramm (1956). *Four Theories of the Press*, Urbana, Ill.: University of Illinois Press.

Singer, E. M. (1968). *Antitrust Economics: Selected Legal Cases and Economic Models*, Englewood Cliffs, N. J.: Prentice-Hall.

Sinkey, J. F. Jr. (1986). *Commercial Bank Financial Management in the Financial-Services Industry*, New York: MacMillan (2. ed., 1. ed. 1983).

Söderlund, E. (1964). *Skandinaviska Banken i det svenska bankväsendets historia 1864-1914* (The Skandinaviska banken in the History of Swedish Banking 1864-1914), Göteborg: Skandinaviska banken.

Söderlund, E. (1978). *Skandinaviska Banken i det svenska bankväsendets historia 1914-1939* (The Skandinaviska banken in the History of Swedish Banking 1914-1939), Uppsala: Almqvist & Wiksell.

SOU 1988:38. *Ägarutredningen,* Industridepartementer. Stockholm: Allmänna Förlaget.

State Planning Bureau of Indonesia (BAPPENAS), 1987, "Perdagangan Imbal Beli (= Countertrade)", Djakarta, unpublished report.

Stewart, R. (1987). Chairmen and General Managers: a Comparative Study of Different Role Relationships. Paper presented at the British Academy of Management, University of Warwick, September.

Stonehill, A. I. and K. B. Dullum (1982). *Internationalizing the Cost of Capital.* Copenhagen: Nyt Nordisk Forlag Arnold Busck A/S.

Svenska Konsultföreningen (1982). Stockholm.

Swedenborg, B. (1988). Den Svenska Industrins Utlandsinvesteringar 1960-1986 (The Swedish Industry's Foreign Investment). Stockholm: Industrins Utredningsinstitut.

Teece, D.J. (1976). *The Multinational Corporation and the Resource Cost of International Technology Transfer.* Cambridge Mass.: Ballinger Publishing Company.

244 REFERENCES

Telesio, P. (1979). *Technology Licensing and Multinational Enterprise*. New York: Praeger.

Terpstra,V. and K. David. (1985) *The Cultural Environment of International Business*, South-Western Publishing Co. Cincinnati, Ohio.

Thomsen, H.B. (1974). West-European Approach on the Acquisition of Technology Through Licensing", Regional Seminar on Know-how about Licensing Arrangements, Manila, Philippines, 30 May-6 June 1974, UNIDO.

Thorelli, H. (1986). Networks: Between Markets and Hierarchies", *Strategic Management Journal* 7: 37-51.

Thunman, C.G. (1988). *Technology Licensing to Distant Markets.Interaction Between Swedish and Indian Firms,* Acta Universitatis Upsaliensis Studia Oeconomiae Negotiorum **28:** Stockholm: Almqvist & Wiksell.

Toyne, B. (1989). International Exchange: A Foundation for Theory Building in International Business. *Journal of International Business Studies,* Spring, 1-17.

Toyne, B. and P. Walters (1989). *Global Marketing Management: A Strategic Perspective*. Boston: Allyn and Bacon.

Trade Development Board of Singapore (1987). Countertrade in Southeast Asia. Asian Regional Workshop on Counterpurchase in Beijing.

Turnbull, P. W. (1979). Roles of Personal Contacts in Industrial Export Marketing. *Organisation, Marknad och Samhälle*, **16:** 325-337.

Turnbull, P.W. and J-P. Valla, (eds.) (1986). *Strategies for International Industrial Marketing,* London: Croom Helm.

Uggla, C., (1982). International Means of Payments and Credits: What a Commercial Bank Can Offer. In: G. Bergendahl, (ed.), *International Financial Management,* Stockholm: Norstedts, 71-86.

U.N. (1972). *Manual on the Use of Consultants in Developing Countries*, 72.II.B.10, N.Y.

Vahlne, J.-E. and F. Wiedersheim-Paul (1973). Ekonomiskt avstånd. Modell och empirisk undersökning (Economic Distance. Model and Empirical Investigation). In: E. Hörnell, J-E. Vahlne and F. Wiedersheim-Paul, *Export och utlandsetableringar* (Export and Foreign Establishments), Uppsala: Almqvist & Wiksell, pp. 81-159.

Walter, I. (1985). *Barriers to Trade in Banking and Financial Services,* London: Trade Policy Research Centre.

Webster, F. and Y. Wind (1972). A General Model of Organizational Buying Behaviour. *Journal of Marketing,* **36:** 12-19.

Welch, L. S. (1983). Licensing Strategy and Policy for Internationalization and Technology Transfer. In: M. R. Czinkota, (ed.), *Export Promotion.* New York: Praeger, 5-23.

Welch, L. S. (1985). The International Marketing of Technology: An Interaction Perspective. *International Marketing Review,* **2:** 41-53.

Wiedersheim-Paul, F. (1982). Licensing as a Long-run Relation", *Research Report,* No. 11, MTC, Stockholm, 37-64.

Williamson, O. E. (1975). *Markets and Hierarchies; Analysis and Antitrust Implications,* New York: Macmillan/The Free Press.

Wilson, J. D. (1986). *The Chase. The Chase Manhattan Bank, N. A. 1945-1985,* Boston, Mass.: Harvard University Press.

Woodward, J. (1965). *Industrial Organization: Theory and Practice,* London: Oxford University Press.

Yamagishi, T., M. Gillmore and K. Cook (1988). Network Connections and the Distribution of Power in Exchange Networks". *American Journal of Sociology.* **4:** 833-851.

Young, S., J. Hamill, C. Wheeler and J. R. Davies (1989). *International Market Entry and Development.* Hemel Hempsted: Harvester Wheatsheaf.

Zenoff, D.B., (1970). Licensing as a Means of Penetrating Foreign Markets. *Idea,* Summer, 293-308.

AUTHOR INDEX

SUBJECT INDEX

251